teach yourself®

writing for children

teach ®
yourself

writing for children
allan frewin jones
and lesley pollinger

For over 60 years, more than
50 million people have learnt over
750 subjects the **teach yourself**
way, with impressive results.

be where you want to be
with **teach yourself**

For UK order enquiries: please contact Bookpoint Ltd, 130 Milton Park, Abingdon, Oxon OX14 4SB. Telephone: +44 (0) 1235 827720. Fax: +44 (0) 1235 400454. Lines are open 09.00–17.00, Monday to Saturday, with a 24-hour message answering service. Details about our titles and how to order are available at www.teachyourself.co.uk

For USA order enquiries: please contact McGraw-Hill Customer Services, PO Box 545, Blacklick, OH 43004-0545, USA. Telephone: 1-800-722-4726. Fax: 1-614-755-5645.

For Canada order enquiries: please contact McGraw-Hill Ryerson Ltd, 300 Water St, Whitby, Ontario L1N 9B6, Canada. Telephone: 905 430 5000. Fax: 905 430 5020.

Long renowned as the authoritative source for self-guided learning – with more than 50 million copies sold worldwide – the **teach yourself** series includes over 500 titles in the fields of languages, crafts, hobbies, business, computing and education.

British Library Cataloguing in Publication Data: a catalogue record for this title is available from the British Library.

Library of Congress Catalog Card Number: on file.

First published in UK 2006 by Hodder Education, 338 Euston Road, London NW1 3BH.

First published in US 2006 by The McGraw-Hill Companies, Inc.

This edition published 2006.

The **teach yourself** name is a registered trade mark of Hodder Headline.

Copyright © 2006 Allan Frewin Jones and Lesley Pollinger

Typeset by Transet Limited, Coventry, England.
Printed in Great Britain for Hodder Education, a division of Hodder Headline, 338 Euston Road, London NW1 3BH, by Cox & Wyman Ltd, Reading, Berkshire.

The publisher has used its best endeavours to ensure that the URLs for external websites referred to in this book are correct and active at the time of going to press. However, the publisher and the authors have no responsibility for the websites and can make no guarantee that a site will remain live or that the content will remain relevant, decent or appropriate.

Hodder Headline's policy is to use papers that are natural, renewable and recyclable products and made from wood grown in sustainable forests. The logging and manufacturing processes are expected to conform to the environmental regulations of the country of origin.

Impression number   10 9 8 7 6 5 4 3 2 1
Year   2010 2009 2008 2007 2006

contents

acknowledgements

In the preparation of this book, we received help, support and advice from many people, including those who kindly responded to our research questionnaires. If we have forgotten to list anyone, please forgive us. With thanks to Stephen Aucutt, John and Kate Briggs, Iain Brown, Giles N Clark, Michael Coleman, Suzanne Collier, Peter Clover, Andrew Dalton, Joan Deitch, John Goodwin, Joanna Devereux, Catherine Fisher, Jennifer Flannery, Lisa Grey, Philip Gross, Barry Kernon, Penny Morris, Sue Mongredien, Christopher Norris, Gary Paulsen, Amanda Punter, Brandon Robshaw, Victoria Roddam, Gillie Russell, Andrew Sharpe, Doug Vickers, Sue Welford, Adrian Whittaker and all the staff at Pollinger Limited.

foreword

Many years ago when I was first starting to write, one of those ridiculous writing magazines that tell you how easy it all is had an interview with Gore Vidal. When asked if he had any advice to give young (or new) writers, he said (paraphrasing – it has, after all, been some thirty years), 'Don't do it. The competition is too hard and you'll never make it. Stay out of it.'

Anger at the statement kept me going for months, but in the event he was only being honest. The competition *is* hard, almost impossible – you have about as much chance as selling your first book as winning the lottery. And the second one is harder. Publishers will say one thing and do the opposite, or – more likely – nothing. Agents will fudge the truth, or at least exaggerate horrendously, and movie people ... well, let's just say if you get far enough along the food chain to deal with movie people, prepare yourself for what amounts to life on another planet.

Don't do it. Stay out of it. It's too hard and will break you.

Pause.

If you're still here – as I expect you will be and as I was – and are thinking of sticking with it though you paper your house with rejections, though you spend all your extra time, money, life, on Making It Work; if you are still here then there are three primary things to take into consideration if you're going to write for young people.

Do not write down. (They are smarter than you and will smell it coming and stop reading, which is the very worst thing you can have happen as a writer.)

Do not preach. (See above.)

Do not overwrite. (See above.)

As for all the rest – dealing with publishers and editors and agents and printers and distributors and truck drivers and first readers and second readers and movie people and paper people and proof readers and editorial assistants and your cousin Fanny who read your manuscript and thinks it's '… just precious' – as for all that, read this book.

Gary Paulsen

01

writing for children: an easy option?

In this chapter you will learn:
- that writing for children is not an easy option
- that getting your material published is going to be hard work
- some basic guidelines to help increase your chances of getting published.

Once upon a time, someone had a really brilliant idea for
a story ...

Stop right there! Do you have an idea for a story buzzing around in your head at this moment? Have you written it down anywhere? If not, put this book down *immediately* and go and get your idea onto paper, or onto a computer file – or even as a reminder on your mobile phone. This is not a joke – this is a Red Alert!

Do it *now*. Story ideas can drift in through one ear and out through the other in the time it takes to sign a letter; and there is nothing more maddening than knowing you *had* a brilliant idea, and later being unable to remember what it was. Bear in mind the cautionary tale of the poet Samuel Taylor Coleridge who was interrupted while writing *Kubla Khan* by the notorious 'visitor from Porlock' and who, when the visitor departed, found that the muse had also entirely deserted him.

Thus lesson one is: always have a pen and a notebook within reach, and write down ideas as they come to you.

Okay, have you written down that idea? If so, and you are sitting comfortably, let us begin ...

How to use this book

Everyone knows that today's newspaper is tomorrow's recycling. Books, by their very nature, are different. In the great march of technology, they have thus far managed to avoid being supplanted by computers and digitalization – they are still solid objects with a degree of permanence about them. People are brought up to treat them with care: to turn the page from the top edge, not to fold down corners to mark your place and never to scribble in the margins. A lot of adults treat books as ornaments, reading them once, placing them carefully on a shelf and dusting them every now and then. *This* is not that sort of book. These days many students sit 'open book' examinations, and are taught to see their textbooks as active tools in such a situation. They are encouraged to make marginal notes and to underline or highlight potentially important sections.

This book should be treated similarly, as a study aid.

Exercise 1

Get yourself a highlighter, pen or pencil so you can mark any points in this book that you think will be useful. Identify salient pages with those yellow Post-it® note things, or just go wild and turn down page-corners. You can also add your own notes and ideas in the margins. We don't mind – we want this book to work for you.

We will not be handing out diplomas, but by the time you have finished this book you should be in possession of a lot of practical advice and knowledge to help you polish your writing.

One point: this book is not intended for published authors; it is aimed at those of you who have been quietly creating stories for your own pleasure or to amuse children, but who have not taken that first step towards a wider audience. Or perhaps you have been thinking, 'I'd like to write for children. How do I go about it, and how do I go about getting my name in print?' Or maybe you have been toiling away, completing stories and sending them to appropriate publishers, only to have them returned for your pains with deflating rejection letters attached. Perhaps you are wondering what you are doing wrong and have decided to seek advice.

Read on.

Starting with the basics

As with any textbook, it is impossible to prejudge the level of expertise of a potential reader. This book has therefore been written as a 'beginner's guide', and in the same way that a tutor book for a musical instrument shows a novice the basics, and answers questions like 'Which way up do I hold the instrument?', this book will act as a comprehensive though basic guide to the world of children's writing. Having said that, even hardened veterans of children's writing might just learn something new.

There is no right or wrong way to write for children, but you will need to understand some basic guidelines which, if followed, should increase your chances of being published. The idea is that, by using this book as your study aid, you will be able to achieve your aims more quickly than by the tortuous route of trial and error. In preparing this book, questionnaires were sent to a great many published authors, publishers and other professionals involved in the world of children's books. Response times varied from return e-mails to next-day letters; and no-one took more than ten days to respond. This makes one thing very obvious – people in the book business want to help new writers, and are willing to share their expertise, not to mention their mistakes and failures. (It needs to be pointed out, though, that response times for submitted manuscripts will not generally be anything like so swift. Reply times can, in fact, vary from days to many months.)

The responses to the questionnaires ranged from the unprintably funny to the grimly sober. Many encouraging and useful pieces of advice will appear in italics throughout this book. We have left the authors of these gems unedited and anonymous to protect their own interests, but have included their names in the Acknowledgements.

Dear Lesley

Good luck with the book. J wishes a certain agent would send him some bestsellers so he can buy a mansion and a yacht on the Cote d'Azur [sic].

Hope this [completed questionnaire] is helpful.

Best

[US publisher]

Mythbusting

First the gloomy news: if you thought writing for children was an easy option, forget it! It is probably more difficult to write the text of an 800-word picture book and get it published than it is to sell an 80,000-word novel for adults. These days it is tremendously difficult for a new author writing in any area to get their foot in the door, and the children's market is certainly no exception. Large book store chains will usually have a central buying policy which inevitably means that variety and choice become more limited because books are bought in large numbers and profits must quickly be shown. Therefore, books by established authors, or those receiving a great deal of publicity, will get preference. And as chains of book stores merge and are bought up, this effect can only become more prevalent. Supermarkets and similar outlets are also in the book-selling game – 'stacking 'em high and selling 'em cheap' – which is great if you are a recognized best-selling author, but it does trap first-timers in the proverbial catch-22 situation: if you have not yet been published and have no track record or identifiable readership, how do you get a publisher to give you your first chance? It is the same principle that applies to any job-seekers: no experience equals no job; no job equals no experience.

Myth 1: Writing for children is easier than writing for adults

Some people, including a number of well-known authors of books for the adult-interest market, think that writing for children may be easier than writing for adults.

Wrong!

Even famous authors of books for grown-ups have found that their fame does not transfer easily into the children's market. Writing successfully for children calls on special and specific skills from its practitioners.

Renown in one area of celebrity does not necessarily smooth a path into an entirely different zone – as blink-and-you'll-miss-them 'faces' have discovered once the media spotlight ceases to play on them and their spin-off publishing deals evaporate. It's also a very badly kept secret that many celebrity books – even autobiographies – are not actually written by the person whose face appears on the cover, and such books are at best only going to be one-hit wonders. In other words, if you're a *Big Brother* winner, stop reading this book right now – just take the money and run. But if you want to learn how to do it right – stick with us.

When writing for adults, there are almost no limits to the language you can use. You can adopt whatever style takes your fancy and produce a script on literally any subject. *And* there is a very wide range of book publishers who will consider publishing your script.

These things are certainly not true of the children's market, where considerable thought must be given both in terms of what kind of story you tell for what age of child – and then what level of understanding (story-wise and language-wise) – has been achieved by the age-group which you are targeting; not to mention the fact that the number of publishers you are able to approach is significantly reduced.

Even the most skilled authors need a couple of elements working for them to be successful. That indefinable something called *inspiration*, and that even more ethereal something called *luck*. Into this brew, add an enormous amount of persistence, and the concoction is starting to look promising.

Another fact that you might like to mull over is that in the children's market a great idea, badly written, has more chance of being picked up, than a weak idea written brilliantly. A publisher may latch onto a marvellous concept, knowing that the flaws in the writing can be ironed out in the editing process. The same publisher may admire the technical expertise of wonderful writing, but if the story being told does not grab them, the book will not be taken on. In other words, there is no place in children's writing for the abstract, abstruse or overly-complicated; the job of a children's writer is to tell a story – simply and entertainingly.

But is this an easy option? Not at all.

You would hardly credit it, but some people, even those inside publishing who should know better, or writers who have experienced 'crossover' success (children's books which are also read by adults) still view children's books as being of lesser importance than books for adults.

One established writer of children's books actually had an editor come up to him and ask him when he was going to write a 'proper' book. Unfortunately the writer in question was so flabbergasted by this witless comment, that the offending editor was out of earshot before an appropriate reply came to mind. Always the way, isn't it? Take heart, though – in your book, the hero will always be able to come up with a snappy one-liner – even if it takes you two weeks to think of it.

The following is part of an actual letter from an editor who usually works on adult-interest books, in response to the submission of a children's short story:

> *It would do you some good to make heavier demands of your art and yourself. Although you have a gift of writing both poems and fiction for children, and there is no reason why you shouldn't continue to cultivate it, I do worry that you may be clinging to those habits as a form of security.*

What a condescending clown! That editor should be sat down and faced with a panel of those children's writers whose work has been loved and cherished by generation after generation of young people, and asked to explain exactly why he or she assumes that writing for children is some sort of security blanket for those unwilling to fully explore their talent!

> No one should look upon writing for children as a soft option. Yes, it is in many ways far simpler than writing for adults – the books are shorter, the ideas less complex – but you need a particular type of ability to do it well. An ability to become a child, to get right inside the minds of your child characters, to see through their eyes and with their experience – while at the same time, remaining your adult self, sifting and selecting as you write.

Myth 2: The good old days of publishing

Remember the good old days? An editor likes your book: they feel it has something to say, and that plenty of people will want to buy it. They agree to publish it. Success. Unfortunately, editors and publishing houses no longer operate in this way. The legendary leisurely lunches are a thing of the past. Literary merit and an honourable handshake no longer lead to amiable deals and speedy decisions. Business managers and accountants have moved into publishing. (If this sounds a little like Hollywood, it should: the money people have taken over the book world in the same way that they took over the movie world.) Companies have merged, staff have been rationalized and pressure applied to cut costs and increase profits. The good old days have been replaced by tough new days.

Today an editor has to present your book to a meeting of sales people, marketing people and hard-nosed accountants whose sole interest is in profit margins – and all of these 'suits' have to be convinced that your book is going to reach its projected sales target before it will be taken on. Literary merit? – of course it's still on the agenda, but quality talks rather quietly at these meetings while money shouts its head off, especially if that 'quality' does not lend itself to easy explanations.

What these people like is to be told that a new book will be a cross between *Titanic* and *Jurassic Park*, or *Pride & Prejudice* meets *The Lord of the Rings*. This they will understand – this they will 'green light'. Tell them it's a totally original concept, and they'll shrink away from it like snails curling up in sunlight. But don't panic – brand new ideas can still force their way into the light. It's just not quite so simple to sell them to a cautious publishing world.

In such a climate it makes sense to play safe and to publish the tried and tested author, rather than to gamble on an unknown. There will always be the 'hot property' exceptions, but on the whole you need to bear in mind that in most cases *you* are going to be The Unknown.

It is said that everyone has a story to tell. The question that occupies the minds of publishers is whether that story will be of any interest to anyone outside the author's immediate circle of friends and relations.

Myth 3: Only children buy the books

Another thing you need to bear in mind is that, as with children's clothes and children's toys, the majority of children's books are *not* bought by children. They are bought by booksellers and librarians, by teachers and bulk-buying distributors. They are bought by parents and relatives, or by adult collectors and dedicated followers of a particular author's work.

In other words, your children's book or *proposed* children's book has mainly to attract and gain the interest of an *adult* audience. It is absolutely true that the manuscript of Tolkien's *The Hobbit* was handed by the publisher Sir Stanley Unwin to his 10-year-old son Rayner for an appraisal. The boy liked it – and the book got published. These days – no chance. Forget it.

Something else to think about is that there are fewer children in a population than there are adults, so the children's market is obviously going to be smaller than the adult market. Getting the picture? Children's publishing is a very tough and competitive market.

And what if your great idea is for a picture book? Picture books are an even smaller slice of the market, and you also have to allow for a whole number of marketing rules which are out of your control, and possibly subject to a shifting social perspective way beyond your ken. Therefore, your 800-word picture book idea will have to conform to a specific set of rules, and only then will it be able to take a leap into the fiendishly competitive world of potentially publishable material.

Now for some good news! Just when you were contemplating an easier career path, a shaft of light illuminates the gloom: the children's book market is actually healthy and expanding. It is also heartening to know that in a recent UK survey, three out of the top five 'Favourite Books of the Twentieth Century' were actually children's books – how about that, then?

A vital resource

No matter what sparked your interest in writing for children, it is worth pausing a moment to consider how important books are for children. If people do not learn to enjoy reading as children, their chances of picking up the joyous habit at a later age are pretty limited.

It is sometimes said that the printed word is dead, and that the computer screen has taken over. This is not yet true – a quick glance around on a bus, train or airplane soon proves otherwise. People still love the portability and ease-of-access of a book, magazine or newspaper. You do not need to turn them on, nor do you need to insert batteries. You can read a book wherever you like: in the bath; up a tree; on a beach. It is also still far quicker to look up an unknown word in the dictionary than it is to switch on a computer and access the right web page (especially if you are in the bath or up a tree at the time).

How are children intended to gain access to knowledge and information if they never learn to read and write? A reasonable level of literacy is absolutely vital in life. Try playing a new computer game without first browsing the accompanying written instructions, let alone make sense of the actual computer whose destiny is apparently to supplant the printed word. To understand how a computer works, it is still necessary to fall back on the printed word: *Computers for Dummies* manuals, anyone?

How do you apply for a job without being able to fill in a lengthy application form? The ability to write goes hand-in-hand with the practice of reading. While modern society is crying out for increased levels of literacy, these standards are not only failing to be maintained, but in many places are falling, as statistics frequently published in newspaper articles will show. Basic literacy skills are a vital resource for anyone wishing to communicate on any level above the purely verbal.

Many people lament the changes being engendered in standard written English by e-mails and mobile phone text messages, but there is really no problem here – just so long as a clear 'benchmark' system of spelling, grammar and syntax is taught; the fact that young people use slang and truncated word-forms to chat among themselves is nothing new and certainly nothing to be concerned about. Remember, a healthy language is in a constant state of flux, with words dropping out of use and new words entering the vocabulary all the time. Thus, the important thing for a writer to achieve is a *modern* voice, but one which avoids falling into the trap of using the kind of ephemeral street slang that can outdate a book within a period of months.

Not everyone's contribution to society can be as clear-cut as that of a doctor, a lifeboat crew member or a charity aid worker. A children's author may never know how much joy, understanding and information their work has given to children all over the world, and in every situation. If your writing cheers one single child, if it provides escapism for a short time from some harsh reality, or if it teaches one new word or comprehension of a problem, then that is a worthy contribution to have made.

Books are essential for children and have an important and significant role to play. There is no better medium for firing the imagination. Nowadays, humans need the skills of literacy and communication more than ever before. A large part of that learning process and literacy will involve books.

Take heart

Remember the questionnaires we mentioned earlier? Amongst those people we canvassed were prize-winners and full-time professional authors; and one of the questions we posed concerned the most useful piece of advice given to them when they were starting out on their writing career. Their answers make for interesting reading:

> Your readers will only read this <u>once</u>. You've got to get them <u>first</u> time.

> Keep trying, don't give up in the face of innumerable rejection slips. If you really believe in yourself you will eventually succeed.

> Don't try to spot trends in the market or fill gaps. Do something that is absolutely 'you'.

> Learn to cope with rejection. Be yourself. Write what you want to write, and strive to find your own voice, not a pale imitation of somebody else's. Write the sort of material you

*enjoy reading, and ask yourself if you would read with
pleasure the book you have just written!*

*Talking to other writers is really helpful, as well as
interesting. I also used to be part of a creative writing
group where we discussed each other's work every week.
It was terrifying at first, having complete strangers telling
me what they thought of my writing, but getting such
feedback and insight was incredibly useful, and gave me
the confidence to show my work to professional editors.*

The real world

In our experience, a general rule is that it takes any author
about *eight years* to go from publication of a first work to the
point where a living wage can be earned. The exception would
be for someone producing an instant worldwide bestseller. Of
course, if you do not need to go out and earn a living, then you
might be able to carve a few years off the end of this timescale,
but that is all. It is still a lengthy process.

The average author has to *love* writing; it is pointless going into
the writing business with expectations that truck-loads of cash
will shortly be rolling up to your door. It simply does not work
like that.

You will need huge amounts of patience and vast quantities of
perseverance. Those who devote all their time to writing will
also point out that it is essentially a very *lonely* occupation.

If you have a job, keep it: you will need the money. If you are
totally dedicated to writing for a living, explore the possibilities
of job-sharing or part-time work, so that you can be sure of a
regular and reliable income. Writing, like many freelance
occupations, can be a case of swings and roundabouts, feast or
famine. Gradually an author will accrue income from royalties,
advances and so on, which will help through the lean times, but
there is no substitute for the security of a separate safe salary.
Think of that salary before handing in your resignation.

Besides needing some other source of income, you will also need
to get out into the real world to keep the creative juices flowing,
and to keep a balanced view of life. Working with other people,
meeting new faces, experiencing novel or unusual situations and
listening to the experiences of others will give endless fuel to
your imagination.

As one author says:

> *Your own experiences, and those of people around you, are
> a good source of ideas. I find that early writings have more
> resonance if they are based on something you already
> know. Always keep your eyes and ears open. Observe how
> people behave, and listen to what they say. If you want
> your books to be peopled with real characters, you need to
> become something of an expert on human behaviour.*

Exercise 2

With luck, you are already filled to bursting-point with ideas for
stories, and you are only reading this book in order to learn how
best to present them. But wait a minute. You may discover that
your brilliantly original idea is already out there – while you were
putting your thoughts together someone has already written the
book, manufactured the t-shirt and sold the movie rights. Or the
morning may dawn when you stare blankly at a blank sheet of
paper or a blank computer screen with the dull feeling that the
creative part of your brain will never wake up again.

> *Writers are always unconsciously looking around for ideas.
> Anything potentially interesting should be filed away in
> your memory, or preferably in a notebook or on a computer
> file. Bear in mind that an idea is seldom much use on its
> own: you usually need two or three ideas to gel together
> before you even get the glimmerings of a plot.*

So, if you do not have one already, you will need a small notebook
and pen. Computers are very handy, but pen and paper are much
more transportable. Take a notebook everywhere with you and get
into the habit of being an 'ideas detective'. Look, listen and learn
from everything that is going on around you. Make especial use of
any contact with real children and of things to be found in a child's
world. Watch children's television programmes, buy children's
magazines and check out Internet websites aimed at children. But
be sensible about how you use the Internet – browsing websites
aimed at children is fine, but never involve yourself in young
people's chat-rooms or anything of that nature, even if your
interest is for research purposes and entirely innocent.

Visit toy shops, take slow meanders around a shopping centre at
the weekend or during school holidays, and even dare to board
buses at school finishing time. (The last suggestion is for the
brave-at-heart only – massed school kids on buses take no
prisoners.)

Snippets of conversation overheard in queues, fast-food restaurants or on railway platforms will no doubt open your eyes. But do remember that although editors are always asking for 'reality' – they don't really mean it in the raw. Children communicating with other children can use language that would never pass even the most liberal editorial censorship test – so learn how to take the harsh reality of street-talk and turn it into something that can be published. Similarly, observed behaviour between children can reach startling extremes of cruelty and violence and casual abusiveness – not to mention jaw-dropping snogs on the back seat of buses – and although these are all 'real', they will not find their way into published form unless there is a very good reason. Even then, books with such content may well be banned from schools and libraries and so on. In other words – get real, all right – but remember the strictures of the market and the behavioural limitations of the society in which you live.

Train yourself to observe the differences in behaviour between children. Do boys behave differently from girls? If so, in what ways? And why? Do girls behave differently in front of boys than they do with other girls, and vice versa? Do they all behave differently with adults? Jot down ideas in your notebook, whether they come from an immediate experience or from the recesses of your own memory; the most unlikely ideas can later blossom into extraordinary storylines or a non-fiction idea.

> I get my ideas from books, places, TV, from myths and legends and from using archetypal storylines. I have a notebook, nothing else.

Alongside your notebook, you should start a scrapbook – a cuttings file which will become your 'Ideas File'. A large envelope would do the job, an empty drawer, or you could go crazy and set up an alphabetical or cross-referenced subject filing system. Or you could open up a computer file, or a computer folder with a number of different files for ease-of-access. Into your chosen system you can put newspaper or magazine clippings – eye-catching headlines or entire articles, pictures of people, buildings, scenery, cartoons, work by an inspirational artist – anything, in fact, which you think might be a future source of work. If you have a scanner, you can even transfer these scraps straight into your computer – or you could spend a little time each week, transcribing your favourite clippings onto a file. Do whatever works for you.

For character ideas, I cut out photos from magazines/ papers/catalogues. I make a pinboard for each book, with notes beside pictures for age, character, links with others, etc.

Keep notebooks, diaries, random jottings. You may not recognize 'a writing idea' – one that will grow and develop – until much later. Things lie dormant, waiting to meet up with another idea or occasion.

Later in this book we will start suggesting uses for your 'Ideas File', so it is best to start gathering material now. The larger your collection, the more useful it will become. Think about it: a picture in today's newspaper of a child being rescued from a burning building may be the kernel from which a whole book could grow; an article about curriculum changes in education may be the seed for a non-fiction work; a face in a magazine may awaken in you the entire personality of a central character for a book.

As we said right at the beginning, if an idea comes to you, note it down while it is still fresh in your mind. Then put it somewhere safe. The back pocket of a pair of jeans that are heading for the wash is not a good place. File it away in your 'Ideas File'.

For many years I have kept an 'Ideas Folder'. Whenever an idea comes to me, even if only a snippet, or a funny or intriguing remark I have heard someone say in the street, I immediately put it in my folder. Ideas can linger therein for years before finally being put to good use.

The electronic age

Advances in technology inevitably change the way you work. Sadly, whether you like it or not, the pencil and paper is redundant.

Writing on a computer has proved invaluable. All my notes/ideas/drafts/research are there on one file, only a finger-click away.

Something remarkable has happened in the last ten years. Way back in 1995, when we started organizing our thoughts for the first edition of this book, it was by no means the norm for people to have their own personal computer at home, and the astonishing world of the Internet was still very much in its infancy. But all that has changed. Computers are now a quite

ordinary piece of equipment in very many homes, the price
having gone down in real terms to the extent that in many
households, it is possible for children to have computers of their
own in their rooms. Broadband has speeded up access to an
astonishing universe of information and research material. In
the words of one publisher:

*These days, for writers, the computer is no longer an
optional extra – it is a vital tool.*

As with all technological advantages, this can be both a good
thing and a bad thing. Those disenfranchised from the
computer/Internet revolution for whatever reason, find that they
have an additional hurdle to overcome. These days the vast
majority of communication between an editor and a writer will
be via e-mails. The book you are writing may not actually ever
appear on paper – in 'hard-copy' form – until the finished and
published book lands on your doorstep; the whole process will
very likely take place on a computer – with copies flying back
and forth via e-mails as the editorial process is pursued. And
contracts increasingly include the proviso that the writer must
submit the work '... on an IBM PC-compatible disk or as an
e-mail attachment'. In other words, unless you have a computer,
you may not even get a contract.

But the computer and Internet revolution has had enormous
benefits for a writer capable of taking advantage of it.

*I would never have written novels, I suspect, before
word-processors. Editing – for myself, back and forth
with editors – is really well served by e-mail.*

*You can work on more than one project at a time. A
finger-click and everything's filed away, neat and tidy.
Also, editing has become a dream where it used to be a
nightmare of messy crossing out, tipped and spilled
coffee!!*

You are writing an adventure story set in a remote part of China
– the characters canoe down a river – one of them falls in and
becomes ill – and it might be cholera. Exciting stuff – but you
have to make it seem as realistic as possible. You don't have the
resources to visit China – you don't know a canoe from a
banana and you have no idea of the symptoms of cholera.

In the recent past, all this information would have to have been
painstakingly gathered. Maybe a trip to a local bookshop to get
a good travel guide on China, another book on canoeing, and a

medical dictionary. Or you could try the local library. Or you could ask around friends and acquaintances. Or you could visit or make telephone calls to people you think may be able to help. Time-consuming and potentially expensive ... and even then you may not be able to get the exact information you want.

These days? You get on the Internet and you open a search engine and you type 'cholera + symptoms'. And there is all the information you could possibly want – delivered to your computer instantly and in copious amounts. We just tried this very exercise ourselves – and came up with 620,000 reference hits.

And if you want more tactile information, you can enter an Internet bookshop and buy yourself a 'Lonely Planet' guide to China, and then augment the book by seeking out websites where tourists have posted their vacation photographs of China, so that you can actually see what the area about which you are writing looks like.

Your characters are in China, and you live in the United Kingdom. You know about Chinese food, but you suddenly realize that you don't have the faintest idea what Chinese people eat for breakfast. Into the search engine: 'Chinese + breakfast' – and there you find a comprehensive set of menus for a whole range of Chinese breakfasts. For those of us who have grown up doing this kind of research the hard way, the Internet revolution is tantamount to a modern miracle!

The bottom line here is that the Internet has become an invaluable resource for writers, a tool which allows you access to a colossal and ever-expanding world of information that can come leaping out at you at the touch of a keyboard.

A word of warning, though. It isn't necessarily a good thing to become an 'Internet potato'. You still have to get out there into the real world sometimes and see what real people are getting up to – don't let yourself overdose on the Internet and forget what is happening beyond your front door. Cross-reference your work for accuracy too; a recognized authority's website is more likely to be correct than Joe Bloggs' 'blog' page. (A 'blog' – short for weblog – is a personal or non-commercial website where users can add questions or comments or leave answers to questions and responses to comments, and which usually contains links to other websites along with information about those sites. A blog will probably be frequently updated and can involve groups of people with specific interests such as politics, news, pop culture, or computer issues.)

And in more basic terms, the computer file is an astonishing time-saver. Only a few years ago, any changes to a script would have to be laboriously cut and pasted into the pages of a hard-copy manuscript. If there were too many changes, or if they were peppered all over the script, then the entire manuscript would need to be retyped – a time-consuming ordeal if you were doing it yourself, and an expensive one if you hired a 'ten-fingered' typist.

The editor likes your book but wants the main character's name changed from 'Prudence' to 'Jade'. A nightmare of work a few years back – but now you just press FIND, type in 'Prudence' – press REPLACE – type in 'Jade' – and it's done – in a moment 'Prudence' is replaced by 'Jade' right through the manuscript.

Even in a pre-edit phase of writing your book, you can make big changes very easily. Scenes can be highlighted and moved about in the manuscript. Paragraphs, incidents, conversations, revelations, explanations, can be taken out, rewritten, expanded, tweaked, twisted and rearranged – and all with an ease that would have had Dickens dancing in the streets.

In other words, if you can possibly afford to rent or buy a computer – or if you can beg or borrow one or find access to one for your writing-stints – then go for it! This is a revolution in writing that you really cannot ignore; as one writer expressed it:

I can hardly believe it now, but I used to write everything in longhand and then type it up on a clanky old typewriter! I still can't type 'properly', but nowadays everything goes straight onto the computer; for anyone wanting to be taken seriously as a professional author, a computer is not just useful, it is an absolute necessity – and so far as research is concerned, the Internet has now become my very best friend.

02

a professional approach

In this chapter you will learn:
- how to approach the craft of writing in a professional way
- the importance of research
- how to maintain contact with the children's world and the world of children's publishing.

There are many reasons why people choose to write for children and to pursue the dream of getting their work published.

I used to work in children's publishing, and when I left work to bring up my children, writing for that market seemed a very family-friendly thing to do.

At first, I wrote books so that I could read them – it was only later on that I considered the possibility of any audience other than my own children.

In other words, you might be someone with a good working knowledge of the publishing world – or alternatively you might be someone who locks themselves away at regular intervals because stories are pouring out of you. Either way, you have a wide chasm to leap; and in particular the gulf between writing for pleasure and writing for publication is a deep and wide one.

If you are writing to entertain only yourself, or friends and family, then you have no need for a guide to getting your work published. At most, you would want a book that shows you how to improve your story-telling skills, and even then you can choose to ignore the advice if it doesn't appeal to you. There are a lot of 'amateur' ways of getting your work out there: fanzine fiction has become increasingly popular with the rise of the Internet: stories inspired by fans of *Star Trek* or *Dr Who* or the *X files,* etc., written and read by a small band of enthusiasts. Or you can just print your work out and hand it around to receptive friends – there's nothing wrong with doing that. But in this book, we assume you want to learn how to become a *professional* – how to get your work *published* – and that is an entirely different thing.

As with any profession, you have to learn the rules before you can start work. You would never imagine yourself waking up one day and saying, 'I'd like to be a surgeon – but I'm going to do it *my* way!' You would expect to have to go into a long period of learning and training before anyone slapped a sharp scalpel into your hand and said, 'Cut!'. On a less elevated level, if you enjoy gardening and want to make the most of your garden, you have to understand which plants like which soil – which flowers bloom best in sunlight – which enjoy half-shade and which thrive in full shade. You'd want to know about soil types, pruning times, planting techniques, etc.

Excuse the stretched metaphor here, but turning a seed of talent into a blossom of professionally produced writing involves you spending a lot of time and effort in the garden before you invite anyone in to check out the results. Meaning, you have a long and challenging learning curve to negotiate before you should consider presenting your work to a potential publisher.

Researching the market is absolutely essential. We'll say that again, just to make sure the message comes through loud and clear: *researching the market is absolutely essential.*

In this chapter we are going to look at the sort of research work you should consider undertaking before you even pick up your pen or approach your keyboard. It will not be necessary for you to try everything mentioned here, but it is important for you to know about it all. The more you know of your intended market, the better your chances of getting your foot through the appropriate door and keeping it there.

Research

The main problem that many aspiring authors need to overcome is a total lack of *research*. It is impossible to overstress the importance of research, as every publisher would agree.

> *My advice is to read a lot of children's books, and visit many children's bookshops. Too many would-be writers have no idea what's in the marketplace or what may appeal to their readers.*
>
> *[Swedish publisher]*

The importance of research

You're probably getting twitchy by now. You're reading this book because you would like to write in a more professional way and you're probably asking yourself when does the actual *writing* start? Well, sorry, but not just yet: there is some vital groundwork to cover first.

First you need to take a long, hard look at the market for your work. If you were designing a new invention, you would want to look at the opposition and conduct some market research first, wouldn't you?

Say you have scribbled out the blueprints for the multi-purpose wine-drinker's companion, a handy little electronic device which, at the press of a button, will open a wine bottle and send it trundling around the table to fill your guests' glasses to brimming perfection. Before you pop down to the local hardware store to buy the basic equipment needed to turn this idea into hard reality, you would want to find a few things out. Your enquiries would include checking patent registers to find out if your idea is unique: the 'Glug-o-matic' might already be out there. Then you would need to assess the viability of mass production, materials, branding, advertising and market potential, as well as identifying possible interested manufacturers. Finally, you would work out the most professional way to demonstrate your invention, and to whom it should be presented.

Similarly, if you went to a job interview, you would create a favourable impression by showing that you had done some homework on the employer's company.

Creating a piece of work for children and presenting it to a potential publisher is no different. The authors responding to our questionnaire said:

> The most useful piece of advice anyone gave me was 'Go to the library and see what sort of books other people write. This will give you an idea of what publishers want.'

> Research, read and target your market.

> If you want to get published, then you have to write something publishers are looking for. Find out what is selling (or even better – what is going to sell next year) and then write something which will fit the bill.

> It's important to think about your market, age ranges, current tastes and issues before you start writing.

As well as researching the market, research the publishers. Not all publishers publish children's books. Not all children's book publishers publish non-fiction books. Teenage magazine publishers do not necessarily publish magazines for the pre-school age group. It is a waste of everyone's time to submit a project to an inappropriate publisher. A little research will tell you where your work is most likely to find an appreciative home, and even if you are not successful straight away, at least you will be heading in the right direction.

Where to start researching

The first place to start your research could be the Internet. Surfing the net for information is a very quick, inexpensive and user-friendly way of accumulating information. Virtually all publishers will have websites that you can access – these will give you plenty of information about what kind of books they publish and they will also very likely have a section on how you should approach them with an unsolicited manuscript.

Online bookstores such as Amazon and Waterstone's are worth checking out. Here you'll find out which books are the highest-sellers and what types of books are getting a big promotional push – both useful things to know for the budding professional. You may also be able to read both an in-house review of the book and comments by readers. Although the latter will always be subjective, a book that received unanimous five-star reviews has got to be worth investigating further. Schools also have websites these days, and there's a good chance that you might pick up something useful there. Similarly, many authors have their own websites, and popular books and authors often have official and unofficial fansites where you will be able to learn first-hand from their readers what it is that they love about the writer and the work being discussed.

The Internet can also put you in touch with writing groups and creative writing websites, where you can have online discussions with other trainee writers, and with people who offer teaching services. Be careful before you join any group that asks for fees up-front. And of course, the more you search, the more you'll find as links lead you in random but possibly inspirational directions.

But don't become so mesmerized by the Internet that you forget that there is a real world out there. Take time out to visit your local bookshop or library – you will probably find they each have a website of their own that you can investigate first (the big book store chains will certainly all have this resource). After that, visit every bookshop and library you come across. Widen your area of research as far as you can. If you are away from home, check out any 'book places' you may happen across. There are a few specialist children's bookshops, but it is a good idea to root around in regular bookshops, too, and look at all other retail outlets where children's books are being sold.

Children's books are sold in all manner of places, from newsagents to service stations, from supermarkets to market stalls, from garden centres to mail-order clubs and leaflets, from television shopping channels to online booksellers, from toy shops to school book fairs and clubs. Some publishers sell enormous quantities of stock through home and place-of-work sales via 'book parties', in much the same way as 'party-plan' and direct marketing operates.

Bargain and remainder bookshops are worth investigating, too. They will give you an idea of books which have not sold well, and which are being sold cheaply. There are publishers who produce glossy-but-cheap books specifically aimed at this market, and some titles may have been bought in as 'damaged stock' – these could well be bestsellers. Take the time to browse and observe.

Treat all your research visits as a real learning process. Unless you have already chosen a specific area of writing, look at *everything*. It will help you understand the market.

As far as libraries are concerned, spending cuts have necessitated some unpredictable opening hours, particularly of specialist children's sections. You will also notice that libraries stock far fewer hardback titles and more paperbacks these days. Indeed, many children's publishers do not now produce original fiction in hardback at all. Some hardbacks have been replaced with what are called 'trade paperbacks'; these books are aimed primarily at the schools and library markets. Trade paperbacks are generally the same size as a hardback, but because of the 'soft' cover are less expensive both to produce and to buy.

During your research, if you are lucky enough to encounter a specialist children's librarian, you should talk to them. These people are very widely read and knowledgeable in their field. Pick an appropriate time to approach them, or arrange to go back and speak with them at a more convenient time. You never know, a good library and its staff could prove a gold mine of reference and research if approached in the right way. Also look out for information leaflets, recommended reading lists, competitions and children's events run by your library or visiting library. One author said this:

> *A children's writer's best friend is her librarian – cultivate the local children's library or department, useful for research/publicity/contacts/sales.*

Try and visit book stores at times when they are not crowded out. This might give you the opportunity to approach staff and speak with them. You never know, you might encounter someone with both the time and the knowledge to be a help to you. For example, they may be able to tell you what their best-selling titles are. Many bookshops that are part of a group or chain have central buyers who make the purchasing decisions for the whole group; however, if you come across a person who actually buys the books for the store, you could ask them about their favourites. Ask them what titles or subjects publishers' reps are pushing hardest at the moment and also what kind of things customers most frequently request. That way you can discover both what the publishing world is trying to sell, and what customers are looking for.

You may discover that customers want books on coping with examination stress at school. Are there such books? If so, what form do they take? What age-range are they intended for? Where are they located in the shop? If there are no such books, you may have just discovered every author's potential crock of gold: a gap in the market.

Finding your writing zone

If by now you have chosen a zone of children's writing that particularly interests you, take a good look at books in that field. Do not forget to make notes of what you see. How many pages long are the books? How large is the typeface, and what style is it? Does the font size and type make it easy to read? Roughly calculate the average text length of the books and note the differing needs of different age groups. Do the books have illustrations? Are they in colour or black and white? Full page or amongst the text? Are there a lot of titles by the same author? Do the books form part of a series?

You will come across a lot of 'series' books identifiable by their series titles or visual style. Some series may be about one set of characters and written by a single author – or at least, bearing a single author's name. (A series may very well be written by several authors, but be published under a single 'brand name' for ease-of-identification and bookshelf placement.) Other series may have a specific theme: horror stories, for instance, or romance, or maybe a non-fiction series by different authors, but sharing the same jacket logo, name and style. Series aimed at younger readers – storybooks for instance – may have colour-coded or numbered – recommended reading age guidelines.

Calculating the length of a book

Count the number of words in ten average-length lines of print. Divide the total by ten to give an average number of words per line. Look at several pages of text and note the average number of lines per page. Multiply the average number of words per line by the average number of lines per page. This will give you a rough idea as to the number of words per page. Multiply this figure by the number of pages in the book. You now have a good working idea of how many words there are in the entire book.

Example: 10 words per line × 25 lines per page × 100 pages in a book = a 25,000-word text.

Make some allowance in your total figure for illustrations, chapter openings and where chapters end part-way down the page and so on.

Research on your doorstep

There could be many reasons why you may not be able to visit libraries and bookshops as often as you might wish. To compensate, you may like to investigate the many mail-order book clubs which exist for children. Book clubs often advertise in newspaper magazines, and their leaflets frequently fall out the moment they are opened.

Some book clubs require a certain purchase commitment which you may wish to think about, and the advertised prices in the catalogues (although usually lower than those in any bookshop) are unlikely to include an amount for postage and packing. Any books or audio tapes that you do order are likely to be invaluable for your research, and the regular book club catalogues will give you a good idea of current popular titles, including design fashions and prices. Do not forget to keep your receipts or invoices for purchases made in connection with your writing business, as these expenses may be offset against tax (see the section, 'Tax and accounts', in Chapter 12).

There are a huge number of websites dedicated to children's interests, books, reviews, literacy, activities, education and so on. However, it does help to know how best to use the Internet for research purposes. If the words you type into your search engine are too vague, you could end up wading through hundreds of thousands of hits before finding what you want.

How to search the Internet effectively

- Use several search engines regularly, such as Google and Ask Jeeves (ask friends for recommendations): this will help you get to know their strengths and weaknesses. Use web directories such as Yahoo! and Vivísimo, when you are searching for general concepts or organizations. (Yahoo! is also a well-known search engine.)

- Use double quotes when search for a particular phrase; for example, "children's books and toys".

- Think laterally about your query: do not just enter "children's books" and expect to see a small number of relevant pages. You might perhaps, add extra search terms; for example, "children's books" + non-fiction + UK, to exclude websites that are pertinent only to other countries, such as Australia or India. All search engines have similar ways in which you can narrow down the results you need. The Google "Refine search" page explains some simple ways in which Google searches can be made more relevant, and many other search engines use exactly the same conventions: http://www.google.co.uk/help/-refinesearch.html.

- If one search using a particular set of key words does not give the results you need, simply search again with slightly different key words, until the results match your hopes and expectations.

- Read the search engine's help pages. These are invaluable guides to any extra features that a search engine offers.

- Do not feel you have to look through all the search results returned. Often you will find an appropriate site within the first page of results.

- Try entering the phrase for which you are searching as a web domain address. For example, if you were looking for a site that was about writing books for young people, try entering "writingforchildren"; sometimes you might strike it lucky!

- Look at the link pages on related websites and blogs. For example, http://www.direct.gov.uk/Homepage/fs/en would offer a set of relevant links for anyone looking for further information on children's education in the UK. Also, Yahoo! provides an interesting list of popular book blogs at http://uk.dir.yahoo.com/Computers_and_Internet/Internet/-World_Wide_Web/Weblogs/Literature/.

There are also various magazines aimed at teachers, parents and buyers of children's books. You may consider these worth subscribing to as they contain author interviews, reviews, news of awards and event details. The reviews, for example, cover a vast array of subject matter and, among other things, may prevent you from embarking on a project which someone else has just had published.

Other trends to keep an eye on include those in toys, merchandizing, clothing, film and the media. This is known as 'riding the zeitgeist' or – more plainly – giving the audience what it wants. But beware: you must avoid writing a book on a subject that is all the rage *now* but which will be out-of-date by the time it hits the shelves. Contemporary writing needs to be able to survive short-lived fashions and to avoid becoming rapidly dated. In other words, follow the latest trends, but do not be mesmerized by them. It can take a couple of years for a book to reach publication. Micro-scooters and merchantable character crazes may reach epidemic proportions every Christmas, but in two years' time a book devoted to the craze is likely to be unsaleable as new fads are promoted. Keep attuned to what is happening in the marketplace and, if possible, think of what might be coming next.

Educational periodicals are good sources of information if you are thinking of writing non-fiction or entering the educational market. Such publications discuss issues and trends in education, as well as containing reviews and details of educational websites. Some newspapers review children's books and materials, and have occasional children's book supplements.

Radio, television and the magazine market can keep you fairly well informed. Listen to and watch children's and teen-based programmes, as well as broadcasts for schools (often shown during the day). You should be interested particularly in book reviews, readings from books, and dramatized shows on terrestrial, digital, cable and satellite television. Set your video or recordable DVD machine to catch programmes that are broadcast at inconvenient times so that you can watch them at your leisure. This will also allow you to hit the pause button if you are making notes. Tape relevant radio shows for future play-back – radio is more word-heavy than TV, and you may miss something important or useful in a single hearing.

I have a lot of contact with children through family, friends and regular visits to schools. I find it enormously important to keep a feel for the way children talk and behave and think … and also to know a little about current trends and interests. Watching television is particularly useful.

Buy a variety of children's and teen magazines on a fairly regular basis. Look at the letters pages and features. If you are not familiar with today's teen magazines, you will probably be surprised or even shocked by the topics covered, but if you do not immerse yourself in the cutting-edge and scarily savvy world of modern-day children and teenagers, you are unlikely to be able to communicate effectively with them. Remember – these kids are a lot more worldly-wise than you were at their age. Talk down to them at your peril.

Exercise 3

We realize that the weight of all this research is making you itch, so we suggest you pause and try this exercise for your imagination.

Take a newspaper or turn to a 24-hour TV or radio news channel, or open a news page on the Internet. Take two totally random headlines or stories. For instance: 'experts meet to save sea turtles' and 'retired civil servant spends lifetime eating roadkill'. Believe it or not, these two items appeared at the same time on the same day on two Internet news sites.

Ask yourself a relevant question, such as: what were those sea turtles doing crossing the road in the first place? Or: was the civil servant involved in some secret government experiment researching food alternatives?

Now write a paragraph-length synopsis of a story linking the news items that have caught your eye. Or you could try a very short story, or even a poem or limerick incorporating your news items.

Seems a bit arbitrary? It certainly is – and the less relevant the two items are to one another, the more fun you can have coming up with ways to link them together.

This technique of randomly selecting unrelated ideas can also oil the pistons of a seized-up imagination.

Those more interested in writing non-fiction can use an encyclopaedia, or technical website. Randomly select a heading and write down all you know on that subject, even if very little, before comparing your piece with the entry. If you select two headings, stimulate the brain cells by seeing if you can form a connection, however tenuous the link.

By the way, if you haven't got another person to hand for any of these exercises, remember that you may find a writing buddy via a local writing group, or an online writer's website.

Meeting your audience

Some authors claim to have very little contact with children, yet are still able to produce marvellous work time and time again. They are able to remember their own feelings and experiences and access their 'inner child' to create works which are avidly read and which garner ecstatic reviews. These authors clearly recollect what it is like to be a child, and how children think and comprehend the world around them.

I think contact with children can be overrated. The important thing is to remember what it was like to be a child. Their environment may be very different from yours, but their emotions aren't. Children still laugh at the same things you did and cry for the same reasons.

I have little direct contact with children other than visiting schools to do book talks. I don't actually know any children and have thus come to conclude that it is not important. More important is to be flexible in your thoughts, keep abreast of modern trends and perhaps above all to go back and become as a child.

I teach in a primary school and see children a lot. It is important, especially if you're used to reading aloud to them, so that you know how they respond to books. Having said that, I don't think about the reader much at all when I write, being so caught up with the story and satisfying myself! But the knowledge of probable responses must be there deep down.

What of the publishers of children's books and their staff? You may be surprised at how little contact many of them have had with children since they themselves left school. Many young people work in editorial, production and marketing positions, and do not always have families of their own, so their recent experience of children can be very limited. And it is often the case that these young editors will come from a middle-class Oxbridge graduate background where their attenuated knowledge of street life may colour their attitudes. Publishers will point to the years of experience that senior editors have in the world of children's publishing – and to their great knowledge of what works and what doesn't – but the reality is that you may find yourself facing a very inexperienced editor who, for workload reasons, has to make critical decisions with limited knowledge and very scanty senior advice. Some enlightened publishers do send staff into schools on a regular basis and use this to get feedback on potential projects. However, an editor's possible lack of child contact and experience should be borne in mind when working with a publisher, or coping with rejection letters.

You may be one of those people who seem to have a sixth sense for what will appeal to both children and publishers but, on the whole, successful children's authors whom we contacted felt that it is very important to keep in regular contact with children and their world.

I need to stay in touch with children. Language, tastes and outlook change all the time.

Have as much contact as you can stand!

How do you know what children like to read if you don't have contact?

You may have children of your own, in which case you can use them as a starting-point. Do not be beguiled into thinking that a bedtime story which proves a roaring success will necessarily interest an outside audience. Most children love to be read to, and simply enjoy the attention and experience. A young child might well be perfectly happy to have an attentive parent's lulling voice intoning names from a telephone directory prior to lights out.

My elder two children always said, 'I loved that book, Mum. You're really good.' The youngest is more critical. I like the first reaction best!

Children's schools and interests

The friends, hobbies, schooling and interests of your own children can be very useful. Authors with children (and grandchildren) will already know what clothes, books and toys are appealing, as well as what films and television programmes are popular. They will also know what is 'hot' and what is definitely 'not'.

Your social situation will narrow your field of experience. Unless you have lived with and worked amidst a broad cross-section of society, you are almost bound to have a limited understanding of other lifestyles. Therefore, it makes sense to write about situations you understand rather than experimenting with those you have never encountered. The former will always ring truer to the reader. For example, if you have daily contact with pre-school children but seldom encounter young adults, it may be a mistake to try to write realistically on teenage subjects. The language and attitudes of young adults change rapidly. Finding out what they read and watch will broaden your experience.

> *Sadly I don't have much contact with children, very important from the view of listening to speech patterns and current colloquialisms.*

Your own children may have grown up and there are no grandchildren to hand. In this situation, it may be hard to remember the language and abilities of a toddler. A good parenting book or website will provide the answers. For example, say your story idea concerns the activities of a naughty 12-month-old baby: such a parenting source will remind you that some babies are talking at this age while others are not, and some are walking when others are still zipping about on all fours.

If your children are of school age, then it is relatively easy for you to join in and meet other children from a wide range of backgrounds. Most schools and playgroups welcome parental assistance. An hour or two when you get the chance will provide you with a great deal of information. You could choose to listen to children reading, and will discover the enormous range of reading and language abilities. You will find out about favourite books and topics, humour and concerns, as well as getting an insight into your local education system. You will learn the way children are taught to read, and the reading schemes and methods used. If the non-fiction area interests you, then it may be possible to help or work as a classroom assistant on project work. This will help you to understand the educational curriculum requirements, the texts children presently work from and their ability to tackle practical work. You will also find that teachers are a valuable source of information and opinion.

> *I think contact with children is vitally important. I have my own, plus the children I meet at the school book club I run.*

Some schools may welcome help from you even if you are not a parent, but they will need to obtain references and other official clearances to reassure themselves that you are an appropriate person to work with children – for reasons that will unfortunately be all too obvious to you. If you have no children and are unable to get to a school during working hours, then there are plenty of other organizations which would welcome your involvement. These range from your local church youth group, or differently-abled organizations, to outdoor activity movements or first-aid organizations. A few hours on a regular basis may give you all the feedback and inspiration you require for your writing.

Should you be interested in the young adult market, then an educational course could provide the answer. Attending a school or college-run course in a subject which teenagers are taking or retaking will give you very interesting company. You could be learning keyboarding skills or how to use graphics software while gaining an insight into modern study methods and the social behaviour of young people.

In the previous chapter, we mentioned the importance of becoming an ideas detective. Watch, listen and learn when you are out and about and ideas will come to you, as the following author discovered:

> *I was stuck on a story about goats! Two months later I was walking past a bus stop where a gang of aggressive-looking bikers in full leathers was standing. I was a bit nervous, and could see plenty of things dangling from the belt of the ugliest one who had a brass studded leather cap. As I tiptoed past, I heard Studded-Cap say: 'Yeah, I was scared to cut my budgie's toenails in case I hurt his feet, so I took him to the vet. It doesn't cost much ...' I realized that the things dangling from his belt were a pair of nail clippers and a bottle opener, not knuckle dusters. A biker with a heart of budgie feathers brought my story to a riotous conclusion.*

Listen to young people, but try not to choke in horror at some of the subjects they cover or the language they use. Nonetheless, if you produce a book filled with the same undiluted street-talk, you will discover that despite wanting realism, publishers have their limits, and the sort of language that could strip paint off a battleship, real as it may be, is unlikely to find favour. We know that strong language and extreme behaviour occur in life, but the adult book buyers may not necessarily want to condone it in print and every society has its legal and social methods of censoring the things that are seen as stepping outside accepted conventions – either by not publishing them in the first place or by them being banned at point-of-sale subsequent to publication. It is true that a bit of outrage by 'concerned citizens' can boost sales – all children will be drawn to something that they are told is 'bad' for them – but this is not an area to approach lightly and could prove disastrous for your career. Courting controversy is not necessarily a good career-move for the hopeful first-time author – especially as today's controversy can easily become tomorrow's big yawn.

The publishing world

There are many societies and organized events which you will find useful. Details can be found in the weekly book trade magazines, writers' reference books, libraries and so on. You will be able to subscribe to most of these societies (although some will require that you have had at least one book published). Your membership will usually bring you regular mailings of information about the world of publishing as well as the latest developments, conferences, lectures and services.

Many lectures and talks will be free to members, and not too expensive for non-members, and some conferences can be very good value. Not only will you learn a lot, but you will get the opportunity to meet other people with the same interests, and also those working in the publishing industry. Some conferences organized by professional bodies can prove very expensive; these might include, for instance, conferences on technology developments and intellectual property rights in the electronic publishing world. Fairly esoteric stuff for the beginner, and you should think carefully before committing a lot of money to such an event. Consider whether the outlay will be justified by the potentially useful information or contacts gained.

Book fairs or educational/game/computer/merchandizing fairs can prove invaluable research venues. You will see the latest trends and developments in the publishing and related industries. You will discover who are the biggest companies and the breadth of their product ranges – and you will get a look at the sometimes daunting competition. You might find that your latest brainwave is already on the production schedules of half a dozen other companies. Or you may spot a gap in the market. Whatever you find, there is no need to be intimidated by the sheer range and quantity. All you need to know is that the majority of material is of a very high standard, and has been thoroughly researched as a saleable commodity before it was put into production. These fairs will teach you that publishing is big business.

You need to understand exactly what is going on at a trade fair or exhibition. Basically, the exhibitors are selling their products to each other, not to the general public. They could be selling books, e-books or online content to distributors and retailers, or 'rights' (paid permission for translating a book, or any other selling area different from the original printed work) to the home or overseas markets. In any event, your presence, while encouraged as a potential individual customer, is not always entirely welcomed by busy sales people working under great pressure and within strict time limits. Try to take everything in while keeping a reasonably low profile.

The Bologna Children's Book Fair is the largest of all specialist children's book fairs and has been held in northern Italy in April for over 40 years. More than 1,200 exhibitors and 4,500 publishing people attend from over 70 countries. See http://www.bookfair.bolognafiere.it.

Other trade professionals who attend Bologna include authors' and illustrators' agents, senior book buyers for major selling chains and book clubs, printers, designers, card, film and television producers, poster and multimedia manufacturers, all looking to buy or sell Intellectual Property Rights, or to view forthcoming products. Every hotel and flight is booked solid by the publishing trade from one year to the next and there is a tendency for prices to treble during the week of the fair. In other words, this fair may not be the best place for a budding author to visit.

('Intellectual Property' is a term used in the commercial exploitation of copyright. For instance, your book is your Intellectual Property and anyone who wants to use it as a basis for a movie or a TV or radio programme or series, or for a computer game or a board game or a jigsaw or a t-shirt or baseball cap or any other spin-off merchandize you might care to imagine, would first have to acquire the Intellectual Property Rights in order so to do.)

A similar story can be told of the Frankfurt Book Fair, which takes place in Germany every October. Here, the entire range of book and related product manufacturers meet for the same purpose. The fair in Frankfurt is truly frantic and frenetic. See http://www.frankfurt-book-fair.com/en/portal.php.

It may well be worth attending a national event such as the London Book Fair, which is held annually in March, especially if it is within travelling distance and your budget. See London Book Fair: http://www.lbf-virtual.com/.

Some dos and don'ts when attending fairs and exhibitions:

- Book fairs and other children's product-related fairs will be advertised in the trade magazines: do try to get tickets in advance by contacting the exhibition organizer. They can be free or cheaper if obtained prior to the commencement of the fair. Large fairs may also organize discounted travel, accommodation and entrance packages if you live too far away for a day visit.

- Attend on a Sunday if possible – Sunday is generally the best day for the public.

- Do wear very comfortable shoes.

- Do take a bag or rucksack to carry home all the free catalogues and information exhibitors give away. Be selective about what you take – if you are not, you could end up crawling out on all fours under a mountain of paper. At the end of the last day, some exhibitors sell off display material at bargain prices.

- Do look, listen and learn. Note potential publishers for your work. If possible, go with an interested companion, so you can discuss what you see.

- Do not interrupt staff who are obviously in the middle of a business meeting.

- Do not try to sell your work to anyone. The chances are that you will be speaking to the wrong people anyway and, in any event, 'cold-calling' at an exhibition is considered unprofessional and could make you very unpopular.
- Do not be intimidated by the seemingly crowded nature of the market. Publishers are always on the lookout for new talent with innovative ideas.

How to annoy publishers

We asked publishers what they hated most about the unsolicited submissions they receive. The replies were universally similar. Read and remember!

Anthropomorphic animals, absolutely! Anything with a heavy-handed message. Several ideas on a page, requesting an opinion on which of them are worth working up.

People who have no idea how high the standard of writing is nowadays, and who assume because their text is for children, poor quality writing doesn't matter. People who, in their submission letter, say how much their own children, or their neighbours' children/class at school/etc. love the story (of course they do!).

The most ridiculous stories we receive usually involve the animation of inanimate objects (characters generally have alliterative names): Elmer the Elevator whose day has its ups and downs; Bertha the Bathtub who is worried about her bathtub ring; or the chocolate bar who runs down the street and melts on the sidewalk.

A story starting with breakfast in the summer holidays. Elves, pixies and fairies. Things like Cuthbert the Cucumber, Larry Lighthouse, Freddy Foghorn, Oscar Ozone – all actual examples, I'm afraid.

You have been warned! No twee stories with animals in clothes doing human things. No old-fashioned stuff because it reminds you of books you loved as a child. And while you're at it, you can roll up that 'Teddy the Table-lamp' manuscript and use it as a firelighter.

Exercise 4

For the next chapter you will need a sample of your writing. ('At last,' you may say.) We are not concerned with style or content just yet, so if you do not have something obvious to hand, then a letter to a friend or a diary entry will do, or your comments on a book you have read recently, or even your opinion on a news item. It does not matter what the subject is: just aim to write or type about two pages of stuff.

03

getting started: the tools of the trade

In this chapter you will learn:
- how to prepare yourself and your environment for writing
- how to gather and file storyline ideas.

Write it down

You have an idea. It could be for a picture book. It could be for a storybook. It could be for a full-length book. It could even be for a series. It could be fiction or it might be non-fiction or educational.

The question you are asking is this: 'How do I get this idea out in the open?' Telling your family and friends about it is easy. With an e-mail you can even send it to people all around the globe. You could open a web page and write it there. Famous writers have been known to write Internet-only books – selling them to fans one chapter at a time. But you are not a famous writer and few if any people are going to pay you to have your book downloaded onto their computers – even if they manage to find it in the first place. The bottom line is you still need a publisher to help you get your work across to your potential audience – to all those people who might find it interesting, entertaining or educational. In order to present it to a publisher, you have to write it down in one form or another; and to do that you will need some basic equipment.

Although the first items of equipment you need are a pen and a notebook, or a handy computer, before you kick-start your brain and send your pencil scurrying across the paper, or your fingers flitting over the keyboard, you need a good grasp of the language in which you will be writing.

You will probably be writing in the same language as the prospective publisher of your work. (Occasionally a book is first released by a foreign publisher in another language, but we don't need to worry about that right now.) Later on we will be looking at the way in which different writing areas require differing tones, styles and contents, but right now you need to address the level of your own language skills.

Words, words, words

Are you writing in a language that is not your native tongue? There may be areas in which you are going to need help. There may be other reasons why your language is not as skilled, nor your command of words as extensive as you would like it to be. You are going to be writing in words, phrases and sentences that must convey your message to a wide variety of people, all of whom need to understand what you are trying to say.

Language works on many levels. It ranges from eloquence to street-slang, from: 'Good morning, and how do you do this bright and sunny day?' to 'Yo, bro! Wassup?' From ancient to modern. From 'Hail and well met, good fellow!' To 'Hiya!' As we mentioned before, language is in a constant state of flux, with old words falling out of favour, the meaning of words changing and new words entering common usage every year. Just take a look at some old movies to see how significantly language has altered over the past few decades. In the 1930s, a female movie star could blithely enquire of a man sitting and talking to her, 'Are you making love to me?' In the 1970s she might ask, 'Are you chatting me up?' – and these days it's unlikely she'd bother saying anything at all, as she'd just as likely be the one making the running.

Different fields of expertise each create their own jargon and every passing year throws up new buzzwords, some of which slip into general usage and some of which remain a closely guarded secret, or at least, impenetrably opaque to anyone outside a small number of 'experts'. A few years ago, those with an ignorance of what goes on under the hood of a car might listen in baffled silence as people chatted together about the torsion on the grimble-shank or how the left-handed cam-spindle is an improvement over the right-handed valve-shaft. These days it's more likely to be computer-talk that leaves you standing there with your mouth hanging open and your brain heading for the hills. Although this jargon is handy for those in the know, it is useless for widespread communication. The purpose of language is to communicate to the widest audience possible – and hopefully to continue to do so for a reasonable length of time. Thus, some common ground needs to be found – common ground that will allow your work to survive. For this you will need to know how to use correct language, with accurate grammar and spelling.

Another thing to keep in mind is that, especially if writing for younger children, your work will form part of that child's education. An enthusiastic person with poor language skills may get far, but probably not so far as they might if their language skills were better. These skills give confidence both to the user and to the person on the receiving end.

At the publishing house the person who receives your work is likely to be someone educated up to, and possibly beyond, university level. Their language knowledge should be good, and their expectations high. A submission littered with spelling mistakes and grammatical inaccuracies will fare less well than a professionally produced piece. To be taken seriously, you must adopt a professional approach.

Almost every publisher we contacted commented on the spelling and the grammatical content of the scripts and the covering letters they receive. Here are some of their comments:

> *Call me pedantic, but it's immediately off-putting to receive a badly presented, misspelt, grammatically incorrect manuscript. Ask someone to check your spelling!*

> *Badly written letters, or proposals containing poor spelling and punctuation usually get rejected. If a writer is incapable of checking an introductory letter then there's precious little chance that he/she is going to take care over a manuscript.*

> *Spelling mistakes. It makes my blood boil when I see really common mistakes like there/their and apostrophes in the wrong places.*

Improving your language skills

In Exercise 4, we asked you to produce a piece of writing. What we would like you to do now is to show it to someone whose language skills you trust. This person may be a friendly teacher whom you know, or someone with an indigenous language degree, or similar expertise. Give them a couple of pages of your work and ask them to go through it, highlighting with absolute honesty any problem areas they find. Explain to them that it is not the *content* that you would like them to examine, but the grammatical accuracy.

If you have no school or college qualifications, are dyslexic or already aware that your writing lacks polish, then there are various ways in which you can get help.

Further education

First, there is further education. There are adult education language courses to suit everyone's ability and pocket. These may be run through local schools and colleges. In such classes you will find people of your own level of ability who are willing and enthusiastic to learn. You will also meet teachers who really *want* to teach you. If you have grim memories of your own schooldays, just remember that every student you will encounter is there because they want to be there and because they want to *learn*. Not only will you be polishing your craft, but you will be meeting new people and storing up some new experiences for your 'Ideas File'.

If, for any reason, you are unable to attend classes outside your own home, then there are correspondence and online courses available. These are advertised in newspapers and magazines, and on websites, and range from private companies to recognized correspondence universities with radio, television and summer-school lectures. Private editorial help is also available through writers' magazines, directories of freelance editors and children's writing organizations. But beware of expensive proof-reading services or creative writing courses with high fees up-front – especially those that try to seduce you out of your money by making grand claims about how much they will help you. Spending large amounts of money at this stage may not be in your long-term best interests.

Always try to check the credentials of any person or organization to whom you submit work. Word of mouth is obviously the best recommendation, so ask around to ensure you are getting value for money.

We said earlier that writing can be a lonely business, but you will have noticed by now that the world of writing is teeming with possible contacts and with people from whom advice and encouragement can be obtained.

There are also creative writing organizations and societies that run workshops, lectures and creative writing weeks. Writers' groups and adult education creative writing courses may also be taking place near where you live. These can be wonderfully stimulating and beneficial: you may be set tasks, be asked to read out your work in front of the class, discuss your own and others' work, and have your writing corrected if it needs it.

There are also MA and BA courses in creative writing in colleges and universities, and you might wish to explore these as a potential way of learning the 'proper' way to hone your craft. Even if later on you decide to move away from the accepted norms of story-telling, it is vital to know what the rules are before you start breaking or ignoring them.

If you have been writing in private until now, the thought of presenting your work in public may be very daunting. On the other hand, you may be eager to get up in front of an audience and share your work with them. Either way, you are going to need to develop a thick skin. Your writings are your *babies*, the fruits of your heart and soul, the result of days, weeks and months of effort. No matter how you view your writing, it is certainly going to be very personal to you and revealing it in an open forum will be a major – and for some, traumatic – experience.

How good are you at dealing with criticism?

Throughout your writing career you will *have* to deal with rejections and put-downs. Think carefully before you choose to present your work in public. Perhaps you need to give yourself a little more time to hone your skills and temper your spirit. Do not run before you can walk, and do not allow a potential talent to be crushed before it has the chance to blossom.

In a creative writing class, you should always keep an open mind about criticism and advice. But at the same time, make sure that the advice or criticism you are receiving is pertinent to your situation. If the person advising you has had only the one book published, say, 40 years ago, on techniques in postmodernist beekeeping, then you might wonder whether he or she is really in any position to comment on your brilliant new idea for a young adult novel or pre-school picture book.

Believe in yourself, but keep in mind the needs and requirements of the market. If you have an absolute brainwave of an idea, do *not* discuss it with other people: they might very well sneak off and write it themselves whether deliberately or subconsciously. The benefits to be gained from further education or from creative writing classes will be to have your writing skills checked and improved as well as stimulating your creativity, *not* to give away your best ideas.

It is not enough to feel confident of your language; you also need to be able to present your work in an acceptable fashion. Stories circulate occasionally of some *idiot savant* whose barely legible scribbles on the back of breakfast cereal packets are snapped up by a publisher and transformed into a novelty bestseller. As far as *this* book is concerned, such unusual events are irrelevant to the fact that *your* work *must* be presented to a publisher in a professional way.

Can you type?

It's a sign of the times, but these days, when people want to communicate non-verbally with one another, they are more likely to reach for a keyboard than a pen. Don't bother watching the skies for the planet-wide invasion – the take-over has already happened – we've been colonized by computers and we're rapidly becoming their slaves. No, don't panic – it's not all bad – computer files and e-mails are wonderful tools for the budding writer.

You will need to present your work to a publisher in a professional form. This means either in black type on white A4 paper or as an e-mailed computer file or disc. The finer points of professional presentation will be dealt with in Chapter 9, but meanwhile, can you type? If you cannot, then life is going to be very difficult, and it will definitely benefit you to learn.

Certainly you could employ a professional freelance typist to produce your final copy either on paper or computer file, but this approach has distinct disadvantages: it is expensive; it means you will not be able to do any last-minute fine-tuning; and if the manuscript needs to be revised, either a fresh paper copy will be required or you will have to go back to your typist to amend the computer file – meaning yet more expense.

You may have a friend who can type. Three or four manuscripts/revisions down the line, you may not! On the whole, it is far better for you to acquire the skill yourself. Typing and keyboard skills courses are available through adult education classes, schools, correspondence courses, software packages for computers, and from teach-yourself-at-home workbooks. You will be able to learn at your own pace. (If you are presently a two-fingered typist, you could improve your keyboard skills, speed and accuracy and, moreover, prevent the very real risk of repetitive strain injury.) It may mean going back to basics, of course, and unlearning all those bad habits, but the results could be worth the effort.

Basic equipment

Your work might begin with notes scribbled on slips and scraps of paper. You might have a notebook or a sheaf of lined writing paper, but however you get down to the business of writing out your ideas, you need to make yourself comfortable both in terms of your environment and the tools you use.

Roald Dahl would exile himself to a shed at the bottom of his garden. Gary Paulsen uses a laptop on his boat. J. K. Rowling used a series of cafés when she started out, and J. R. R. Tolkien commented that he could not put a word to paper until he was all but obscured in a fug of pipe smoke.

Pen and paper

If you choose to write initially in longhand, then you may have a favourite old pencil, or a fountain pen or black ballpoint pen. Use whatever instrument suits you best, but remember that this method of working can only be temporary – at some point you will have to use a keyboard.

If you use lined paper, then leave a gap of at least one line between your writing. This will help you when you come to revise your work. It may help to do revisions in a different colour pen, as this will show you how your work has developed. Provide yourself with wide margins and write only on one side of the paper: the reverse will give you additional space for alterations and additions.

Computers

A computer is not as cheap to buy as a pen and notepad, but you will find very quickly that the benefits far outweigh the cost, especially if you have children or other people in your household who will be able to take advantage of the computer in your down-time.

Once again, before you dash out with your credit card/cheque book/sock full of cash, you need to do some research. For a start, introduction to computer courses are widely available and will help you get some idea of the kind of system most suitable to your needs. On the other hand, if you have children or know anyone else who has children, they will very likely have become computer-literate at school and will quickly be able to get you up to speed on the basics.

The first step in buying a computer is to find yourself a reputable retail outlet with knowledgeable staff and a good after-care service. Word of mouth, once again, is as good a recommendation as any. You should buy the best system you can afford. It is also possible to get very good second-hand or re-conditioned equipment. Do not allow yourself to be intimidated by computers – for your purposes at the moment they are just typewriters with big brains. All you initially need to know is how to create a computer file and how to save your work when you take a break, and how to store it so that you can find it again. And the really great thing about computers is that they check your spelling for you as you go along and will advise you if your grammar is a bit suspect.

Learning to use a computer is no different to learning how to drive a car, or figuring out how a new food-mixer or DVD player works – and once you have mastered the basics, you'll find that a whole world of possibilities opens up to you.

Laptop computers also have their advantages – they are portable for a start, meaning you can work perfectly well when you are away from your normal work-space, and they will give you the same access to e-mails and the Internet as a desktop computer. The only thing to bear in mind is that, on the whole, a laptop will be more expensive than a desktop – so you need to weigh portability against expense, especially at this stage.

Once you have learned how to open and use a computer file, your next step should be to discover the delights of e-mail and the Internet. Trust us – within days you will be wondering how you ever lived without them. As we mentioned before, the Internet is a source of worldwide information that you have to explore to believe. All you need is a search engine – and the rest is virtually done for you. Want to know the average annual rainfall in Peru? It will take you about 30 seconds to find out. (In case you're interested, it's about 1 inch in the arid west, 34 inches in the cooler areas and an alarming 160 inches on the eastern flanks of the Andes – and it took us less than a minute to come up with the question *and* find the answers!) A whole world of knowledge, both mainstream and unbelievably obscure is literally at your fingertips once you master the Internet. And with the advent of broadband, you can now use a single telephone line to access the Internet while someone else makes a telephone call at the same time.

Sorry, but that word *research* is going to appear again – there are many Internet Service Providers out (ISP's) there, and each of them will offer a slightly different package, so you should find a provider who will give you what you want at a price you can afford. This can range from 'pay-as-you-go' packages – meaning you pay for the exact amount of time you spend online – to 'flat-rate' monthly one-off payments with no additional charges. But read the small print before you decide – your cheap one-off payment will have conditions attached, and you may find that only a certain number of hours a month are 'free' – and that you will incur extra charges if you go over your proscribed limit. You will also find that you are offered different speeds and different extras in different packages – again you must decide which best suits your needs, and you may want to start small and upgrade at a later stage.

The ability to send and receive e-mails is also becoming essential. Although it is still normal for unsolicited manuscripts to be presented to publishers in 'hard-copy' (paper) form, you may well find that correspondence from an interested editor will soon take the form of e-mails and attachments – especially when you get to the editing and revising phase. That said, publishers still expect and prefer new writers to submit their work on paper – round-robin e-mails sent to every publisher you can think of will not endear you to anyone, so make the effort to get your initial submission down on paper.

The day may well come when you get an urgent e-mail requesting biographical details and a photograph by return so that these can be submitted to a committee discussing your book and deciding whether or not to go ahead with it. For this, nothing but e-mail will do the job. And as your career progresses, you may even find it worthwhile to build your own website to publicize your work worldwide and to keep in contact with fans.

One final word – make sure your computer is protected against viruses and other problems by investing in a recognized virus checker, spam filter (to avoid unwanted junk mail), and even a 'pop-up' blocker – many are available for free trial periods from the web. The last thing you want is for something to infect your computer and destroy days, weeks or months of work. Finally, a power surge-breaker for your plug sockets will also prevent potential problems caused by a disruption to the electricity supply.

Save your work!

When using a computer, it is vitally important that you remember to save your work. Most computers have an automatic saving system that will save at regular intervals without you needing to take any action, but at the end of each writing session, you *must* copy your work onto a separate backup disc which should then be labelled and dated, and/or printed out, or transfer your data onto a USB pen. Keep your work disks, USB pen, and your printed typescripts in a safe, element-proof place. That way, even if you suffer a catastrophic hard-drive crash, your only immediate concern is finding an alternative computer on which to continue working.

Insurance

You should have accident insurance cover for your computer. Some household contents policies may cover such items, but some do not. Also, some buildings insurance policies do not cover your home if it is also your workplace, especially if you occasionally receive business visitors, or your name is published. Authors, check your cover!

It is also important to have your computer insured in case anything goes wrong with it. Purchase an extended service warranty when you buy your machine, and renew it when the cover runs out. The last thing you need is an inoperative machine and the prospect of a large bill to get it repaired, not to mention the delay and inconvenience of finding someone to repair it. Remember, it is important to get your computer up and running again as quickly as possible – without it you may not be able to work.

Reference books

There are many books available which can help you with your writing. Authors' societies may have recommended reading lists. You may wish to start off with one or two 'beginner's guides' and then expand your collection as your interests and needs evolve.

Three books will be of particular value.

A dictionary

A dictionary is essential. If you can afford only one book, then it should be an up-to-date dictionary. Do not borrow your great-uncle's school dictionary: language changes quickly. A simple contemporary dictionary should be sufficient for your writing needs, and some browsing through the pages may well open your eyes to what words are now in common use and are considered an acceptable part of the language.

A thesaurus

A thesaurus can be very useful when you are stuck for the exact word you need, or if you want to avoid repeating a word or phrase. A thesaurus will provide you with lists of alternatives to keep your writing sharp and sparkling with interest. Seek the advice of a bookseller or librarian on which thesaurus will best suit your needs.

A writers' reference book

Any one of the annually updated writers' reference books contain enormous amounts of useful information, from publishers' and literary agents' addresses, to prize awards and guidelines on copyright.

You may find that these resources are also available online, but we would still recommend that you buy the books – you will find that it is easier for you to place Post-it® notes into the pages of a book to mark relevant words or suggestions or passages than it is to be popping in and out of web pages all the time.

With particular regard to writers' reference books, it is vital that you buy or access the most recent edition. Information about publishers and agents and so on changes rapidly, and you do not want to be sending your submission to someone who has not been working at your chosen company for a couple of years.

This is another reason for not trusting what you read on websites.

Spell-checkers

Ode to spell-checkers
I have a spelling checker
I disk covered four my PC.
It plane lee marks four my revue
Miss steaks aye can knot see.
A checker is a blessing.
It freeze yew lodes of thyme.
It helps me right awl stiles two reed,
And aides me when aye rime.

— Author unknown

A spell-checker on your computer is a great asset. However, these are not always sufficient or workable. For instance, a spell-checker cannot differentiate between words such as 'bear' and 'bare' which could be potentially embarrassing, not to mention 'there' and 'their'.

It is also as well to check whether your system has an American or English spelling list. Many words are spelt differently in Britain and America. You can set the spell-checker dictionary to the appropriate language and terminology.

Also, if you are checking a long piece of work which contains made-up words or names, or a non-fiction text full of abbreviations or unusual words, then a spell-checker will go mad highlighting the whole lot and you will be left to laboriously explain to your machine that all these words are OK, and to add them to the dictionary.

Never rely totally on your spell-checker for accuracy. You must always read carefully through your work.

Raising funds

One young author on a very limited budget asked her friends and family to help her by supplying her with writing materials in lieu of birthday and Christmas presents. An idea like this is not only very helpful, but such a show of support will lift the morale of any ambitious budding author.

If you are unable to afford a computer, then perhaps you can borrow one or have access to one through work, a library, or a school or college – or even via a friend when the time comes to type up a completed work.

Keep all your receipts for anything you spend money on in direct connection with your writing work. This not only includes paper, ink and so on, but also Internet access, work-related telephone calls, travelling expenses if, say, you visit a museum for research purposes, or for any books you may purchase to help you with a writing project. (See the section 'Tax and accounts', in Chapter 12.)

Bursaries

Bursaries may be available from arts councils, associations or charitable trusts to enable authors to complete a specific project. Conditions vary: money may be made available to a new author, or to an established author who wishes to concentrate on a particular project which would be considered to be of great potential value to the reading public. A fairly detailed explanation of the planned project would be needed, along with some supporting references from people whose opinion would be taken seriously by the judges in the relevant decision-making panel. Such grants and bursaries can be quite large sums of money, enough to enable an author to give up a day job for several months in order to complete a project.

Details are available through libraries, authors' magazines, in writers' reference books and on many websites.

Door-to-door

Recently one of us opened the front door to discover a 'would-be' young writer standing on the doorstep, selling her autobiography from door-to-door. The idea was for you to pay for the book up-front and then to receive it through the mail in a couple of months' time. In this way, the author hoped to make enough money in advance to cover the cost of having the book printed. Always being on the look-out to help young hopefuls, money passed from hand to hand and two months later the book duly appeared. The plan had obviously worked! Now we're not suggesting that this is a great way of getting your book published – it isn't – it's hard work and will give you only a very limited audience, depending on how much shoe-leather you're prepared to work through. But it does show that there are alternative ways of financing your work.

Writing time

You have set up your 'Ideas File'. You have done lots of research. You have learnt to type, and you now hopefully have access to a computer. So, what do you need next before you can start work?

Two things:

- space in which to write
- time in which to write.

The ideal situation would be to have your own writing space, an area used for nothing else. Some authors have a spare room they can use. Others convert lofts or sheds into an organized (or disorganized) office: computer on desk, comfortable writing table, typist's chair and bookshelf with dictionary, thesaurus and other books at arm's reach. (To many authors, this scenario would be paradise on earth!)

Whatever space you can squeeze out of the general maelstrom of your life, try to make it as comfortable and convenient for yourself as possible. You cannot be creative if you are too hot, too cold, too cramped or crammed into an uncomfortable chair or trying to write on a washing machine in spin mode.

Some authors conduct their business from bed; others work at the kitchen table or a desk in a hallway or under the stairs. Wherever you work, aim to make it somewhere as peaceful as possible so that you are able to concentrate (even if your idea of peace includes Wagner operas or hip-hop as background music).

Quite a few full-time authors and illustrators dislike the solitude of working from home and find that a better working environment is created for them by renting a desk in the corner of a busy office – which proves that peace is a pretty flexible concept. Other authors need absolute silence and solitude if they are going to be able to function at all. The least interruption can close the brain down for hours.

The telephone can certainly drive authors crazy. Imagine: you are in the middle of a complex piece of writing when the telephone rings. You pick it up, have a conversation that lasts only a couple of minutes, and then return to your desk only to find you cannot remember for the life of you what was going to happen next.

Make it clear to friends and relations that working at home does not mean you can be called up every half-hour for a quick chat. A five-minute telephone call can result in the creative part of your brain being scrambled for an hour or more. If you have a real problem with this, then you might be wise to disconnect the telephone for the duration of your writing-stint. Alternatively, put the telephone out of earshot, bury it in the garden or, if you can, buy an answerphone or messaging service and let it take messages until you have finished work.

If you are able to allocate a regular daily or weekly time for writing, then make sure *everyone* is in no doubt that at those times you are to be left alone, short of winning the lottery or the house catching fire. Ask friends not to drop by for a chat. Tell your partner or your children that you require to be *invisible* for *x* amount of time. If all else fails, insert earplugs and lock yourself in your room.

> *I have to be disciplined about answering phones and glancing at e-mail: responding to something here-and-now is so much easier than the long-term rewards of writing. Don't fall for the myth that you can just 'get everything out of the way' before you start: you never will!*

Create a space where you can leave your work and know it will be unmolested. It could be somewhere as simple as a drawer or an out-of-pets-and-children's-reach shelf. Wherever it is, keep it as organized as you can: it does you no favours if it takes you half an hour to get yourself sorted out every time you want to return to your work. Get into the habit of putting everything away in an orderly and accessible fashion every time you stop working.

You do not want to lose the scrap of paper on which you jotted the brilliant but complicated best-selling idea that came to you in the middle of the night. Keep it somewhere safe. Similarly, you do not want your finished manuscript to arrive on a publisher's desk covered in coffee stains, muddy paw-prints or smears of marmalade from a midday snack. An organized approach should prevent all the above problems.

> *Finding time for writing is very difficult – especially as I have three young children! I would say that frequency of writing is more important than the total number of hours put in. I try to manage an hour a day – after the children have gone to bed, and there are also a couple of mornings where I go to work late and I can write for an hour or so after the kids have gone to school. I always put in a good stint on Sunday mornings while my wife looks after the kids – then I take them out in the afternoon.*

You should treat writing in the same way as you would treat studying for an examination. Create a writing routine. If you try to fit it in now and then, you will probably find the 'thens' outnumber the 'nows'. Pick a time when your mind is at its most alert. If your brain is a seething cauldron of creativity first thing in the morning, try to set aside an hour before you go to work, or before the rest of your household awakes.

Perhaps your mind sparks best when you return from work: try to devote an hour or so to writing before you do anything else. Perhaps your inventiveness peaks late at night – a time when you are less likely to be derailed by telephone calls or ringing doorbells. Perhaps weekend mornings provide you with the peace you need.

Your individual circumstances will dictate when you can write; the important thing is to fight for your writing time and to make it an absolute habit, breakable by friends and family only on pain of swift retribution.

Some authors make it a point to produce one finished page per day – about 250 to 280 words. That may not sound like much, but do that for one year and you are looking at a 365-page book. Other full-time authors set themselves specific deadlines, this being the only way they can push themselves to complete a piece of work.

Deadlines can be very helpful because they force you to plan your work systematically, If you are one of those people who have to make time to write then a deadline is invaluable – it makes you put everything on hold while you do the work.

A deadline definitely helps me ... knowing I have to write a certain number of words each day or week or month does get it done.

The ideas mine

Authors get their ideas from absolutely everywhere, but it may help if we divide the harvesting areas into three main categories.

First-hand

First-hand ideas include things experienced by you personally, or things which happen to people very close to you. They can be events from your own childhood, or from any time in your life, where the experience would relate to something which you could use as the starting-point for a project – for instance, sibling rivalry between you and a sister/brother, or between you and close friends. These experiences will range from the traumatic to the hilarious, but the important thing for you to do is to swim back though your life and try to revive your feelings of the time.

- You spilt red ink on your mum's favourite cushion while she was out. You put it into the washing machine and then into the tumble drier. Black smoke poured out of the tumble drier and when you opened the door the kitchen was suddenly full of burnt feathers. Not funny at the time – but now it would make the basis of a cute comic short story!
- Your best friend came to school with unexplained bruises on her arms. What was going on at home? It may be that you never found out – but now it could form the spine of an emotionally engaging story.

- Your parents separated. How did you cope? What did you feel? Include it in a story.

Use your own life as an 'Ideas File'. Delve back and into yourself: your experiences may one day help another child to understand his/her own situation, and to realize that other people have had the same problems.

Perhaps you notice that your own child is afraid of thunderstorms. What might help? A picture book, possibly, which explains exactly what thunder and lightning are and why there is no reason to be scared.

If you are a parent, or have regular contact with children, the important thing is to see things from a child's perspective. Adults frequently believe that *their* wishes and opinions should take precedence over those of a child. If you are going to write for children, you must forget all about that. The priorities of children are quite different from those of an adult. Not less important, just *different*.

For example, children perceive time in a very different way from adults. Half an hour can seem like an eternity to a child. The agonizing, anticipatory wait of two whole weeks for a birthday party to take place can reduce a child to a tearful, gibbering wreck on the actual day. You must try to remember what this felt like if you are going to speak believably to children through your work.

Books for young adults often explore the gulf in understanding between parents and children. You can tackle this only if you enter the world of the young person and address the conflict from his/her point of view. Try to remember the battles you had as a teenager with those adults who wielded authority over you, be they parents, teachers, the police or whomever. How did *you* feel when these people tried to impose their will on you?

Remember your own feelings of enchantment when you were a small child. Think back to the time when quite small things held an entire world of fascination. A walk in a wood where *anything* could be lurking. A secret tunnel known only to you and your friends. The first time you noticed the shadows on the moon. Faces in flames and the shapes to be found in clouds. Desperate alliances and sundered friendships.

The lives of children teem with imperatives. Who is your best friend? Who do you hate most in all the world? Children live on the brink of triumph and disaster minute by minute. You need to live it with them. Never be squeamish: dive in!

Second-hand

Second-hand experiences are those that are repeated to you or observed by you, but which do not directly involve you. Such experiences could include, say, an overheard conversation between children on a bus or a train, or happenings related to you by friends or relations.

Obviously you are going to be one step removed from the intensity of such experiences, but your job as an author is to soak up all the elements, be they comic or tragic, and to tuck them into your 'Ideas File' for future reference.

It may be that a single aspect of someone's anecdote sets your story antennae twitching, a throwaway comment that is hardly relevant to the main thrust of the story but which strikes you as having potential. A word of warning here: not everyone relishes the idea that everything they say to you is just grist for your writing mill. If you hear a story which you just *know* is a sure-fire winner, then make some judicious changes. Adapt it, maybe by changing the sex of the main protagonists, altering the location, making changes in their social background. Create new characters from aspects of several different people. Edit the story so that the heart of it – the spark that ignited your interest – is still there, but construct around that, a world created in your own imagination. (We will mention libel in Chapter 09.)

Perhaps you notice some piece of social behaviour between children which you find interesting, intriguing or amusing. Jot it down and file it away.

Be particularly aware of the rhythm and dynamics of speech. A good rule of thumb for an author is to keep the mouth shut and the ears open. Listen to the way people speak.

Take an 8-year-old child: how does he/she speak to friends? How does he/she speak to children he/she does not know? How does he/she speak to older children? To younger children? How does he/she speak to adults – parents/guardians/authority figures? It will not take long for you to notice that children use a multitude of differing modes of speech, adapting themselves to their circumstances in a very sophisticated way. A sweet-faced little cherub may be very polite and biddable in front of adults, but may mutate into a bullying, screaming banshee once let loose among his or her peers.

A few words of advice concerning dialogue. The only way you are going to be able to write convincing dialogue is by listening to real people talking to one another. Do not try to learn this from books, television shows, films or radio. In all these media, a filtration and editing process has already taken place. You need conversation in the raw, untouched by any other writer's hand. When you have written a piece of speech, read it aloud to check if it feels right in your mouth and whether it sounds natural when it hits the air.

Third-hand

The third-hand areas from which you can get ideas are those where you have no personal contact with the story at all. They split into two sub-headings.

Reported

You may notice an item on a television news programme which takes your interest. You may read the report of an incident in a newspaper, or hear of a real event via the radio.

> *A missing 8-year-old boy was rescued today from the basement of a part-demolished building following a two-day search. He was exhausted but unharmed, having fallen through rotting floorboards whilst exploring with a friend. The delay in discovering the boy was due to the fact that his friend was too scared to tell his parents of the incident as they had been specifically told to keep away from the demolition site.*

This story is adapted from a real incident reported in a television programme. From an author's point of view, it has several areas of interest. There is the incident itself, of course, written as a kind of adventure, but an author will be interested in what was going through the minds of the two boys at the time. One trapped in the dark, the other just as trapped by the fear of recriminations. And then you have that moment when the second boy finally had to tell his parents what had happened. Powerful stuff!

How about taking the lives of the two boys on a few years, and writing a story of them as teenagers? What sort of effect would that incident have on their future relationship? How will the second boy be coping with his feelings of guilt that his delay in telling the truth could easily have been the cause of the other boy's death? What if these two boys are interested in the same girl? Might the boy who was trapped use the story to put the girl off the other boy?

As you can see, the possibilities are endless, and all this from a fleeting snippet of news, jotted down and filed away when everyone else had forgotten all about it by the next day. Similarly, headlines, web pages, odd paragraphs and photographs clipped from newspapers and magazines can prove to have enormous potential.

There is a phenomenon called 'cab driver's eye' which is used to explain the way in which a cruising taxi driver's eyes are constantly swivelling around in search of a potential fare. You should learn to cultivate 'author's eye'.

Refried

Whereas the previous section on reported events concerned itself with real incidents reported through the media, the *refried* third-hand area is where you glean ideas from other authors.

We need to be perfectly clear what we are talking about here. Stealing other people's ideas is not only cheating, it is also illegal. It is called plagiarism and must be avoided. However, this does not mean your own imagination cannot be sparked by something that happens in a book, play, movie, television or radio programme you happen across.

For example, one author wrote a book which told the story of 'mad' Mrs Rochester from *Jane Eyre*. Mrs Rochester was a shadowy figure kept incarcerated in the attic of the house; her main contribution to the story comes when she escapes and burns the house down. Having read *Jane Eyre*, this author found herself wondering what it must have been like to have been that locked-away woman, and thus her book was born. (*Wide Sargasso Sea* by Jean Rhys.) Likewise, a playwright took a single, almost throwaway comment in a Shakespeare play and wrote a play of his own based upon it. (*Rosencrantz and Guildenstern Are Dead* by Tom Stoppard.)

Consider myths, legends and fairy tales. These tales have survived because they tell a riveting story which has the ability to transcend changes in society, sometimes over many centuries. If you are short of ideas, you could do a lot worse than read a book of Greek, Japanese, Aztec or Russian folk tales and legends.

'Sleeping Beauty' could be brought up to date and written as a story of a girl in a coma and how her boyfriend copes with the situation. 'The Ugly Duckling' is the universally understood story of any child who learns to throw off some burden and be themselves. One editor to whom we spoke commented that Verdi's opera *Rigoletto* had provided at least two storylines for a well-known American teen-fiction book series.

By now you will have realized that every single thing that you see or hear can have potential for your work, be it in the world of fiction, non-fiction or education. All you need to do is reach out and grab it, file it and personalize it.

Hunter/gatherer

Have you considered investing in a pocket digital recorder or in a mobile phone that allows you to leave yourself reminder messages? You may find it more convenient to simply *speak* an idea into such an electronic device rather than write it down. Otherwise, a small notebook or diary will do the job as an initial holding-pen for your daily observations, thoughts and ideas. Whatever method you use for recording your fieldwork, you will ultimately want to bring your findings home and make use of them in your 'Ideas File'.

Dr Johnson said that there are two kinds of knowledge: the knowledge which a person carries around in his/her head; and the equally important knowledge of where to *find things out*. One of the points of your 'Ideas File' is to save you the trouble and potential heartache of trying to carry everything around in your head – but it is also important that the material you have accumulated is easily accessible.

Be professional in your approach to storing your 'Ideas File'. We mentioned earlier the possibilities of a drawer or large envelope. This is all very well if your research is minimal and based on a single project, but if you are (and you *should be*) engaging in a permanent general trawl for ideas, then you will very rapidly find yourself with a towering heap of paper which takes an age to delve through.

The perfect 'hard-copy' solution to this problem is, of course, a proper filing cabinet with a sophisticated index system. This may not be as far out of your reach as you might think, providing you have the space. Ex-office filing cabinets, from small, two-drawer affairs to five- or six-drawer giants, can often be purchased relatively cheaply in second-hand office-supply stores. Or again, you could take a look at one of the many 'selling' magazines. An office clearance could land you a real bargain.

Failing this, a drawer in a desk would do the job, or even a drawer in an ordinary cabinet or chest of drawers, provided everyone is told that the said drawer is not to be stuffed with socks, pieces of motorbike engine or any other old junk. There are also box-filing systems available in stationery stores, in which a fair amount of information can be kept tidily.

Of course, by far the most convenient way to store your ideas is in your computer. Open different folders for different topics. New Work. Current Work. Old Work. Then put carefully titled files into the appropriate folder – preferably with a date on them: 'New Book – working copy – third edit – 12-01-2007 – so you can instantly see which is the latest version of files that have gone through several incarnations. This is particularly vital if you are working with a publisher and various copies of your book are flying back and forth with different layers of editing on them. Keep all the versions – just name them accordingly – you never know, an idea edited out at an early stage may need to be re-inserted later on.

If you invest in a scanner or a digital camera, you can scan or photograph items or objects that will be of use to you and have them in a clearly labelled folder for ease of access: 'New Book – newspaper clippings', 'New Book – research photographs'.

The important thing is to implement a system which you understand, be it alphabetical, numerical or cross-referenced, on paper or computer. You should have files for specific projects and files of general-interest items. A separate file for pictures and another for newspaper cuttings. Files of character ideas and files of storyline jottings.

If your project is a non-fiction or educational one, you may wish to subdivide your work into topic or chapter headings, and store information that way.

Remember, careful planning at this stage will save you a lot of trouble in the long run. If you planned on decorating a room, you would need to get everything in order before you started – unless you found it entertaining to take a trip down to the local DIY store mid-work with a length of pasted paper in your arms and a perplexed expression on your face. Writing is exactly the same. Some well-considered preparatory work will help you enormously when you come to actually sit down and get the project started.

Exercise 5

After all that concentrated information, a pause for some light relief. One author told us that to get ideas, he often turns common situations on their heads, or headlines from newspapers or television back to front. For example, a newspaper headline, 'Lottery hoaxer fools family' becomes 'Family fools lottery hoaxer', and a storyline is born! Or you could juggle those fridge-magnet words until something interesting emerges. Write out some ideas (fiction or non-fiction) or cut out headlines, chop them up into word-sized chunks and juggle them around. This is an excellent activity if you have a creative block. If an idea emerges, sketch it out now, before you read on.

04

what to write and who to write for

In this chapter you will learn:

- how to choose the genre of writing best suited to your talents and aspiration
- how to shape your work for the market
- how to organize your work.

You may already have very definite thoughts about the areas in which you want to write. You may have specific ideas for the fiction market: an intergalactic octopus which crash-lands in your hero's bedroom; girls from witch-school who use magic to spy for their country; a gritty urban update of *Little Women* or *Winnie the Pooh*. Or you may want to write a factual book which explains the human respiratory system in words and pictures; or possibly an exciting pop-up book on glass-blowing as a leisure activity. Whatever your reasons for choosing a particular field of work, there must have been some initial spark which made you sit bolt upright in bed one night or suddenly go glassy-eyed in the middle of a conversation and realize you wanted to *write*. The task before you now is to nurture that initial spark and to turn it into a blazing bonfire of controlled creativity.

But first, a word or three about the astonishing diversity of the children's market. You will already be aware of the most obvious division – the one between fiction and non-fiction – but there's a lot more to it than that.

Fiction

How is fiction defined? One renowned author was asked by some intellectuals to define 'the novel'. They were probably hoping for some obscure observations which they could take away with them to ponder at length. However, the author thought for a moment and then came back with the comment, 'It's telling a story.' The delightful thing about this response is that it pricks pomposity as well as nailing the truth.

The point of fiction is to tell a story, any story, in a way that will hold the attention of the audience. Story-telling is as old as humanity itself. No matter how far back you research into human history, you will always discover the relics of story-telling, from the aboriginal cave paintings in Australia to the hieroglyphs on the walls of Egyptian tombs.

In many cultures the tale-bearer was an important person. In ancient Rome, poets would be hired to tell elevating tales of the behaviour and misbehaviours of gods and goddesses, as well as recounting, in verse, the deeds of more earthly heroes. In those days, oratory was a great skill, especially in cultures where the average person did not read or write, and the maintenance of a cohesive social structure was reliant on people who could tell stories which bound people together by way of a common story-telling ancestry.

The earliest stories, as far as we know, were usually attempts at explaining events and phenomena beyond ordinary understanding. You could almost think of them as *science fiction*: they were attempts at making sense of the world in a way with which the human brain could cope. How do the seasons of the world change, and why? What forces are at work changing the shape of the moon? What are earthquakes? Who tows the sun across the sky and where does it go at night? If you sail beyond the horizon, what will happen to you? What wonders or terrors lie beyond the sealed doors of death?

On the white, outer edges of old maps were written the words 'Here be dragons', but someone somewhere first had to invent the idea of dragons, just as someone somewhere created the idea of flying horses, magic rings and gorgons with serpents for hair. Equally, someone else invented androids and 'warp-drive' and little grey aliens who abduct people and experiment on them in interstellar spaceships. You never know – maybe you will invent something that will fascinate readers 500 years hence. After all, *someone* has to come up with this generation's marvels. There is one thing in this world that flies beyond all boundaries, and that thing is the human imagination.

Without getting too philosophical, the idea of the difference between 'fact' and 'truth' can be explored within the bounds of fiction. A myth or legend concerning the activities of Greek gods may not be factual, but it contains an enormous amount of *truth*. It is apparent in many ancient religions that the gods and goddesses frequently behave in ways that are all too human. They are capable of being devious, brutal, aggressive, compassionate, arrogant, loving, angry, stupid, thoughtful, selfish, brave and cowardly.

Myths, legends, parables and fables all have a similar root: they seek to enlighten while entertaining. And the more an audience is *entertained* the more likely that audience is to remember the kernel of truth at the heart of a rip-roaring yarn. This balance between enlightenment and entertainment leads us neatly on to a very salient point in writing for children: the best way to convey a message is to give the impression that no message is being conveyed.

You may be deeply concerned about the environment, or wish to warn young people about the dangers of drug abuse; you may think a little morality needs to be introduced into children's behaviour. Children can spot didacticism and moralizing from miles away. You would be amazed at how speedily a child can vanish if someone is telling them something that is perceived as 'being good for them'.

A story can be of value, even if it contains no social message or moral at all. It can be valuable as pure escapism. It can simply be *fun*. Children's writing certainly forms an aspect of their education, but that does not mean children should not read simply for pleasure. After all, even if the story is just a piece of escapist lunacy, the child will still be absorbing aspects of grammar, punctuation and syntax.

> *Anything can spark an idea. A conversation with a child, an item on the news, a random 'what if?' thought, a dream ...*

> *The unexpected coming-together in the same place or at the same time of a number of things that I feel strongly about, or that I find particularly fascinating.*

> *Useful plot starters are folk and fairy tales, legends and stories of old.*

The great thing about myths, legends and fairy tales is that their universality gives them the power to be constantly reinvented to suit each new generation. Ghost stories have lost none of their impact despite the attempts of science and physics to prove (or disprove) their existence. In past days, ghosts haunted the wild woods or distant, crumbling towers; these days, they lurk in office buildings and drive spectral cars down twilight streets.

In brief, the business of fiction is to present an audience with something that is 'truthful' (that is, believable or at least capable of creating a willing suspension of disbelief), but not based on *fact*. The Greeks had Ulysses; the Norsemen had Beowulf; the Anglo-Saxons had Robin Hood – mythic heroes all. The 21st century has the reinvention of favourite modern characters such as Batman, Spiderman and Dr Who, and favourite stories such as *Star Wars I, II,* and *III, The Lord of the Rings, Sin City, The Incredibles* and *The Fantastic Four.*

Categories of fiction

Fiction breaks down into several categories. Publishers are always on the look-out for modern-day humour. If you can write page-turning contemporary stories that make people laugh, your chances of being published are really quite healthy.

Then there is fantasy, sword-and-sorcery, horror, scary/ghost stories and science fiction. The common thread in these areas is that they take the audience outside the accepted laws of nature, to an elven city, a wizard's chamber, a werewolf's lair or a desert planet beyond Betelgeuse. A word of warning: the market is already saturated with such books – you will need to come up with something startlingly original if you want to get published in this category.

Historical fiction is another category of fiction (but think twice before embarking on yet another telling of the legend of King Arthur). A story of children caught up, say, in the French Revolution will need to be heavily researched and very accurate. Even then, the most meticulously researched and presented story may not find a publisher in such a limited area. If the area of history you have chosen is being studied by children at school, your chances of interesting a publisher increase. However, in historical fiction the story must come first. The text should not read like a documentary with the addition of token fictional characters.

Romantic fiction can draw a large young-adult audience, as can thrillers and crime stories. Research your market, looking at different publishers and their series to get a sense of the range of acceptable styles and limitations. Romance can range from growing friendship to potential parenthood, from historical to contemporary settings. But in a book that includes thrills and chills, or involves gangsters and criminals – you will need to know how far you can take the gore factor and what level of violence is allowed.

Books with a school setting have always been very popular – children can readily identify with such instantly recognizable surroundings, empathizing with characters as they encounter everyday problems presented in a page-turning way. Similarly, books following the adventures and misadventures of a group of friends always go down well – although once again you will need to come up with a compelling new angle if you are to hold a publisher's attention.

Publishers are also always on the look-out for 'series' ideas (that is, an idea in which a regular cast of characters will appear in a succession of books). There are enduring favourites such as the Beatrix Potter tales, Flower Fairies, and Mister Men books. Now Lemony Snicket, Alex Rider, and many more series such as Rainbow Magic which sell a lot of books by allowing an audience to follow the ongoing exploits of well-known or established characters.

Series books follow the adage of 'giving the public what they want', by variations on particular themes. Such books can safely be bought in the knowledge that they will involve known characters in known situations.

There is also a call for poetry and plays for use in schools, as well as themed poetry collections for the general trade market. Poetry has never been an easy area for new authors to make their mark. You may need to establish yourself on the poetry scene first (via competitions, readings, poetry circles, etc.).

In the young-adult market you will find a certain amount of *issue fiction*, in which contemporary social issues are explored. Such books have to be of a very high standard if they are to find a home in the limited market area.

Non-fiction

The range for non-fiction work is enormous: it can cover anything from a short piece in a magazine to a multi-volume encyclopedia.

You may have noticed that your own children are interested in watching tadpoles transform into frogs. You decide to write a piece explaining the various stages of the transformation and outlining the optimum ways of looking after them. Add some information on amphibians in general, a few thoughts on their dietary habits and the environment in which they best flourish; mix in a series of diagrams, illustrations and photographs, and you are well on the way to developing one of those 'How To Look After Your First ...' books that are found in bookshops, supermarkets, libraries and pet stores everywhere.

Alternatively, you may be an expert juggler. How better to pass on your skill and knowledge to children than by writing everything down in an article or a short book? Juggling could be put into a wider context – the performing arts, for instance. Your piece on juggling could become but a single chapter in a book about street theatre or the circus. A skilful juggling mathematician could even incorporate juggling into an explanation of the laws of probability and calculus. A biologist could use juggling to introduce a work on how it is that the human body is capable of such dexterity.

Any and every activity under the sun is capable of generating its own non-fiction guide. How to play football. How to use face-paints. How to make cookies. How to find bugs and where to keep them. How mobile phones work and how to use one. How to build a magic castle out of empty toilet rolls and discarded egg-boxes. How to cope with the measles and why you became ill in the first place.

History

Who built the great pyramids of Egypt? Who invented gunpowder? What sparked the American Civil War? When did men first travel to the moon and back?

Geography

Where is Egypt and why did its ancient peoples rely so heavily on the annual flooding of the Nile? What is the Great Wall of China and why was it built? What happens when an agricultural society clashes with an industrial one? Why do earthquakes happen?

Science

How were the pyramids built by a society that had not even invented the wheel? What are the component parts of cement and how does it hold buildings together? How did people manage to get a rocket to the moon? Why are many scientists so worried about the depletion of the ozone layer – and what exactly *is* an ozone layer anyway?

As you can see, non-fiction subjects can be viewed in many ways, and each viewpoint will give an enquiring author a fresh angle from which to go about their work (be that person a teacher, an interested parent, an expert, or just someone who wants to find something out for themselves and then share their knowledge with others).

It is a famous observation that most creative writing starts off with the phrase, 'What if ...' What if there was a book for children explaining DNA (deoxyribonucleic acid – the building blocks of life) in an entertaining, amusing and informative way? Is there?

Areas of non-fiction

It is admittedly early days in this book for a lot of technical information about publishing practices, but it is worth pointing out that non-fiction divides into two main areas: trade non-fiction and educational non-fiction. An author would need to investigate both markets before embarking on any project, as they both have quite different and separate requirements.

Trade non-fiction includes those books or articles in magazines (including specialist magazines – *Sewage Pumpers Weekly* or *Penguins for Pleasure and Profit Monthly*, etc.) which you might buy for home consumption. Trade non-fiction includes everything, in fact, from *Living in Space* to the hugely successful, fun non-fiction titles of the *Flaming Olympics* and *Horrible History* variety. Trade non-fiction will appeal to the general market, as well as school purchasers.

Educational non-fiction is primarily bought by schools and colleges for educational purposes. These can range from reading schemes to foreign language workbooks. These books will have been commissioned with the school curriculum needs specifically in mind.

Faction

As this hybrid word suggests, 'faction' is the skilful combination of fiction and non-fiction. Most people will have encountered this method of story-telling via films or television mini-series which dramatize the life and loves of Marilyn Monroe, or the lives, loves, divorces and beheadings of Henry VIII's six wives. Anything which purports to shed light on a historical character or event in a dramatized form is actually 'faction', be it the life of Gandhi, the Battle of the Bulge or the events surrounding the 9/11 terrorist attack on the Twin Towers in New York.

Books in the faction area include historical 'I was there'-type works in which the author 'sees' great events through contemporary eyes. This can be a very effective way of bringing historical subjects vividly to life, although, as with all non-fiction areas, thorough research is vital. Having an Egyptian child riding a bicycle to go and watch the building of the Great Pyramid of Cheops would not endear you to a potential publisher. Neither would a Roman mother calling:

'Clytemnestra! Agrocrytes! Come on in – your pizza is ready!' Or *did* the ancient Romans eat pizza? Find out before you write about it.

Dramatized biographies can also bring past lives into sharp focus, as can dramatized versions of catastrophes or extraordinary events: the Black Death, the Asian Tsunami Disaster or the life story of the inventor of the jet engine can all be made more real to young people by giving them a contemporary, dramatized voice – although beware of writing a fictionalized account of a *recent* disaster or you may be accused of exploiting the suffering of others. Similarly, a book for very young children about going into hospital, starting school, ballet lessons or learning to swim, can benefit from the faction approach.

Just when you thought the range for children's writing had become bewildering enough, we now throw a few more thoughts at you. What about comic strips? What about children's magazines? How about sticker and activity books, puzzles, painting and colouring? What about original material for first publication on the Internet? By now you will have realized exactly how diverse the world of children's writing actually is, and where your book, *The Trousers of Destiny – Leg-wear Down the Ages*, will find its warmest welcome.

Suiting the language to the child

Time for a bit of role-playing. You are 7-years-old and are spotted by your peers reading a book clearly labelled 'For readers aged 5 and 6'. Your friends fall about laughing. What do you do? It's a no-brainer, isn't it? You dump the book and make sure you never touch anything like it again – no matter how tempting it may actually look. Or it's just as likely that you won't need peer-group pressure to help you decide to avoid books specifically shown as being aimed beneath your age or literacy range or, more to the point, below your 'cool' range! And it's just as likely that you would even keep away from books that are aimed at your *own* age-group. You are far more likely to 'read up' – to go for books in which the main characters are a few years older than you are.

Many publishers divide their children's lists into very specific reading and interest ages, particularly those aimed at the younger readers. They do this in a variety of ways, from the deliberate inclusion of a target age on the cover to colour-coding or age-coding labels on the jackets, all of which are intended to push their product into the correct pair of hands. Whether this type of categorization is a good idea or not is open to debate, but while such methods are being employed, it is important for an author to understand what is going on.

The main reading age-groups have often been divided by publishers in this way: 0–2, 2–5, 6–8, 7–9, 10–12, 12+. Some publishers may take a more broadly defined colour-coding or series jacket design approach which liberates children from an age-based reading straitjacket. As times and trends shift and change, these divisions and approaches are altered, abandoned, re-thought and then embraced again by publishers – and you will need to follow the current developments and tendencies as you go along.

Children throughout the world learn to read at different times, at enormously varying speeds and in very different ways. Remember that a book written and published in England could easily end up being read in Russia, Belgium, Korea or Zimbabwe. The majority of children start full-time schooling around the age of 5 and will usually be reading alone and silently by the age of 7. But children's education and reading abilities vary enormously for many reasons, and text which one 7-year-old will discard as too simple may well cause problems for a child of a similar age but of a different reading level. The task of the author is therefore to aim their work squarely at the middle of the appropriate age-group and to pick up the average child.

The requirements of publishers for the language and level of books vary so widely that an author must research (yes, that word again) the market and aim his/her work accordingly. For instance, picture books for the very young may consist only of 12 words. Further up the reading scale, an illustrated storybook may consist of 2,500 words, and a book aimed at the young adult market could be up to 80,000 words. There are exceptions to this rule, but it is unwise to present a potential publisher with a book aimed at 12-year-olds which weighs in at 250,000 words.

Another useful tip, as we pointed out above, is that children like to read of the exploits of people slightly older than themselves. So, whatever age-range you are seeking to write for, position the leading characters either at the top end of that group, or slightly above it. For readers aged 8–12, the age of the protagonists in your work should be 12+, and a book aimed at 7–10 year-olds should have characters aged mainly between 9 and 11. This is simple psychology and no more demanding than choosing a birthday present that is just a little older than the child for whom it is intended. (Young-adult magazines appearing to target an audience in its mid-to-late teens are actually aimed at and read by children as young as 10.)

Fluent readers are going to devour everything from picture books, sometimes with a very adult subtext, to books that would generally be thought beyond their ability or interest. C. S. Lewis, the author of the Narnia series, observed that his childhood was spent in a house teeming with books of every type, form and nature, some intended for children, and some emphatically not, but that he was denied access to nothing. Given half a chance, an inquisitive 8-year-old could have a field day with a copy of *Bridget Jones' Diary* in much the same way that an 80-year-old might still enjoy the exploits of Ratty, Mole and Mr Toad.

Exercise 6

The average child's ability to understand written information changes as that child gets older. As a writer for children, you must be aware of those changes and judge correctly how to approach children of varying ages. To this end, as a useful test of your ability, write a series of letters, all on the same subject and each aimed at a different age-group. The subject can be of your own choosing, but make it something that would be of interest to children of all ages – a description of a forthcoming event, pop concert, party or holiday.

First write your letter in such a way that it can be read to a pre-school child by a parent or some other adult.

Next, write the same letter for an 8-year-old.

Now write it for a 13-year-old.

Finally, try writing it for a 17-year-old pen-pal from another country whose first language is not your own.

Points to note:

- Try not to 'talk down' to your audience. A 13-year-old is unlikely to see the funny side of being written to as if they were only 8, and a 17-year-old, despite any limits on grammatical comprehension, will expect to be treated as an adult, so ecstatic descriptions of jellies and finger-painting will not necessarily be appreciated. Similarly, something which may be of great fun to an 8-year-old (a disco tent at a fête, for example) is unlikely to have much resonance with a 4-year-old.

- Your use of language should alter, from being simple and lucid for the youngest audience to more advanced and complex for the older readers. Correspondingly, your terms of reference must shift in perspective to suit the reader's interest level.

- If possible, you should get a parent, teacher or indeed a child of the appropriate age to 'criticize' your letters. The last, of course, is the best way of discovering whether you have hit the mark, but in any event, seek out someone whose opinion has some authority or experience behind it, and then take heed of what you are told. You should then attempt the exercise again – taking on board all the hard-learned advice, comments and criticisms. You will see a marked improvement in your work. You are on the way to being a professional writer.

Styles

He often changed his residence: and during his various travels, while he visited the most celebrated parts of the south of Europe, his admirers in England were indulged with the productions of his powerful and versatile muse: sometimes proudly soaring into the pure regions of taste, breathing noble sentiments and chivalric feelings: at other times, descending into impure voluptuousness, or grovelling in sheer vulgarity.

This extract is a quote about Lord Byron taken from a book of biographies published in 1845. What clues are there to place that huge sentence in its native time? Its labyrinthine length, for a start. The writer is producing work for an educated minority readership for whom the style of the description is as important as the information being conveyed. There is also a very particular moral tone being struck.

We spoke to one author who described being accosted by the chairman of a school's board of governors (and would-be author) and told very effusively how much this interlocutor liked semicolons, and how he lamented that modern publishers tended to erase them and break an elegant single, multi-clause sentence into several smaller parts. It probably never occurred to him that these despised modern publishers were concerned more with making books reader-friendly than they were with the elegant preservation of ponderous prose.

Two thoughts:

- always keep your audience in plain sight
- brevity is the soul of wit.

Your job is to communicate, not to construct soaring conceits of grammatical whimsy. Say what you want to say as lucidly and briefly as you can. (This does not mean blandly, of course.) Telling an engaging story in 800 words is a lot harder than stretching out the same story over 30,000 words.

Exercise 7

You might like to explore the above point by describing the area immediately surrounding you in a sentence of not more than ten words. Take your sentence to another person and see if they can get any real feel for the place that you have described.

This is not as easy as it sounds, and you may wish to try a number of different approaches as you attempt to grasp the essence of the area being described.

Back to Lord Byron: the sentence we quoted was very much of its time. How might a modern, thumbnail biography approach the same subject?

> *He travelled widely in southern Europe, house-hopping continuously and pausing only to send back his latest works to his English admirers. These works ranged from the lofty and noble to the decidedly earthy.*

The above modernization retains all the information of the original and manages it without a single colon or semicolon, while halving the length of the original.

A children's author must keep abreast of how language changes. You need to speak directly to a modern audience without falling into several traps. These traps take on two main forms. First, there is the use of contemporary 'slang'. You should be very cautious in your use of idioms. Cool slang expressions are abandoned with surprising speed, and having a character say

'See you later, alligator' may have sounded very hip in 1962, but today it just sounds weird (and a few years ago, we might have written 'odd'!). For some time children have used the word 'loser' to describe anyone they despise or pity – or indeed, anyone they wish to insult ('What a *loser*') – and a casually tossed-off 'whatever' is a great way of expressing indifference or boredom. But are they still being used as you read this book, or have they already fallen out of favour? You need to find out. Think about your language before you people your books with youngsters who use contemporary slang in their dialogue. Your work still needs to make sense in five years' time.

Debates are currently raging as to the inroads that texting and e-mails and chat-room shorthand are making into the levels of literacy that children attain. It is an interesting question, and one which you should think about. The knee-jerk reaction of older people is to throw their hands up in horror at the way words and sentences are telescoped and abbreviated, and to fear that this effect is going to shrink children's vocabularies and grammatical expertise away to virtually nothing.

The bottom line is that in a modern society people have a tendency to want to get their point across as briefly and succinctly as possible. In the hit movie *Pirates of the Caribbean: The Curse of the Black Pearl* there is a pertinent exchange. Will Turner accuses (pirate) Captain Jack Sparrow of cheating in a sword fight. Captain Jack just looks quizzically at him and says 'Pirate!' Everyone watching the movie knows what this one word means – it means: 'Of course I cheated – I'm a *pirate*!' So, ask yourself – does this reduce language to rubble, or is it just a quick and neat way of getting your point across?

In other words, are texting, e-mailing and chat-rooming creating huge problems for language skills – or are they just quick ways for a perfectly literate child to communicate with friends? As a writer, you need to get involved in this debate, because your books will form part of the educational matrix of these children's lives. R U up 4 it – or do you deplore the paucity of semicolons in modern children's literature?

The second trap to avoid when writing is to presume that the moral climate in which you are living is the only acceptable one from which to view events. The biographer of Lord Byron did just that. Take another look at how pompous those words sound to today's reader.

You do not have to delve far back into the 19th-century to see how social opinion has changed. Look at the children's books written in the two or three decades after the Second World War and note the behaviour of the girls and boys portrayed in those classic stories. Television series, too, were equally 'guilty' of stereotyping male and female roles. Women and girls cooked and cleaned, while men and boys fought enemies and aliens!

Times have changed, but how often do you read an adventure story in which the hero is in a wheelchair? Or a story where one of the main characters is deaf, not deaf because the deafness is integral to the plot, but simply deaf in the way that people are in real life?

Like the brush-stroke technique of an artist, many authors can be identified by their style, and often the more famous they are, the more obvious will be their stylistic quirks. As an author wishing to be published, you must be wary of 'copying' these individualistic traits. Of course, you can always *learn* from other authors, but the trick is to read widely enough that you avoid stylistic plagiarism (albeit subconsciously) and seek through myriad voices that surround you to find a separate and complete voice of your own.

Organizing your work

For the amateur writer, hitching your creativity to an interesting idea, inviting a couple of fascinating characters on board and heading off into the unknown is all part of the joy of writing. You may start your story with a vision of a small shark rising from someone's bathwater and politely but sheepishly asking its way to the Indian Ocean, but without much of an idea about what is going to happen next; for the professional this is an indulgence you will seldom be allowed to get away with.

Even if your introductory letter piques a potential publisher's interest, it is likely their response will be for you first of all to send in a detailed synopsis ('chapter breakdown') of your book, accompanied by some sample chapters. This is fine if you have already written the book – although it may mean you scrambling together a hastily written synopsis after the event, and possibly finding that when the plot is laid out in this form, certain problems of which you were unaware suddenly become glaringly obvious. (Oh, no – Uncle George couldn't have met the kids at the railway station that day – he was on an aeroplane over Antarctica at the time!) On the other hand, if you are floating a concept for a potential book, you will need to be able to show where it is going. You cannot simply say: 'Pat, George and Freda are teenaged friends who have a whole lot of great adventures, but come out of it OK.' You will have to be a bit more specific than that.

And even if we forget publishers and editors for the moment – you do not want to waste your time in charging headlong into a book which stays on track for the first two months of writing, but which then does a spectacular nose-dive off a cliff because the creative rails have suddenly run out. Putting together a synopsis would have saved you all that wasted time and effort – and will possibly have revealed how a few judicious tweaks and twists at an early stage of the story could have prevented you from crashing. Besides which, it will aid you enormously with polishing your story-telling skills to sit and write out point-by-point exactly what is going to happen through the book. It will help you to clarify ideas and to highlight structural weaknesses before you get started.

Your synopsis for a book could be as simple as a page or two of bullet points, outlining the salient events of the story in the correct order, or it could stretch to a detailed chapter breakdown, set out scene-by-scene and chapter by chapter, incorporating not only the main story-threads, but including proto-dialogue snippets, character and plot back-stories for your own benefit – and alternative possibilities which may or may not come to life once the actual writing gets going.

Many full-time authors are invited ('commissioned') to produce particular works; that is, they are paid a sum of money (an 'advance') on signature of a contract in which they agree to write a specific book (or a number of books) usually on a particular topic for a particular readership and of a particular length. Obviously a publisher will want to know what they are getting; hence the author will usually be asked first to submit a proposal and then more detailed outlines of character and intent.

Following this, a publisher will usually ask for a full synopsis of the story so they can see exactly what the author intends to write, and so they can make editorial comments early on, thus preventing the problem of a major rewrite at a later stage.

Synopses are not only of use to publishers. You will, by now, know that books in all age-groups have quite tight word-limits. It is taking a real chance for a writer to start a book for 11-year-olds without much idea of what is going to happen, but with the hope that whatever does happen will resolve itself exactly to the word limit. In other words, a professional author *has* to have a pretty good idea of where a piece of work is going, if only to make sure it gets to its conclusion at the right time and not 2,000 words short or 5,000 words over the acceptable length of the book.

Some authors sit down in a locked room and write and write until the story is all there in front of them. Some write thumbnail sketches then wander off for a while to let their ideas simmer and stew. Others use the 'tumble drier' approach, in which the plot is allowed to rumble around in their heads until it resolves itself.

Still others take a long walk to thrash out complicated plot lines. Others use the 'orienteering' approach, in which individual ideas are run up mental flagpoles in a more-or-less straight line from chapter 1 to chapter whatever; the task then being to map-read your way from flagpole-to-flagpole.

Then again, the plot may come to an author piecemeal and out of order, starting life as a heap of scraps which need to be sorted out before a coherent pattern emerges. A plot may start from a single observation which clicks with something that has been languishing in your 'Ideas File' for months. Marry them up and see what happens.

A synopsis presented to a publisher is not written in stone, and plots can be altered as you progress when better ways forward present themselves. Do not be afraid to make radical changes if second thoughts turn out to be better thoughts. And be prepared to have to rewrite existing chapters if a brilliant idea suddenly hits you halfway through a book but requires 'seeding' earlier on. (A computer makes this sort of rewriting a total breeze!)

Some authors accost their friends, family or partners and use them as sounding boards or alternative brains when plots are being devised. If you have no children of your own, then the children of a friend could prove an invaluable source of ideas. A couple of hours with a child can produce better results than six months of staring at a blank sheet of paper or screen.

Some authors like to keep their synopsizing to a minimum, simply sketching out the plot and leaving the details for the full writing process. Others will write formidably detailed, scene-by-scene, chapter-by-chapter outlines that leave nothing to chance.

The fact is that you must discover the plotting method which best suits you, but we emphasize that you must not be afraid of changing things in midstream if new thoughts occur. Very few authors really know exactly how they plan on getting from A to Z: after all, the journey is all part of the pleasure. We will cover this more fully in the next chapter, when we discuss plot structures.

Checklist

- Target your market.
- Make sure that your idea fits the target audience for whom you wish to write.
- Make sure the level of language and so on suits the age-group for whom you are writing.
- Similarly, make sure the length of the work is suitable for the market.
- Write a full and coherent synopsis.
- Do not include dialogue or material which is unsuited to the age-group you are targeting.
- Try to get into regular contact with children of the appropriate age.
- Do not use transient slang.
- Try to make your work as 'timeless' as possible.
- Aim for the average ability level of the age-range for which you are writing.
- The age of your main characters should be at the top end of the intended reading age-group.
- Be frugal with those adverbs and adjectives, and aim to keep the narrative bright, lucid and engaging.
- And, lest you forget, enjoy yourself!

05 the basics of writing fiction

In this chapter you will learn:
- the essentials of story-telling: storylines, plotting, character and situation, structure and narrative voice
- how to hone your style
- how to revise your work and overcome writer's block
- how to create a publishable work of fiction.

You don't need to be a mechanic to drive a car.

Meaning what, exactly? Theatre critic Kenneth Tynan once remarked that a critic was a person who knew the way but could not drive.

Our point is that a good author can be a person who knows how to drive the English language but who has only a basic working knowledge of what actually goes on beneath its figurative bonnet. In other words, you do not need a Master's degree in English in order to be an innovative, successful and published author. Of course, you need to be gifted with an eye and an ear for language and an ability to present your personality on the page in an engaging way, but that does not necessarily mean you need to know why a pluperfect is a pluperfect, nor why a phrase is not a sentence, nor why the plural of 'foot' is not 'foots'. A highly academic knowledge of your language may help you to produce a very polished piece of work – but no matter how grammatically perfect it is, it may still bore your audience to tears.

A good eye for words on paper and a highly tuned ear for conversation will take you a lot further than years of technical tutelage. As long as you have mastered the basics of your language, you should become your own teacher and your classroom the world around you. An author, particularly of fiction, is selling his/her personality via the medium of the printed word. Your job is to make the ink and the paper or screen dissolve away from your reader and to leave only the pleasure of a well-told story.

Storylines

It is widely said that there are only three basic plots in fiction, subdivided into seven classic plot lines derived probably from the Greeks and later used by the likes of Shakespeare *et al*. We decided to track down a more definitive answer to this 'rumour' and ended up posing the question on the Internet. Replies came back from all over the world, from university professors to librarians. Here are some of the responses:

1. *Cinderella (rags to riches)*
2. *Faust (the debt has to be repaid)*
3. *Achilles (the fatal flaw)*
4. *the eternal triangle (man plus woman plus X)*

5. *the spider and the fly (good versus evil)*
6. *Romeo and Juliet – a tragedy (boy meets girl, boy loses girl, boy gets girl back)*
7. *the great 'romance' (X meets Y, they hate each other, then they fall in love, then they live happily ever after)*
8. *the twister – at the end of the book, you realize nothing was quite what it seemed.*

Several of the respondents claimed that there are in fact up to 36 dramatic situations, and provided lists to prove it.

Nevertheless, however many archetypal plots there may actually be, one publisher boiled the whole affair down to this: 'There is a problem. The problem develops. The problem is solved.' This is known as the 'beginning', the 'middle' and the 'end', without which story-telling ceases to function in any coherent way. For any plot to give satisfaction to its audience, these three simple elements have to be presented in appropriate proportion: for instance, you do not want the beginning to drag on until about three-quarters of the way through the book, and for the middle and the end to get crammed into the final couple of chapters.

This may seem pretty obvious, but one agent told us of a manuscript they received in which the *actual* story did not get off the ground until the final chapter; the book seemed, in fact, to stop dead just as things were getting interesting, having wasted thousands of words on totally unnecessary introductions to a whole bunch of extraneous characters and events. Publishers and agents often receive manuscripts with 50-page introductions or very promising picture book stories which fall badly out of balance when the author tries to wrap the plot up in the final couple of sentences. This kind of thing happens when an inexperienced author dives head-first into writing a novel without giving much thought to where they are going with the story or why they are going there. Pause here to remember what we said in the last chapter about the importance of walking through the plot in synopsis form before you start writing.

So, ask yourself a few hard questions before setting pen to paper or finger to keyboard.

What do you want to say, and why do you want to say it?

A work of fiction must be inspired by *something*. Even if the idea seems to have sprung fully formed from the depths of your imagination, you can bet your life it has been gestating away in there for a while – inspired possibly by some snippet or scrap in your now fully formed 'Ideas File'. Having brilliant ideas, though, is only the first part. Next you need to get your brilliant ideas into some coherent form.

The importance of this exercise is two-fold: firstly, to see whether your idea or mix of ideas has 'legs' – meaning, is it big enough to fill your intended word-length – and, secondly, to find out if you have the creative passion and enthusiasm to follow it through in detail over a period of weeks or months.

A point worth pondering over: if the idea of rigorously thinking your story through and writing it out in synopsis form sounds a bit tedious, then perhaps you are not quite so passionate about the whole thing as you think you are.

Story lengths

Remember what we told you about the way publishers approach their market? Books for young adults are generally longer than books for the 'middle fiction' range. These are, in turn, longer than storybooks, and storybooks are longer than picture books. In other words, if the characters or events you have come up with steer you towards a young-adult audience (12+), you need to draw the plot out to cover about 50,000 words, or more. If your characters and the things they do better suit a 10–12-year-old audience then you are looking at approximately 40,000 words – and so on down the age-range.

You may think that a length of 50,000 words gives ample scope for 'off-the-ball' episodes and character studies, but bear in mind that the modern world is full of distractions, and a 14-year-old is no more likely to put up with long, dry, uneventful passages than is a 6-year-old. In longer books, plots may become more involved and convoluted, but always keep your 'average' reader in mind and never get carried away by whole chapters that will only confuse and frustrate your audience.

Plotting

Mystery is one thing, profound confusion quite another. It is perfectly acceptable to string a reader along with clues and red herrings, but in the end everything must make sense. The reader of a crime thriller or mystery story must be able to look back over the book once they have come to the denouement and wonder how they were so dumb as to not spot all the clues strewn across the preceding chapters.

Like one of those three-dimensional pictures, in which the image leaps out at you when you look at it in a particular way, a thriller, mystery or crime story must, in the end, have a clarity of plotting. Of course there *are* books and films which do not seem to supply all the clues, or provide all of the answers, or may be deliberately oblique. While these may seek to provoke our imagination, they can also be tremendously frustrating and unsatisfying.

Murder/mystery/crime-type books need to be very carefully thought out. For example, the usual method of plotting crime stories would be to start with the initial 'event' (murder, theft or other crime), then leapfrog to the 'resolution' before starting on the laborious process of working out how the two ends of the story are to be linked together.

A murder mystery

Professor X is found dead in her study with an axe embedded in her skull. That is your event; the purpose of your story is to discover who did the embedding and why.

Your hero or heroine will be the person who unmasks the villain. Your villain will be the murderer, who leads your hero a merry dance right up until the last page, when the hero turns, points an accusing finger and says, 'That person did it, and I will now tell you how and why!'

Exercise 8

You are writing a detective novel. Your lead characters are a girl and a boy aged about 12. A theft has taken place at their school: the charity box has been raided.

The two youngsters have a pretty good idea who the thief is. Come up with thoughts on the following:

1 Who stole the money and why?

2 Why do the youngsters suspect the thief?

3 Why do they seek to solve the crime themselves rather than pass on the information to the authorities?

Here are some obvious answers:

1 The money was stolen by the headteacher to feed a secret gambling habit.

2 The youngsters saw the headteacher coming out of the room where the money was kept only a few minutes before the theft was reported.

3 They dare not tell anyone because who would believe the word of two students against that of their headteacher?

So as not to make things too easy for yourself, now come up with three different ways of setting up that plot without the headteacher being the villain.

Your hero need not be particularly clever, nor young, nor sighted; your hero could be an engaging, affable but slightly dim person who discovers the truth by accident while looking in entirely the wrong direction. Your heroine need not be a member of a police force, or from a police officer's family; she could be the caretaker's daughter, who saw something odd on the morning of the theft but to whom no one will listen.

One of the problems with thrillers or crime stories where children or young people are the lead characters is that ingenious methods need to be thought up to explain why adults do not take over the whole investigation. It is your job as a children's author of such plot-driven books to come up with plausible reasons why your protagonists do not tell any adults what is going on.

Another style of story-telling is the 'twist ending' – where a reader's assumptions about the book they have been reading can be totally upended by some stupendous revelation on the last page. Without giving any plots away, books of this type which you might like to investigate would be *The Turbulent Term of Tyke Tyler* by Gene Kemp or *Waiting For Mermaids* by Sue Welford, or if you would like to investigate an adult novel that brilliantly undermines at the end everything you assumed was happening, try Iris Murdoch's *The Black Prince*. Children can derive a lot of fun from finding that their preconceptions were all wrong – but this kind of story-telling needs to be done with great subtlety and skill if it's going to work – and bear in mind that if you hope for a second reading, there will need to be more to your book than a sneaky ending.

Characters and situations

Let us go back to the original questions of 'what' and 'why' for a moment.

What are you writing?

Has a fascinating character come to you? Someone whose life and adventures you are desperate to write about because the person in your head is so interesting? Archetypes have been Toad of Toad Hall from *The Wind in the Willows*. A. A. Milne's Piglet from the *Winnie the Pooh* stories, Long John Silver, Pippi Longstocking, Heidi and Peter Pan. These characters are so strong, rounded and well defined that they have survived for decades and the books which feature them are still being reprinted and read today. But as well as being great characters, they all have something else in common: they are all attached to an engaging plot.

Strong characters in interesting situations

Has an amazing adventure come to you when travelling or in a dream or while you were watching television? It could involve helicopters, frantic rescues from underground caverns or from spaceships careering into the heart of the sun. It could involve the protagonists in fearful perils and extraordinary split-second rescues from massive explosions – but even a plot stuffed to the rafters with action and thrills requires an additional element. It requires the reader to *care* about what happens to the people to whom all these amazing things are happening: if two people are skydiving with faulty parachutes, the reader has to want them not to hit the ground with a nasty splat. Even the most thrilling, nail-biting plot needs to be peopled with characters whose safety and survival is of some concern to the reader.

If, as sometimes happens in plot-driven stories, the characters are fairly two-dimensional, then they have to be placed in a situation where their actions are important on a wider scale. For example, animal rights warriors have released thousands of infected and mutated rats from a mad professor's lab. Josh Blank and his team must recapture all the rats before they infect the whole population, and millions of lives are lost. Josh and his gang may be of relatively little importance in such a book, but their actions will be of vast importance to the reader if disaster is to be averted.

So, here are some basic equations:

> Characters without a plot = nice people – shame they've got nothing to do. Yawn.

> Plot without characters = plenty of action, no involvement. Where's my PlayStation®?

Think of all those 'disaster' movies in which you have paid to see a major catastrophe and lots of spectacular special effects. First, though, you will be introduced to the characters whom the disaster is going to affect. The more you care for and believe in those victims, the greater your emotional involvement.

Far too many scripts arrive on publishers' and agents' desks in which the covering letter points out that the enclosed novel has 'something for everyone'. Wrong! For 'something for everyone' read 'written in a totally unfocused way and probably completely unmarketable'.

Different approaches

Different types of fiction require different approaches. For instance, a thriller should end most chapters with a cliff-hanger, so that the reader is desperate to find out what happens next. A character-led book should have chapters that end with some dilemma facing one or other of the characters, again so that the reader is forced to start a new chapter in order to find out how the problem is resolved.

Short chapters are generally a good idea. A reader may see a five-page chapter and think, 'I'll just read one more chapter before I put the light out,' whereas they would put the book down for the day if they saw that the next chapter was 25 pages long. Psychologically, bite-size chapters can easily draw a reader into gobbling up much more than the few pages they intended.

Chapters do not need to be of a uniform length, although their lengths should not vary too wildly. A chapter needs to encompass a scene or series of interlinked scenes which have some basic cohesion and, as we said above, they should end at a point which leaves things unresolved. Then the *next* chapter should end with a vital point unexplained so that the reader just has to start reading the following chapter, and so on right through the book.

Dialogue has the effect of breaking the page up and of avoiding big blocks of narrative. Have your characters do most of the talking, if possible, and limit your narrative asides to scene-setting and to important explanations.

If your book follows several characters all doing different, perilous things at the same time, you could leave Tania hanging off a cliff for an entire chapter while you show what her pal Eddie is up to. Then you can drop a piano out of a window beneath which Eddie is standing and leave him in imminent danger of being squished while you go back to see how Tania is getting on, still clinging grimly to her cliff-edge.

Why are you writing this story?

Presumably you have an idea or a series of ideas which you believe others will find fascinating. Inside your head, these ideas may well be totally stunning, but the test of your writing skills will be how well you can present them to your audience. As with most things, first impressions are vital. Most agents and publishers will tell you that they can spot a 'winner' within the first paragraph or, at worst, within the first three pages.

So, how do you kindle their enthusiasm?

In a work of fiction you will need to introduce your characters, put them in some sort of context, and give some inkling to the reader of what sort of book this is going to be. However, you cannot hope to achieve all of these things on the first page. Page one needs to involve something that will grab your reader by the lapels and absolutely *demand* that he or she carries on reading. Most of your background detail can be sketched in a few pages later.

For instance, the book can begin with a knock on a door. The door is opened. The dialogue makes it clear that the person inside the house knows the visitor but is shocked by them turning up so unexpectedly.

The first chapter can then continue by describing the reaction of the various people inside the house to the new arrival; and during these exchanges the relationships of the various people can become clear. The chapter can end with a decision having been made as to whether the visitor is allowed to stay in the house or is thrown out again. (The unexpected visitor could be an errant teenager returning to the family home after an unexplained absence of several days/weeks/months.)

With the situation and the main characters now firmly in place, the second chapter could take a reflective look back at how the situation came into being.

Start with a bang

Start your book with a bang – an effect often called the 'crash-start', and explain the reason for the bang later on. Look at how action/thriller films get into gear. (Observing how a well-written, popular film is put together is just as relevant as dissecting books.) Very often such films start off with the main character involved in some unexplained action. Or the action may not even include the main characters at all – for instance, the movie *The Fellowship of the Ring* kick-starts with a huge battle between good and evil that took place thousands of years before Frodo and Sam were even born. This is an excellent way of grabbing an audience's attention from the very start, and also leads nicely into the relatively slow and quiet manner in which the main characters are then introduced. If the action is gripping, the reader will be prepared to wait a while to find out more on who, what, why and where. And if you are looking for ways to give your chapters a nail-biting end, watching the last few minutes of television soap operas can show you how to construct breath-taking cliff-hangers.

It is not always necessary to set the scene before the action starts, and in a lot of cases, it is far better to leave the explanations until later. If the plot centres on one climactic scene, then maybe a flash-forward could be used as a teaser. For a book involving an earthquake, you could always preface the start of the book with a few pages describing the first few minutes of the quake, before going back into real time and covering the days leading up to the quake.

(Flashbacks can serve a similar function as flash-forwards. The book could start with the 17th-century burning of a witch, then fast-forward to the present day and the lives of people living in the same village, and how the echoes of that ancient event affects their lives.)

Exercise 9

Write the opening paragraph for a book.

Your opening lines should be more interesting than 'Once upon a time' or 'It was a dark and stormy night'. Something tantalizing might include:

- (For a picture book.) The duck crashed through the window and landed in Gemma's breakfast cereal.
- (For middle fiction.) On his way home from school one day, Barney was picked up and carried off by a space ship piloted by an intergalactic octopus with a bad head-cold.
- (For young adult fiction.) Mum was always saying, 'Wear clean underwear. You never know when you might get hit by a bus.' As I lay on the hospital trolley, I didn't know which worried me more: my mum, my underwear, or the fact that my 10-year-old brother, Simon, had been driving the bus!

Question your motives

Why do you want your work to be published? Do you have an overwhelming urge to entertain people? Do you want to share some information or knowledge, or do you simply want to be rich and famous?

Perhaps you have an idea for a series or sequence of books. To be honest, your chances of hitting on a perfect idea or formula without a lot of experience and research are pretty limited. You may have read one book of a successful series and thought to yourself, 'I could do that.' Too late! Someone else has already done it. There is no point in labouring long and hard to reinvent the wheel. You need to come up with an entirely *new* idea, and it will have to include a formula with the potential to run and run. Similarly, it is no good having a great idea for a six-book series which peters out after two or three books because by then you have explored every possible area of interest.

The gulf between being an aspiring writer to being the author of a successful series is immense. But don't discard those brilliant series ideas – just be prepared to be patient. Few publishers are likely to commission an unknown author to produce a series, but the situation may well be very different for an author with a few published works under his/her belt.

What other motives could you have? Maybe you are trying to work your way through some personal problems via the printed word; maybe you have an autobiographical tale to tell; or maybe you have a moral point to make. All well and good, so long as the end-product is *entertaining*. Tales of personal angst, no matter how universal the cause, still need to be 'page turners' (and you need to remember that publishers have their own motives and criteria). Here are some of the questions which may run through a commissioning editor's mind once they have read your story:

- Will it be profitable/inexpensive to produce?
- What are the views of the editorial, sales and marketing departments?
- Will it sell?
- Is it complementary to our list?
- Do I have a slot for it in my publishing schedule?
- Is it a new approach to a subject?
- Who is the author, and what are they like? Will they be good at publicity, interviews etc.?

These considerations should not dictate what you write, but it is as well to have an idea of the thought processes that will come into action if your work is liked by a publisher.

Something else to consider are the constantly shifting fashions within the book industry. A topic which publishers may be falling over themselves to purchase one year may be totally passé two years later. Part of being a successful author is the ability to maintain that vital balance between the personal and the professional. Write what has meaning for you, but keep one eye on the marketplace.

Finding your voice

Is your book going to be written in the first person, or the third person? Is it going to use past tense or present tense? Is it going to include the thought processes of your characters and, if so, how many minds are you planning on giving the reader access to?

We shall deal with these dilemmas one at a time.

First person

First person is where the entire story is narrated by one (or more) of the characters in the book – usually a single, dominant character. In this format, the voice of the author is subordinated to that of the lead character. *Everything* in the book must be written in the voice of the chosen character. All the events in the story must be filtered through the mind and voice of this character. The reader can only know and experience things that the main character knows and experiences.

Obviously, a strong, well-thought-out and rounded character is needed for this technique to work. Similarly, the author of a first-person book has to shade and colour the narration so that it comes across as being within the purview of the age and experience expectations of the speaking character. A 10-year-old narrator will have a different version of a series of events than would a narrator aged 8 or 16.

In a broader context, consider how horseplay between some 10-year-old children which results in a valuable vase being broken will be viewed by the children themselves, and then by the adult who owns the vase, hears the crash and comes to investigate. Try writing this scene in the first person, initially from the child's point of view, and then from an adult perspective.

Here is a start for you:

> Child: *We were only* playing. *I mean, a person is entitled to play, aren't they? And if that vase is so totally priceless then Mum was a bit daft to leave it there in the first place …*

> Adult: *I've told and told you until I'm blue in the face: don't horse around in the living room, you might break something! The moment I heard that crash* I knew *what had happened.*

Can you add a third voice, that of an older brother or sister who has been left in charge of the children? How would that person react to the breakage?

A problem with writing in the first person is that it can be a little tricky to include information which is vital for the plot, but which the narrator does not know. In first-person stories, the reader knows only what the narrator relates (although devices such as, 'I didn't know this until later, but what happened was …' can help out in some cases). Another problem occurs when the story involves several different characters all doing different things. The reader can only learn what has been going on via the narrator being told by these characters. To solve such problems, it is usually preferable for events to be recounted in the narrator's presence, so that information is passed on in a conversational form, rather than leaving your narrator to regurgitate information in large, hard-to-digest blocks of prose.

However, it is possible for a first-person book to be narrated by someone who is not directly involved in the action: 'I'd like to tell you about something that happened to some friends of mine ...' In this format, a coherent but uninvolved overview can be constructed in which the opinion of the narrator may not coincide with the opinions of other characters in the book. The courting activities and rituals of a bunch of 13-year-old girls and boys could be amusingly narrated by a younger sister or brother of one of the protagonists: 'Don't ask me what my 13-year-old big brother Matt sees in her, but he's started getting really stupid over the girl who delivers our morning newspaper.' The benefit of this format is that it 'personalizes' a story. The narrator 'speaks' directly to the reader, rather than through the imposed voice of the author. Thus the narrator becomes the reader's 'friend' in a more immediate way, and if it works well, the reader will feel as if they are having the story related to them in much the same way as friends tell each other stories in the playground.

Third person

The third-person format is where the narrator of the story is separated from the action, and the word 'I' does not appear except in dialogue. The reader is one step removed from the characters in the book, whose activities are related by a 'storyteller'. This kind of story-telling goes back into the days of oral mythology, when poets and bards would chronicle the activities of the gods and the immortals for their audience. The third-person format is useful when a story involves a lot of contemporaneous activity and when the narrative needs to shift constantly from one set of characters to another. It is easy to switch from perspective to perspective in a third-person narrative. For example, one character could be held at gunpoint by the villain of the story while the other characters could be searching for him or her. The third-person format allows the narrative to shift its perspective rapidly from character to character and event to event in a way that would be much more difficult if the book were written in the first person.

Third-person narratives also allow for an element of authorial intervention. A character being chased across moors by a maniac will hardly have time to look around them and describe their environment. But within such an urgent setting, the author through the third-person narrator, will be able to snatch a few moments to describe the scene, and perhaps even to give a voice to the maniac. In some cases it may be vital for the reader to know the reason behind the chase, even though the character being chased does not. This style allows the author to tell the readers things which the leading characters in the book may not know. In a suspense thriller, it adds a lot of tension if the reader knows there is a dangerous maniac in the closet which an oblivious lead character is about to open.

The problem with the third-person format is that it can separate the reader from the characters, although it is perfectly permissible for a third-person narrated book to include the private thoughts of as many characters as the author should choose. Presenting the 'thoughts' of a character can be a useful device, but you need to be careful over exactly how many brains to include to which the reader is allowed access. It will not take long for the reader to work out who the villain is in a 'whodunit' story if they learn the thoughts of all the characters, or all characters bar one. It is usually best to limit reader's access to one or two lead characters, and use the 'thinking' device only when there is no one to whom the character can vocalize their reactions. Dialogue is always more lively than narrative, so when using the third-person format, be sure to allow your characters to 'talk' the plot along as much as possible.

The advantage of the third person is that the author is able to narrate events in their 'own' voice (or in the voice of a disinterested and unbiased third party). It allows for the motives of several different characters to be explored without prejudice and for a number of simultaneous plot strands to be followed simply by dint of the narrator scene-hopping in a way that a first-person narrator would find very difficult.

Exercise 10

Try writing the scene with the broken vase again, this time in the third person. Write it first in the context of a children's book and, therefore, from a child's view, and then from an adult perspective. The two versions should come out quite differently. Explore the differences and think about what you have learnt from this exercise.

Multiple narratives

You can write a book narrated by two or more first-person characters, but be wary of including too many voices – this will just become confusing – or of giving your voices unequal 'talking time' in the book – or of adding a voice halfway through which disappears again without explanation.

A simple device for this sort of multi-voice story-telling is for successive chapters to be headed with the name of the character whose voice is being heard. In this way, you could describe a romance between two teenagers and how characters react to the same events with no authorial overview at all. An evening at the movies for Justin and Sarah might be seen as a great success by Justin. He may tell the reader what a great time he had, how he held Sarah's hand all through the movie and how he is looking forward to their next date. Sarah might have a totally different story to tell. She might tell the reader how utterly bored she was, point out that Justin wore aftershave which was overpowering and had clammy hands, and make it quite clear that she has no intention of ever dating Justin again. Successive chapters could then chronicle the 'romance' from those two sides, with neither of the characters actually having much idea of what is going through the mind of the other while the reader knows *everything*. How might the story be enlivened? What if Sarah gradually realizes her first impressions were wrong and that she really likes Justin after all? And what if Justin, dejected by Sarah's rejections of his advances, decides she is not worth the effort and stops asking her out on the very day that Sarah decides she will finally agree to a date? Such a story could, of course, easily be written in the third person, but think how much more lively and immediate it becomes when the only voices being heard are those of Justin and Sarah.

A favourite first-person format is the *diary*. A number of very successful books have been written in this style, so you would be expected to come up with something quite new and exciting to awaken the average publisher's interest. A particular problem with telling a story in diary format is that it is virtually impossible for events to be given anything other than a very immediate perspective. The writer of a diary is not going to be in a position to explain events of immediate relevance if the explanation does not occur for a few more days. In some types of story it does no harm for the reader to know only what the narrator knows; in others, this lack of an overview, or at least of hindsight, will make the story virtually impossible to convey coherently.

A story can also be written so that it alternates between the third person and the first person. One way of doing this is by the inclusion of letters from one character to another within the general third-person framework. This can help to present the opinions and attitudes of a particular character in a way that would otherwise be less vivid. Returning to the Sarah and Justin story, the date could be described in the third person and without any particular insight into how the two characters felt. This could be followed up by Sarah writing a letter to a girl pen-friend, describing her feelings, and Justin to a friend, telling him how it all went (or at least how he thought it went). The story could even be given a further twist: Sarah could be writing to a male pen-friend, in which case the reader will have to decide whether the things that Sarah writes describe how she really feels or only how she wants her pen-friend to think she feels. Alternatively, how about writing the story so that the reader only thinks the letters were written by Sarah, because they had her name at the bottom, but finds out later on that they were not written by Sarah, but by Justin for his own entertainment, and were his assumptions of how Sarah might be feeling. There's the twist ending we mentioned earlier.

By now you should be realizing that giving a book a voice and format is a complex and open-ended task – much like everything else in the writing world.

Books can also include time shifts. For instance, the first chapter could be set in the present day, but the second goes back six months to follow a different plot strand, or to explain how the present-day plot strand came about. In this manner, the entire book could time-hop through its story – with you keeping the audience up to speed by starting each new scene with a date and time in which the events that are to follow take place.

As part of your ongoing research, approach books, TV, radio drama and popular movies in a more analytical way: note how these media use multi-layer viewpoints – revealing the same events from different perspectives. For instance, in *Harry Potter and the Prisoner of Azkaban*, the action towards the end is a puzzle until both the characters and the reader/viewer realize that a magical time-slippage has occurred and the three friends are in two places at the same time.

Non-human voices

Up until now, we have really been discussing formats for different *human* voices. Yet it is possible to write books in voices that are not human. Here are two obvious examples.

Aliens

You might choose to write a story from the perspective of a creature from another planet. If your chosen creature is a messy green blob from Mars, then you may have difficulty in rounding out the character, but something reasonably humanoid or at least with a reasonably human attitude may allow for a whole sequence of amusing incidents based on misunderstandings between species. An alien race may land on Earth whose method of communicating is via hitting each other over the heads with saucepans. How would this go down among humans?

> *The silvery spaceship comes to ground in the park and a door panel slides silently open. A being appears, clutching a saucepan. The creature proceeds to spell out 'Hello, how are you, my name is Ftunnng' by beating a rapid tattoo on the head of the leader of the welcoming committee with the saucepan.*

A word of warning: success in this format is very difficult to achieve, and you will very likely hit up against the 'get rid of the guy with the pointed ears' attitude, so called because that was the verdict of a high-ranking TV executive when shown the pilot to the original *Star Trek* television series – he wanted Spock dumped because he didn't think watchers would be able to empathize with an alien. The point being missed was that human behaviour can often be thrown into sharp focus when viewed by an 'alien', and Spock turned out to be the hit of the show!

Animals

Anthropomorphism means giving animals human thoughts, motives and rationalities. This is a format to which you must give serious thought before embarking on any work. Unless you are planning on turning yourself into an animal, you will have to stretch your imagination to its limits if you are going to present a book in a first-person animal voice. Really, it is best not to try unless you are absolutely certain of your market.

The one exception to this rule involves picture books. In this context, publishers can find it very useful to have the main characters appearing in animal form, especially in co-edition books (books that are commissioned and published in several countries at once) where, for instance, the colour of the main characters' skin may potentially be problematic in a highly illustrated book to be simultaneously published in France, Senegal and China.

Several very successful books have been written in the third person, chronicling the adventures and activities of animals or groups of animals. Richard Adams' *Watership Down* is one such – he did an enormous amount of research work on the way rabbits behave in real life in order to give his book a semblance of 'reality'. He had to humanize the thinking processes of these animals, but their day-to-day lives were depicted in the same way as an average rabbit's. As an aside, the other classic tale about this famous book is the number of times it was turned down by publishers before finally finding a home.

Animals in clothes are not winners. Animals that live in houses, drive cars or play golf are not winners. The fact that you may be able to cite several books in which animals do exactly those things is irrelevant. Trust us, publishers do not look kindly on books where animals are just furry, hairy, spiky or scaly humans. A clever, well-written animal story can be a real winner, but have a good look around the marketplace to assess the competition before you get to work.

While we are on the subject of non-human voices, there is one area in which we received an almost universal shriek of horror from all the publishers whom we contacted: investing inanimate objects with sentience, emotions, self-propelled movement and voices. True, there have been some notable successes in this field, but generally publishers will run a mile when confronted by 'Fiona the Friendly Frankfurter' or 'Terrance the Talking Table'. The following titles are from a list of stories submitted to a publisher and, to make things worse, handwritten on lined paper torn from a shorthand notebook:

- Greg the Gnome
- Simon the Sea Gull
- Carly the Cat
- Bluey the Budgie
- Charlie the Chimney

- Betty in Bunnytown
- Violet the Vacuum Cleaner

Need we go on? The recipient editor probably read no more than the first page of *Greg the Gnome* before reaching for a rejection slip. One final thought on the talking animals front: on the whole, animals talking to each other is fine; animals talking to humans is not, unless handled with a great deal of skill.

Past, present or future

Past tense, present tense and future tense. Yes, yet more ways to format that story of yours.

Past and present tense

The past tense is the usual way in which to tell a story.

> *He ran across the road. She followed him, dodging the traffic as she tried to keep him in sight.*

Effectively, the storyteller is relating a series of events which have already taken place, and putting them in that context by using past tense.

People will fall naturally into using the past tense when relaying anecdotes, although in some cases, a kind of urgency or immediacy can be maintained by the use of the present tense:

> 'So I say to him, I say, you come one step closer to me with that gherkin, and I'll have the law on you, so help me, I will. And he looks at me with his eyes all kind of narrowed-up, and I think: he's going to do it. And then he comes for me, and I run down the street, yelling my head off, and he chases me, waving his gherkin and shouting, stop! Stop!!'

Or:

> 'So I'm saying to him, I'm saying, you come one step closer to me with that gherkin, and I'll have the law on you, so help me, I will. And he's looking at me with his eyes all kind of narrowed-up, and I'm thinking: he's going to do it. And then he's coming for me, and I'm running down the street, yelling my head off, and he's chasing me, waving his gherkin and shouting, stop! Stop!!'

Now let us try it again in the past tense:

'So I said to him, I said, you come one step closer to me with that gherkin, and I'll have the law on you, so help me, I will. And he looked at me with his eyes all kind of narrowed-up, and I thought: he's going to do it. And then he came for me, and I ran down the street, yelling my head off, and he chased me, waving his gherkin and shouting, stop! Stop!!'

Or a different sort of past tense:

'So I was saying to him, I was saying, you come one step closer to me with that gherkin, and I'll have the law on you, so help me, I will. And he was looking at me with his eyes all kind of narrowed-up, and I was thinking: he's going to do it. And then he was coming for me, and I was running down the street, yelling my head off, and he was chasing me, waving his gherkin and shouting, stop! Stop!!'

So you can see how both present and past tenses can be used in different ways to create different effects. And that is not only true for first-person narratives:

'You come one step closer to me with that gherkin,' she said, 'and I'll have the law on you, so help me I will.'

He looked at her with narrowed eyes and she realized he was about to pounce.

She ran down the street, yelling for help while he chased after her, brandishing the deadly gherkin and shouting, 'Stop! Stop!!'

Present tense:

'You come one step closer to me with that gherkin,' she says, 'and I'll have the law on you, so help me I will.'

He looks at her with narrowed eyes and she realizes he is about to pounce.

She runs down the street, yelling for help while he chases after her, brandishing the deadly gherkin and shouting, 'Stop! Stop!!'

Using present tense cranks up the urgency of the piece. It creates the illusion that the reader is actually there while the event is taking place.

The big problem with using present tense is that it is a little unnatural, and requires a good deal of concentration to make sure you do not find yourself slipping back into the much more comfortable use of past tense.

Present tense has an urgency which leads to plot limitations, especially in connection with first-person present tense – not only does the reader not know anything that the narrator does not know, but there is absolutely no way of covering simultaneous action by other characters or clarifying complexities.

Exercise 11

Using the above examples as guidelines – but without the gherkins – write a page-long piece in the past tense on any topic you choose, and then rewrite it using the present tense. Make a note of how the use of different tenses alters the story – paying particular attention to any difficulties or problems which arise.

List a few examples of the sort of stories that you think would work best in past tense, and those that would benefit from the immediacy of present tense.

Conversation

Consider the following. Picture a scene of rolling countryside. A man and a woman stand on the brow of a hill. It is a block-busting generation-spanning tale of love, revenge, sex, money, hatred, money, wealth, sex, power and money, but not necessarily in that order, written by someone called Sapphire Diamond or Jack Ironstone. A rider approaches on a black stallion. The woman speaks.

> 'Oh! Can it be?' Elvira gasped breathlessly. 'Yes, it's Tyler, my adopted half-brother whom Father found in the gutter and brought home to share our good fortune despite what the old gypsy woman said about him being a black-hearted devil. But why is he here? Father sent him to manage the New York office of our multi-national kippering firm and not to return unless something terrible happened. I have not had word from him these past two years, although we were loving playmates as children and in my innocence I always thought we would be married one day.'

As exaggerated as that speech may be, it highlights a common problem with dialogue: translating conversations into readable and realistic dialogue on the page while conveying all the necessary information.

How do people speak to one another? To unravel this riddle you will need to take yourself off for yet another stint of dialogue research. Go somewhere you will be able to overhear people talking to one another. Listen to how they speak and try to analyze what is going on. This could be a party, meeting or anywhere two or more people are gathered in conversation.

Poor dialogue will let a good story down badly: you must get it right. There is a big difference between real conversations and conversations as they appear on television or in books. In real life, people will start a sentence, then change tack suddenly, stammer over certain words, repeat themselves, digress, stop midway through saying one thing to say something completely different, leave observations hanging in mid-air, half-say things, contradict themselves and talk over one another until language seems to turn into some kind of wildly stirred minestrone soup of sounds, sense and nonsense, meaning and meaninglessness.

It is the job of an author to make sense of this mish-mash of dialogue rather than simply to mirror it on paper.

On the other hand, to remove dialogue too far from its natural origins creates its own problems. 'Real' conversation may be incomprehensible, but obviously 'made-up' conversation is no better. A reader has to believe in the characters you invent, and a major part of that belief hinges on your ability to make those characters speak in a natural and unaffected way.

A good rule of thumb is to speak dialogue out loud. Your family and friends may think you have gone potty when they hear you arguing with yourself behind closed doors, but the fact is that the only way to check whether a line of dialogue or an exchange between characters really 'works' is to hear it spoken out loud or acted out.

As stressed in the last chapter, avoid using the fleeting idioms of the present day. You want your book to be read in 20 years' time, so unless the plot has to be anchored in a particular time-frame, you will want your characters to sound fresh and contemporary to future audiences. Street slang should largely be avoided. In real life, a person may say 'know what I mean?' or 'dude' at the end of every utterance, but on paper this affectation will rapidly become irritating to the reader, and the irritation will be aimed at the author, not at the character.

An aggressive person picking a fight may repeat the same bullet-hard phrase over and over to gain attention. 'You talking to me? You talking to me? You talking to me? You talking to me?' Children will often swear for no particular reason and without aggression, simply because such words are considered a normal part of 'playground' conversation amongst their friends. Swearing and bad language are not automatically removed from books for young adults (although they would obviously be inappropriate for younger age-groups), but you should think carefully before having one teenager character tell another to '*get lost*' in expletives. This has little to do with the moral standards of publishers and editors, and plenty to do with selling books: adults do not necessarily want less socially acceptable language to be seen to be authorized by having it presented to their children in the pages of a book. If you want to write a down-to-earth, nitty-gritty, urban-realism type book filled with drug fiends, teenage thieves and social outcasts, by all means do so – but be prepared for the fall-out and do not be surprised if few publishers show any desire to take it on.

A real conversation does to grammar, syntax and language what a one-kilogram club hammer does to a pane of glass. It smashes it into fragments. Your job is to pick up the pieces, discard what is unnecessary, realign what is pertinent, and reconstruct seamlessly what is left. In real life most conversation is of little long-term relevance. Much of it is anecdotal: explaining the day's events to a friend or partner; retelling an amusing incident or an outrageous one; repeating a tale told by a work colleague or school friend; asking for the salt to be passed; enquiring when dinner will be ready or where a fresh shirt is to be found. You know the sort of conversation we mean. Vital as such interaction is in real life, it should not intrude into written dialogue, unless possibly you are trying to show the reader that a character is having a totally boring evening – and even then it should be done very briefly. No one wants to read pages of irrelevant dialogue.

All dialogue has one of two possible purposes: either it is there to move the plot along, or it is there to deepen the understanding of the characters who are speaking and their relationship to one another. Thus, *keep dialogue short and keep it to the point*. And try to avoid bogging down important dialogue by including mundane and irrelevant activities on the part of one or another of the people speaking. On TV or in a movie, having characters doing things while they speak makes for more interesting viewing – but on the page, this just gets in the way and slows the pace down.

At the same time, bear in mind when you are putting conversations down in print that different people express themselves in different ways. A shy person, for example, with important information to convey will express themselves in a different way from someone with a loud, outgoing personality. A single character will use several different modes of speech depending upon their audience.

How are you going to frame your dialogue? Is anything wrong with the following?

Jeanette came running into the room.

'I've seen him!' she gasped breathlessly.

'Who?' Sasha enquired excitedly, leaping up.

'Alvin Knockersbury!' exclaimed Jeanette impatiently.

'What?' Gladys broke in urgently. 'The Alvin Knockersbury? The pop star?' Her face was alive with excitement.

'Exactly!' Jeanette stated sighingly. 'Alvin Knockersbury. My hero!'

'I like him better than you do!' wailed Sasha groaningly. 'And now I'm going to miss him because Mum won't let me go out.'

'Your mum won't know if you sneak out,' Gladys proclaimed whisperingly. 'Who's to tell her?'

'Him!' Sasha complained despairingly, pointing to the 20-stone guard who clutched the other end of the chain which her mother had attached to her ankle.

'Don't worry about me,' the guard observed smilingly. 'I'm Alvin Knockersbury's biggest fan.'

'Hoorah!' Jeanette whooped exultantly. 'Now we can all go and see Alvin!'

And without further ado the four of them raced pantingly for the door.

This is what is known in the trade as 'adverbitis'. It is a similar disease to 'adjectivitis'. The chief symptom is an author's chronic inability to leave nouns or verbs alone. Why write 'she said' when you could embroider your text with 'sadly' or 'gladly' or 'effusively'? Why use 'said' when you could put 'exclaimed', 'ranted', 'quipped', 'declared', 'opined', 'effused' or 'remarked'? All of these words are perfectly acceptable in moderation: if someone makes an exclamation, then by all means say so; or if a person is breathless, then do not hesitate to mention it. However, these words need to be used sparingly and with caution, otherwise the dialogue becomes overburdened and loses all resonance. Bad dialogue can make even a hardened editor cringe, and the overuse of adverbs serves only to make the author's confidence in their work seem rather limited.

Keep interjections between dialogue to a minimum. There is nothing wrong with a simple 'he said' and 'she said', and if the dialogue is between two people and is relatively straightforward, you could even leave the speech entirely to its own devices and give only a guiding 'she said' and 'he said' here and there as reference points. Be careful if you have three or more characters in conversation: a reader can quickly lose track of what is going on if the author does not reference each comment back to its source. It is no good if, halfway down a long tract of dialogue, a reader has to count his/her way back to the top of the page in order to figure out who is saying what.

On the subject of dialogue between several characters, you should try to ensure that, if there are four people present, each of them gets a word in every so often, even if it means sharing dialogue around more than is usual. A reader cannot see a character who is not mentioned or who does not talk. If a character in a scene neither speaks nor does anything, you would be as well to ask yourself whether that person really needs to be there at all. This is especially pertinent when you have a 'gang' who all meet together. Ensure in any ensemble scenes that everyone gets at least one line to say.

Sharing dialogue around has an additional function, especially in stories that require set-piece explanations (such as a mystery story or a crime thriller). What could become a tedious monologue by one character can be greatly enlivened if shared between two or three, more so if the narrative thread of the explanation or exposition is drawn out by a character who asks questions. There is a story-telling rationale behind Batman being teamed with Robin, Sherlock Holmes hanging out with

Dr Watson, and human companions travelling with Dr Who. They are there, at least in part, to draw out explanations and to break up what would otherwise become boring soliloquies.

Another problem with dialogue can occur when an author is very obviously out of touch with young people and the way they express themselves. Should you not have regular contact with the age-group for whom you are writing, you must find some means of occasional access or, at worst, take to watching children's television. The latter is not the perfect solution to the problem, because it means you are only hearing edited and regurgitated dialogue rather than going to the source – but in the early days it will give you an idea of how professional authors approach their craft and it will furnish you with many useful pointers. In the end, though, you ought to be shaping your dialogue and your characters from the world around you, and not through the filter of fellow authors.

Exercise 12

Rewrite the exchange about Alvin Knockersbury with an eye to removing the excess adverbs and adjectives. As with the example of the Lord Byron biography, retain the meaning and interest of the piece while jettisoning all the rest.

Once you have 'weeded' the exchange, you could pause here to practise on dialogue of your own. It is probably sensible to restrict yourself to two characters for the moment (you can worry about convincingly written crowd scenes later on). Set up a scene where two characters are having an argument, pick your own topic, and give the two characters totally opposing points of view. Write a page-long piece of dialogue.

Use only the word 'said' when you are indicating who is speaking. No 'retorts' or 'declareds' or 'proclaimeds'; use just plain old 'saids'. If you can, do not even put 'she said' every time one of the characters speaks. (But remember, never let a reader lose track of who is speaking.)

Read the conversation aloud to yourself – or even act it out. Could a real person actually have said the words you have put into your characters' mouths? Is the sentence structure correct, or would a person run out of breath halfway through? If you have a recorder, use it to listen back to your dialogue. Does it sound realistic? Can you believe that real people would say such things? If not, why not? Where are you going wrong? Does your dialogue come across as being too heavily written? Does it sound like it comes from a page rather than straight out of a human's mouth?

Once you feel comfortable with your page of dialogue, push yourself a little further by placing two characters in a different situation so that you have to take account of their surroundings as they speak. They could be walking along a street, hurrying through a busy park or out canoeing together. Try to incorporate their movements into an unobtrusive, sympathetic narrative as they argue.

Now take the whole piece to another level by adding a third character with yet another point of view. Add a parent who tells the two children to stop arguing. Include the reaction of the children to this interruption. Add a younger child. Add several more characters. See what effect these people have on the argument.

The aim of this exercise is to take you one step closer to that point where, like the novice dancer who suddenly realizes she has stopped counting out the rhythm, you find your invented characters taking over and speaking with their own voices.

Grammar

We have mentioned the importance of having a good working knowledge of the grammar of the language in which you are writing. To extend this, you should know some of the common grammatical errors which drive publishers to distraction.

Apostrophes cause people an awful lot of trouble. Its? It's? Its'? It is pretty straightforward, and you really ought to try and remember it:

- *It's* is short for '*It is*': 'It's time you went home.'
- *Its* without the apostrophe is used when you want to say something like 'The boat skimmed the waves, its sails billowing in the wind.' *Its* refers back to the preceding direct object to denote the noun's possession of the following noun: 'the sails of it [the boat] billowing in the wind'.
- *Its'* does not exist at all (although that fact does not stop people sticking their apostrophes in the strangest places).
- *Do'nt.* Wrong!! It is '*don't*', a contraction of *do not*. The apostrophe in this case denotes a missing letter, 'o'.

- *Can't*: same thing – a contraction of cannot.
- Likewise *shan't* (shall not), *won't* (will not), *isn't* (is not) and so on.

Also be careful when using apostrophes with plurals:

- *Children's books* (books of the children): the plural, children does not end in *s*, therefore the apostrophe appears before the *s* denoting 'of the'.
- *The boy's book*: one boy, owning one book.
- *The boys' book*. More than one boy, collectively owning one book. The apostrophe appears after the *s*, thereby showing that the book belongs to more than one boy.

Something else to watch out for is dated or archaic language. Whatever time period your story is set in, you are writing for children of today. Phrases such as, 'For he thought he was right' and, 'Algernon was one of those people for whom dancing was easy' read as if the author has been dead for 50 years.

Beginning, middle and end

We have already mentioned the importance of balancing your story across the three areas of plotting. You have to get the reader hooked by an attention-grabbing opening chapter, then you can ease the pace a little to fill in the background and put the characters and the action in an understandable context. You will have your synopsis to hand – explaining the series of events through which your story will probably pass on its way to the final chapter.

We included 'probably' in that last sentence on purpose, as it is quite likely that when you get down to writing the full version of your story, you will find that things change in ways you could not have foreseen. This is perfectly OK, unless you have been commissioned to write a book with a fixed plot, in which case changes will have to be authorized by the commissioning editor. However, if that is not the case, and your story is taking you off into unexpected places, be prepared to go with the flow, so long as that flow does not take you up a blind alley. Keep your planned finale in mind. Rewrite your synopsis, taking the changes into account – plot your new way through to the end. Perhaps the book is telling you that there is a better way to achieve your aim than the one you originally intended.

Here are two different ways of presenting a story.

The surprise ending

As we have already mentioned, this is also known as the 'twist' or the 'sting'. A surprise ending makes the reader follow the characters through a series of events without knowing how things are going to work out. Will they all survive? Will someone die? Who? How? When?

In stories of this type, the tension and interest is maintained by adding unexpected twists in the tail of the plot, false endings, shocks and astonishing last-page revelations.

Note when writing this sort of story that it is not acceptable for all the murders to have been perpetrated by Oscar's younger half-sister who has lived all her life in Ulan Batur and whose existence is never mentioned until the detective drags her from a hiding place behind the potted palm. If you are planning great revelations, you must foreshadow them in some way. It is your job to put plenty of clues as to the existence of Oscar's half-sister, otherwise the reader feels cheated and it looks suspiciously like you made her up at the last minute because you could not think of anything better.

Clues and 'hooks' need to be carefully thought out and skilfully seeded throughout the story. The 'hook' is the means by which the 'hero' escapes certain death. An author needs to insert the 'hook' into the narrative in such a way that the reader is aware of its existence, but unaware of how important it will become later on.

An example

Somewhere earlier in your book, in a seemingly plot-irrelevant and off-the-ball scene, you show that Dirk Sox (a 17-year-old on work experience with an investigation agency) has considerable skill with a rope. Maybe you do not actually mention him lassoing things; maybe someone mentions it in passing. (In a narrative section in a book, it could be shown entirely in passing that Dirk's mum's mantelpiece is full of Golden Rope awards.)

Anyway, Dirk gets himself tangled up in a big international diamond-smuggling conspiracy and, towards the end of the book, is set adrift in a boat only 50 metres away from the edge of a 200-metre-high waterfall towards which the rushing, churning waters are inexorably drawing him to his certain doom.

Previously, you will need to have mentioned, again in passing, that there is a length of rope in the boat. A long mooring rope, maybe? Perhaps the villains who cast Dirk adrift threw the mooring rope in his face as the boat floated away from the jetty.

Now you need one final 'hook' in the shape of a tree stump, pointed hunk of rock or some other geographical feature at the very lip of the waterfall.

(One amazing escape coming up!)

Dirk Sox grabs the rope. He fashions a lasso. He hurls the lasso at the tree stump. It misses! Arrgh! He has time for one final throw before plunging to his death. The lasso catches on the stump just as the boat careers over the edge of the waterfall. Dirk swings through the waterfall on the end of his rope. He is saved!

Why stop there? Why not include a map of where the diamonds are hidden? A vague map which says the diamonds are 'under water'. Dirk swings right through the waterfall on the end of his rope and finds himself in a secret cavern *behind* the waterfall. And in the secret cavern he finds the lost jewels! He has not only saved himself from certain death, but he has solved the mystery of the cryptic clue.

The trick when coming up with death-defying escapes is to have made the reader aware in advance of potential escape devices without being blatantly obvious about it.

Hooks are relevant not only to adventures: all plots need their share of clues and hooks if the climax is to be credibly explained.

The known ending

Another way of writing a book is to let the reader know from the beginning, exactly what happens at the end.

Dirk Sox lies dead, shot by a laser-gun in the holodeck of the starship *Zippo*.

Now go back six months and show Dirk beaming onto the starship. The reader is now hooked on finding out which of the characters Dirk meets on the *Zippo* will be the one to gun him down. Will it be Kitty Zaplitter, the half-human half-feline passenger and secret Dirk admirer? Or was it Kirk Karkus, the brooding captain of the *Zippo*? Or Froog, the green-hued alien amphibian from the planet Glugg? Or Thom Katt, Kitty's unrequited love? The only way to find out is to read the book.

You have all your hooks and clues in place, and you have plotted your hero's way to a brilliant climax. But you have still got to avoid the 'one leap and she was free' pitfall. Loose ends must be tied up, good must prevail and evil be punished, but not all in the final paragraph. The end of your book needs to be planned as carefully as the beginning.

In a particularly gruelling or draining book, it might be as well to add a comic or soothing codicil to the final chapter. That is not to say that all books need a happy ending, but most publishers and book purchasers do like readers to experience a 'feel-good factor' in some shape or form between a book's covers.

High drama or fraught emotion can benefit greatly from moments of calm or comedy. Shakespeare knew this, often throwing 'crowd-pleasing' comic sketches in among all the blood-letting and mayhem. Such scenes not only relieve the tension, but help to throw the more serious elements into sharp relief. Many successful television series and feature films have adopted the comedy-drama format, and many heroes are now heard to wisecrack relentlessly in even the uttermost extremity. 'Issue' fiction can deal with traumatic and upsetting real-life situations. While conveying a 'you are not alone' message, or depicting another's experience, but do children really want to read relentlessly depressing material without a glimmer of hope or humour? Even tragedy can contain elements of farce.

This leads us to another topic of particular relevance to children's writing. It is usually preferable for a hero to outwit or outsmart a villain than to clobber the villain over the head with a large rock. Children like plenty of action; they want the plot to take off like an express train and hurtle breathlessly to its climax, but it is part of your job as a *responsible* author to make sure that any violence is put firmly in context. The more down-to-earth the setting of your story, the more important it is to show violence as a painful aberration and one to be avoided if at all possible.

If your story is reliant on some level of violence, then bear in mind that there is a big difference between 'cartoon' violence and real-life violence. Be sure to show the consequences of violent acts, not just in terms of immediate pain, but in a wider context of long-term physical and psychological damage. Whether your work is aimed at the middle fiction or young adult audience, check other books of a similar nature to determine your parameters for potentially controversial areas such as violence, swearing and sex.

Revising

You will be very fortunate if the first version of your story turns out to be perfect. The only 'perfect' idea is the one that sits inside your head. Once you start trying to tease it out into the real world, it will get battered and bent and knocked about until you may hardly recognize it.

Revising? You can't be precious. Be prepared to chuck out stuff, change, adapt and edit. Learning is about letting go.

I find it helps to leave a piece of writing for a week or two after finishing it. You can then come to it fresh and read it more objectively. Even more helpful is reading a story aloud to a child... you can gauge if your pacing and plot are good by the child's reaction!

Even the brightest diamond benefits from a good polish.

Often, published authors later spot sections in their books that could have been improved. An author commissioned to produce a book will be given a deadline by which that book must be handed over. That deadline dictates the point where revising has to stop.

How do you create your own revision cut-off point (or date) when there is no one around to wrest the manuscript out of your grasp? There is no simple answer to this one. Some authors will simply mark a date in their diary and keep to that.

Writing is work. Set a deadline if one hasn't been set for you and live like a hermit!

It helps to arrange a date to show it to a friend.

As with many aspects of the art and skill of writing, you have to develop a feel for 'balance'. On the one hand, you do not want to present a publisher with something that looks half-finished. But on the other hand, editors have a role to play and a particular editor may well have an entirely different view on how your book should be tidied up.

You could easily spend months and months fine-tuning your book until it is a lovely thing to behold, but how are you going to feel when a publisher says, 'We quite like it, but it needs polishing'?

The response is to revise and revise until the book says what you wanted it to say, and says it in as grammatically accurate a way as you can manage. Very, very few books ever enter the bookshops without editorial fingerprints on them. One author said:

> *Revision offers the opportunity of looking at your complete work from a totally different angle. All the groundwork has already been done so you can concentrate on a hard edit. Always take the comments and advice of a professional editor. They are editors for a reason.*

Whether the opinion of every seasoned writer questioned about the editors they have encountered in their career will echo the final sentence above is a moot point, but publishers *certainly* agree with it – so you will need to bear this in mind.

If your book tells a good story in a professional manner and thus grabs the attention of a publisher, you will be given plenty of opportunity to revise it later.

Editors will invariably adopt a 'hands-on' approach to your book once it has been accepted. It is not unusual for an author to be told their book will be accepted on provision that the author is prepared to rewrite large portions. What this means is that the editor has seen that certain appealing 'something' in the book, but feels you have not exploited that 'something' properly. At this point you are entitled to decline the editor's suggestions, but a more *professional* approach is to give very careful consideration to what you are being told. After all, as a new author you must be prepared to listen and bow to professional advice if you want to get published.

> Editor: *I've read your book, and there's a lot in it that I like. Would you be prepared to completely rewrite it for us?*

> Author (thrilled): *Of course!*

> (Six months later)

> Editor: *Well, I've had a chance to read your revised manuscript and I think it's much improved. Now, would you like to go away and rewrite the final two-thirds of it?*

> Author (teeth gritted): *Yes.*

> (Six months later)

Editor: *You're almost there. I've made six pages of comments about the areas I think you need to reconsider, but on the whole I really like it.*

Author (with fixed grin and maniacal stare): *No problem!*

(Six months later)

Editor: *Well done. We'll take it. There, that wasn't so difficult, was it?*

Revision methods

How you go about revising your work will depend heavily on how you approach your work in the first place.

If you are still working in longhand, then hopefully you will have taken our advice and left every other line blank and incorporated wide margins. This will allow you a reasonable amount of space for alterations. If you find you need to insert entire scenes, say, in the middle of page 11, then write the scene on separate sheets and number them 11a, 11b and so on, as well as making yourself very clear, highlighted notes on the original manuscript to remind yourself of where the scenes are to be inserted. Never ever assume you will remember these things. Always leave yourself coherent notes. For all you know, you may not have the chance to go over this work again for months, and by then may have forgotten those great extra ideas.

Using a computer makes the task of revision so much easier – it will allow you to do all the editing you could wish before a hard copy (printed paper copy) is produced. And it will allow you to keep every previous draft of your book on file – just in case you find that a scene edited out along the way, suddenly needs to be popped back in. A computer will also allow you to shift entire sections of the book around at will and effortlessly insert, delete and correct your book to your heart's content.

You may be two-thirds through revising a book when a new idea occurs to you. The only problem being that it will require some judicious back-tracking through parts of the book already written in order to seed properly. If you are on a creative crest you may not want to go back over these points straight away. Make notes in your synopsis of the changes you have come up with and go back to them when you have finished the entire book – you may find that even more ideas will have come to you by then.

At the risk of sounding obvious, do try to be consistent. If you have stated in Chapter 13 that the electricity has been cut off in the house, it does you no credit if a character blithely switches a light on in Chapter 14. If you decide to have a discarded inhaler as a clue, make sure that the person who discarded it has been shown to be an asthmatic earlier in the book. Some authors will make up a card index or filing system for each character and scene. Details will include physical aspects of characters – brown eyes, black hair and so on – and sketches perhaps of the layout of significant buildings along with descriptions. Children have a great eye for minor detail, and will quickly spot any mistakes.

Always reread your work with an alert mind and in one sitting – if you are only half-awake or try to read it over several days, you may miss something glaringly obvious. Check for inaccuracies yourself. Was so-and-so at work on the day of the arson attack, or were they off sick? Does everything make sense? Does it all flow? Might it work better if the scene between Kevin and Dolores took place after the scene where Peter is discovered lurking under the bed in Mr Ponsonby's house?

Sometimes you may find that the simple effort of shifting scenes around will work wonders. Be brave, and be prepared to jettison much-loved scenes if it turns out that they are irrelevant to the main thrust of the story. Nothing need ever be wasted, keep the relevant pages or keep it on a separate computer file – and thus a scene which does not work in one story might well prove successful in another story later on.

Hitting publishers' preferred word-targets takes experience, so the chances are that you will need to add to or take away from your story before it will approach the approved length (not that you should feel that you are chained to a specific length if your book has other ideas). Let the story wind itself out naturally and leave concerns over precise word-targets to the publisher. A good book will not be rejected because it is a few thousand words over or under a publisher's preferred target.

Say you have the whole thing plotted out in synopsis form: there are no glaring contradictions, no gaps, no problems. It all flows seamlessly. Or does it? One of the problems for an author is that you can sometimes be too close to your book to spot omissions which, to a fresh eye, are horribly obvious.

This is where joining an authors' group will come in handy, or you could show your manuscript to a trusted friend. An objective eye may see things that you have entirely overlooked. The old saying, 'can't see the wood for the trees' is especially pertinent here. Putting the script away, rather than rushing to the postbox immediately can also help. Forget about it for a few days (or longer), and then read it again. You may know exactly what happens in your book; after all, you have got the whole thing nicely sorted out in your synopsis. But unless you tell the story clearly on the page, you may find a reader unable to take that 'obvious' step from A to C, for the simple reason that you never actually explained B! Once an agent asked an author, 'How did the diamond ring get in the river?' to which the author replied, 'The swan in the High Street swallowed it!' 'I see,' said the agent, 'but it doesn't say that in the book.'

Exercise 13

Pick a topic, any topic – a recent day out, a description of your home, a birthday party. Anything you like. Now, with the aid of a watch, egg-timer or whatever, write on this subject for five minutes. Do not get rid of anything. Try not to pause for thought. Imagine this as a kind of 'stream of consciousness' exercise. Just go for it!

Now forget all about it until the following day, or at very least, much later the same day. Look at it again and reread what you have written. Spend ten minutes revising it. Note the ways in which the original has been improved. Is it longer or shorter? In either event, examine what you have done and think about why it is better.

Writer's block

What is writer's block? It is that day when you sit yourself down for a quiet stint of creativity and then find yourself, several hours later, still staring blankly at a blank sheet of paper or a blank computer screen.

Writer's block can be caused by a lot of different factors. Often it results from outside stress. If your life is in some major turmoil, the chances are that you are not going to be able to concentrate on your writing.

The first question to ask yourself is whether these external stresses can be removed? If the gas company has decided to spend a couple of weeks digging up the road outside your writing place, can you set yourself up somewhere else until they have finished?

Might the problem be alleviated if you altered your writing routine? Are you trying to write too often? Theoretically you might be able to write for 15 hours at a stretch, but if the creative part of your brain works only for two hours before needing a rest to recharge, then the other 13 hours will be a waste of your time, and desperately frustrating to boot! Two authors made the following comments:

> *If I get bogged down in a storyline, then I sometimes just leave it and switch to working on something else for a while. I go and make a cup of tea, go and talk to my kids, get away from my desk for half an hour and then come back and start on something else. The coming back bit is really important! And sometimes, if I'm writing and I think, this isn't very good, this isn't really working, then I force myself to keep going, and keep churning the words out just to get through that particular section of plot. You can always go back and revise and edit. Just keep writing. It doesn't have to come out perfectly first time.*

> *Going back over what I've already written helps. I usually allow a "block" to take its course; sometimes things just need to settle down. The waiting can allow for some other developments and insights to emerge from the depths of your imagination or memory.*

You could be stuck in mid-plot with no idea of where to go next. Do not worry, you are in good company. By his own admission, while writing *The Lord of the Rings*, J. R. R. Tolkien was stuck in the caverns of Moria for an entire year before coming up with a way forward for his characters. Write one line if that is all you can manage, or put away the work you are stuck on and write something entirely different. A letter to a friend or to a newspaper might be all you need to unlock your creativity.

As one of the authors mentioned above, the 'block' may not be in your imagination, but just as frustratingly, in your inability to get the words down in a satisfactory way. If this is your problem, you might find that just getting the scene finished in a badly written form will be enough. Tomorrow, you can come back to it and work it up into something that you will be pleased with – but if you walk away from it now – the block may still be there the next day.

I find that getting out of one scene and into another can be a nightmare – searching for an elegant and pleasing way of leaving one piece of action and then introducing another can be very frustrating! I generally find that these transitional pieces of writing benefit from being left 'ragged' and then cleaned up later. A book can be like a shark – if it stops moving, it's dead in the water!

For a block of the ongoing imagination, why not a root through your 'Ideas File'. Perhaps a way forward lies hidden in there somewhere. Discuss the plot with a friend or with a group of children: as we said before, a fresh eye can work wonders, and a fresh mind may come up with a solution that might never have occurred to you. Brainstorming sessions can throw up all manner of intriguing ideas.

Of course, if you've taken our advice and worked out your synopsis in advance and in detail, then your creative story-telling 'block' will come at an early plotting stage, and will not intrude into the actual writing of the story.

One word of advice. When brainstorming with someone, do not instantly dismiss their ideas, no matter how feeble you may privately consider them. Friends may very quickly clam up if they get the feeling that you think they are talking rubbish and, you never know, their 43rd idea may be just the one you've been searching for, or may furnish you with a potential springboard for a better idea that you would never have come up with solo.

Another approach could be to open a dictionary or newspaper or website at random until an inspirational word or thought emerges. This may sound a little strange, but we have been told it really does work.

On the other hand, you may find that putting the work aside for a few days will do the trick. Have a change of scene, do something new, go for a long walk. Redundant as this advice may sound, the best bet is to stop worrying.

As one editor put it to us, 'We're not exactly dealing with brain surgery here. It's not *that* important!'

06

illustrations and picture books

In this chapter you will learn:
- how to work with illustrated books, both fiction and non-fiction.

Overview

In this chapter we will be dealing with the craft of linking words and pictures together to make a coherent, convincing and entertaining whole. For starters, the general rule is that the younger the reader to whom you wish to appeal, the fewer words there will be to each picture; as the reader gets older, this equation will gradually be reversed.

Some books, especially those aimed at the middle fiction age-range (8–12-year-olds), may have occasional illustrations, say, at the beginning or the end of chapters, or a few pictures scattered throughout the text, just to enliven the appearance of the book.

In graphic novels (and sometimes in works of non-fiction), the entire story is set out in comic-strip form. Adults are also interested in this type of presentation and there is an increasing number of graphic novels aimed directly at this market.

Any books linking words and pictures requires the author to have some contact with an illustrator. The very least contact you may have would be in a book brightened by occasional line drawings. At the other end of the scale, you may find yourself working from scratch with an illustrator on a joint-effort picture book, where the words and pictures grow up together as your story evolves.

Illustrated books

To go back to the beginning, books for the very youngest start with plastic bath-time books, board books or cloth books. These are deliberately chewable, soakable, scrunch-up-able and carefully manufactured to survive the worst a small child can inflict on them. At their simplest, these books may have pictures and no text at all, bound together to be looked at or sucked as the mood takes. A basic alphabet book could come next, with each letter illustrated by a big, bright picture: 'A for Apple', 'B for Boat', 'C for Cat', and so on.

Following on from simple alphabet books are those books where the pictures are accompanied by a single word: 'House', 'Cat', 'Boat', 'Dog', 'Tree', 'Flower', 'Car', 'Cow' – and there's an eight-page book already.

Writing and having one of these books published is nowhere near as simple as it may seem. For a start, these books will mostly be made up 'in-house'; the ideas will be developed almost entirely by people within the publishing house, or concocted solely by the illustrator – after all, it does not take a particularly brilliant writer to add the word 'cat' to a picture of a cat. For slightly older readers, the wording might be 'The cat sat on the mat in a hat' – and so on up the age-range: 'Puzzledust the wizard's cat wore a pointed hat when she helped her master weave his wonderful spells.' These different texts could all be used to accompany exactly the same picture.

Unless you can come up with something very original, you are going to experience difficulty in finding a publisher for this sort of book. Most ideas in this line have already been thought of, worked out and published. You really need to research the marketplace very thoroughly before expending any effort on these types of book.

Once children pass the 'chew-it-and-see' stage at, say, three years old, we enter the realms of what is known as the '32-page picture book'. These picture books contain a simple story in 32 pages which the child will be able to follow with the help of anyone old enough to read the script to them. Despite their seeming simplicity, these 500-or-so-word books are very difficult to write because there is no margin for error. They usually involve a full-page coloured picture accompanied by a small block of large-print text.

Illustration fashions and tastes change over time. You need only to look at some older picture books to realize this fact; pictures that may have been all the rage 20 years ago may nowadays seem quite old-fashioned and out of date. Similarly, the type of story which may have interested publishers a decade ago may no longer be of interest today. Time moves on inexorably, and no publisher wants to be thought of as being behind the times. Go and look at some recently published works to find out what's in and what's out. Also, bear in mind that different countries have widely differing tastes for illustration styles.

Printing and binding

If you are particularly interested in writing for picture books, you may well find it useful to read a specialist book detailing the printing process. (Such technical background falls outside the remit of this book, and we recommend you research for yourself on how a book is actually made.) With such a specialist title you will learn a good deal about printing processes and thereby gain better understanding of picture books. Very briefly, picture books are constructed in 'signatures' or multiples of eight (hence the name 32-page picture books: 32 being 8 x 4). Thus, eight pages are printed at one time on one large sheet of paper which is folded, trimmed, and bound into book form. As you look at the spine of a hardback book, you will see how these signatures are bound together by being sewn into multiples and then fitted together between thick card covers.

By their nature, hardbacks are more costly than paperbacks. However, in the picture book market, the fact that hardbacks last a lot longer in young hands than paperbacks do means that publishers will produce picture books as hardbacks as well as paperbacks. The sewing together of the signatures also increases the strength and durability of a hardback. The more a paperback picture book is used and loved, the sooner it will fall apart, while a hardback will endure.

On the whole, picture books are larger than books intended for older readers. This takes into account the importance of the size of illustrations. A small child will probably spend much longer looking at the pictures than they will listening to the text being read, and the larger the format of the book, the easier it is for the child to pick out and point to things in the illustrations which are of interest.

Bookshops often display picture books face-out as a purchasing enticement; after all, a book of 32 pages does not have much of a spine to attract the casual browser. From the point of view of the author of such a book, this is very good news indeed. A face-out picture book could easily fill as much visual space in a store as a dozen, spine-out, regular-sized books, and gives excellent visual publicity.

Books intended for beginner readers (that is, those children who are able to read simple things for themselves) will tend to be longer than picture books, but still in the multiple-of-eight format (48, 64, 96 pages) until it heads into middle fiction territory (8–12-year-olds) of 144, 160, 176 pages and upwards.

A modern paperback book is bound in a quite different way to hardback books. The printed and folded sheets are ground flat at the spine and glued into the covers. These days the glue used to hold paperbacks together is intended to keep the book in one piece for over 20 years – and glue technology is improving all the time. Even if dropped in the bath, a paperback should not come unstuck.

Publishers' time

A common question authors ask is why their picture book is taking so long to be printed and published. This is a very understandable query. Publishers tend to plan entire years ahead. For example, an editor might call you in the New Year to say that your book will be published in January. But the editor is not talking about this January; they are projecting into next year – or more likely, the year after. We call this 'publishers' time' and is something you will need to get used to. An 18-month to two-year wait between acceptance of a book and its publication is not unusual.

Why? It is certainly not because the book is sitting around being ignored for months on end. A lot of editorial and production processes have to be completed, and various elements co-ordinated. Your publisher will probably need to have page proofs ('finished' pages) printed to send out to foreign publishers in order to attract interest and money for co-editions. (Remember this term? It refers to a book simultaneously published in two or more countries at once.) The jacket of a hardback book may be printed by a totally different company from the one which is printing and folding the pages. These items need then to be brought together for binding either at the printers or by a separate binder. Add to that the fact that these companies may well be in entirely different countries, and you will begin to appreciate how the time passes.

Until now we have been concentrating on simple picture books, but a quick browse in a bookshop will quickly throw up other varieties. Pop-up books are also published, where the process of opening the page pulls up cut-out sections to create a three-dimensional effect. Lift-the-flap books also proliferate, as do books where the child pulls a tag or turns a fitted card wheel to reveal hidden aspects of a picture. Similarly, cut-out books sell well, as do 'paper engineering' books in which older readers are shown how to make trains or houses or whatever out of pre-pressed-out and coloured shapes.

Again, think hard and take a good look around the market before you embark on such a project. Although successful 'activity' books sell well, they are very expensive to produce and a publisher will need to be convinced that a large audience exists before they will take on a book of this type. At the time of writing this book, we were able to find only a couple of companies in the whole of the UK who were prepared to print a lift-the-flap book, and even they observed that a cheaper quote could be found in countries where the high level of manual labour required is cheaper.

Colour printing and co-editions

Colour printing is a very expensive process and consequently publishers will be wary of what they are prepared to produce. Indeed, publishers will often take samples of text and some illustration layouts or spreads to foreign countries and book fairs in the hope of bringing out one or more co-editions (that is, a joint production) funded between two or more companies in order to keep costs down.

It is important to understand the significance of these co-editions. It is all to do with keeping 'unit costs' low. The more books a publisher can print in one run, the cheaper each book will be to produce (the unit cost). It is exactly the same process whereby supermarkets are usually able to sell items more cheaply than a corner shop. They buy in bulk at a discounted price, and the saving can be passed on to the consumer.

In exactly the same way, if a publisher can be assured of good international sales of an expensive-to-produce book, then they will be prepared to print a large number and thereby keep their costs down. Co-editions guarantee a market in at least one other country, and could mean doubling the initial print-run of a book. If a publisher, of any book, can find a foreign publisher to come in with them, then translations can be made, and the books for both countries can be printed together by the same printer. The finished copies can then be sold and shipped to the publisher ready to go straight into the shops in that country.

Full-colour printing (also known as 'four-colour printing', because virtually all colours can be derived from a combination of four basic colours) is expensive, especially on the sort of good-quality, glossy paper that does justice to the illustrations. Hence, a publisher will need to be totally convinced that your picture book idea has co-edition potential and is therefore financially viable before going ahead with the project.

Text for picture books

If you are still undaunted by the difficulties of breaking into the picture book market, let alone the constraints of writing very short stories, then you will need to know what sort of text lengths are required. A 32-page picture book can have as few as fourteen words or as many as 1,000, depending upon the age-group targeted.

Here is an example of a 32-page spread. This gives you 12 double-page spreads in which to tell your story, once you have discounted the end-papers, the page with publisher's information on it and the title page. So, as you can see, in a 32-page picture book, your story probably will not begin until page 6, and might have to be wrapped up by page 29 if there is a repeated end-paper. Your narrative will have to be spaced fairly evenly through these 12 spreads. You should not have a big chunk of prose on one spread followed by only a couple of words on the next (and yes, there are always exceptions). The story needs to balance out, and this can be very difficult.

Your text can appear on these spreads either in a block in some 'empty' space (space deliberately left by the illustrator) or along the top of the spread, or along the bottom. It can even appear in two blocks, one on each page of the spread, or entirely on one page with the weight of the illustration dominating the other. (Check out the design layouts of popular, and/or award-winning picture books.) It is easier for children who are learning to read, or those with sight or learning difficulties, to read typeface printed on a white surface, rather than type which is overlaid on a coloured background.

All these things will need to be taken into consideration when constructing your story, although once your initial idea has been accepted by a publisher they will then employ someone to work with you and the illustrator on the general design of the book.

Think visually

It is essential, too, to think in *pictures*. Anything that can be *seen* by the child need not be mentioned in the prose. You do not need to describe characters, scenery or action which is going to appear in picture form. However, pictures, no matter how action-packed, are a static medium. They can only capture the instant. Your task as the author is to link those static moments together into a coherent narrative. Use the few words you are allowed to push the story on and to explain to the reader how they get from picture A to picture B and so on. A successful author thinks visually.

You will probably have very definite ideas about what your characters look like or how their surroundings should be depicted. These details can be conveyed separately. Write down all such information and present it with the manuscript. You may also have thoughts on the layout and type of pictures you would like, but be prepared for a publisher to have their own ideas and a 'house style' to follow.

Then again you may have no thoughts at all of how the illustrations will mesh with the text. This is not a problem: an illustrator's job is to visualize your words. But you still need to keep your eyes on the beginning-middle-end balancing act.

On the whole, the middle of your story should take up as much space as the beginning and the end put together, if not slightly more. In a 32-page book, this would mean the beginning should take two or three spreads, the middle would take six to eight spreads, and the end another two to three. These are only guide-lines, but it does serve to give you an idea of the sort of balance for which you should aim. Another thing to avoid is the gabbled ending, where the story suddenly goes into over-drive because the author has not left enough room to bring it to a well-rounded conclusion.

Balance has to be achieved through the pacing of the text as well as the pacing of the story being told. In a 500-word, 12-spread book, you should try to accompany each spread with about 40 words.

Picture book stories need plenty of movement. There is no room for long static conversations between characters. Just as we wrote in Chapter 5 about the importance of ending chapters with cliff-hangers, in a picture book every spread has to be a cliff-hanger in its own right.

The really successful picture books are those which manage to include a kind of 'subtext' which will engage the attention of the adult reader as well as the basic story which absorbs the child. Take a look at a book such as *Owl Babies* by Martin Waddell (the subtext story is a child's natural fear of being left by its mother) and the Ahlbergs' books (where many 'jokes' are told in the detailed background illustrations). Also check out *You're Too Big* by Simon Puttock and Emily Bolan (about feeling different at nursery school) and *Penguin Post* by Debi Gliori (the arrival of a new baby for a sibling). If an adult is going to be repeatedly made to read a much-loved picture book to an insistent child for 365 consecutive days, the successful ones will be those with glorious illustrations, or storylines which never cease to appeal to their audience.

Varying the scenery

The view needs to vary, meaning that your story cannot be set wholly in one place, unless some pretty extraordinary *visual* things happen, or the place can be viewed from several different angles in an imaginative way. The scene must be visually stimulating on every page. The best way of learning how to do this is to read published picture books. Observe how text and illustration blend together in these books. Or try a different approach: block out the text with your hand or a sheet of paper, and see how much of the plot you can follow simply by looking at the pictures.

In a well-plotted picture book, the pictures should almost tell the story on their own. The same kind of effect can be achieved by turning the sound down on a television while watching cartoons. See how much of the story is carried by the pictures. Your text need only convey about 50 per cent of the story; let the illustrations do the rest. That is what they are there for.

Example

Text: *Mum was late!*

Picture: *Harassed-looking mum with gaping handbag, open coat and hair all over the place is pulling child out of house. The child is fully dressed, but Mum is still in her nightie and slippers. By the expression on the child's face, Mum clearly does not usually take him out in her night-clothes.*

The effect of this on the reader is to whet their appetite for what is to come next. Why is Mum late? Why does she have a nightie on out of doors? What happens when she realizes how she is dressed? Will the little boy tell her that she has forgotten to get dressed, or leave her to realize on her own? Where are they going?

All conveyed by three words and an intriguing illustration.

Or the same picture could be accompanied by something quite different:

'Kevin had the feeling that this wasn't going to be just another ordinary day.'

This is a significantly more complex text, intended for an older reader. You need to establish a context and some interesting characters as soon as possible. If the story is to be told through the eyes of a single character, then that character must be shown from page one.

In a ghost story, the first picture may be of Martha in her haunted bedroom. This establishes her as the heroine. On the other hand, the ghost may be the hero, and Martha merely an interloper. Such a story could begin with the ghost peacefully lying on the bed and reading, and continue with the ghost being rudely disturbed by Martha charging in wearing hobnailed boots, swinging a football rattle over her head and shouting loudly. The reader would instantly sympathize with the ghost and would appreciate that the story was to be told from the disturbed ghost's point of view.

A mouse, living in the skirting-board, has its life made a misery by the endless conflict between a well-established ghost and a young ghost-hunter. The story would then revolve around the mouse's attempts to get rid of both the ghost and the ghost-hunter – or possibly to come up with some way of convincing them into peaceful cohabitation.

Exercise 14

Write a text for a 12-spread story in as few words as possible. Your challenge for this exercise is to have the story begin in one place and end in that same place: it could be a garden, in a submarine, beside the dinosaur display in a museum, or wherever. The other spreads must each contain a different scene for visual stimulation. Your aim is for a coherent story, which moves along, as well as keeping to that good old beginning-middle-end structure.

No, it is not easy, but if it is any consolation, a successful picture book text could earn an advance as large as that of a 40,000-word novel!

Important points

Voice of the narrator

When writing for the youngest age-groups, it is best to keep the voice of the narrator well out of the picture. An example to avoid is having text which says 'Can you guess what happens next?' or 'Can you see where Squishy the Squid is hiding?' Small children find this kind of text very difficult to comprehend, especially those still learning to read.

Tense

Similarly, avoid complicated use of tenses. Keep the story in a single tense and keep the sentences short and to the point. There are some very lyrical picture books out there, but they are generally aimed at older readers and you should be aiming for lucidity rather than for the poetic. In picture books especially, adjectives and adverbs should not be as necessary – the illustrations will deal with all such flourishes. If a heroine is wearing her favourite red scarf, the only comment needed in the text is that it is a favourite, and not that it is red. If a hero is entering a building with a sign outside saying 'Swimming Pool', then there is no need to write: 'Zac was going to the swimming baths for a swim.'

Internationality

In remembering the importance of the international market for the viability of these books, it is worth knowing that publishers may be reluctant to take on a book which is understandable only in its country of origin. A book published in the UK may not be acceptable to other countries if it is filled with things such as people delivering milk to the house, police officers with their traditional domed helmets or animals such as hedgehogs. Such details are not universally understood.

Likewise, in the UK the post is generally delivered through a front-door letterbox by a postman/woman, but in the USA the mail is more usually left in an external mailbox by the mailman/woman. This is a small point, but to say to an American that the post has arrived will conjure up visions of a length of wood being delivered rather than letters. Similarly, acceptable phrases, words, jokes, homilies and superstitions in one country, may be meaningless or even misunderstood by another. A black cat that crosses your path in the UK is considered a lucky omen. In Italy it is seen as a very unlucky omen. (In the UK, adult books are those of any subject aimed at adult readers; in the USA, the words 'adult books' refer to those of an erotic nature.) Babette Cole's picture book *The Trouble with Mum* has a universally understood subject – parenthood! *Guess How Much I Love You* by Sam McBratney and Anita Jeram is also known worldwide and *The Gruffalo* by Julia Donaldson and Axel Scheffler, although completely in rhyme, was liked so much by foreign publishers that they translated the text – and it has become a bestseller.

Such prejudices work in both directions, and a UK publisher may well not purchase a foreign picture book which deals with things that make little sense outside the country where it was written. The thing to keep in mind when writing your story is that it should not be too parochial. A child on the other side of the world should be able to grasp the significance of what is going on as well as a child who lives two streets away from you.

Fashion trends

Fashions and trends of acceptability change, and you would do well to take time out to research what is not acceptable in a picture book. Violence, sex, gore and general mayhem are obvious taboos, but these days there is also a reluctance to publish books where the boys go out doing adventurous things while the girls stay at home with their mother preparing lunch for them in between washing dolly's clothes and vacuuming the house.

Ten years ago we would have told you to avoid anything involving dragons – not so now! At the moment, dragons are definitely in demand again. But watch out – a few years on, and they could be publishers' poison again. As mentioned previously, the use of animals as main characters can work well in international co-editions. For instance, an animal can take the place of the child in a story and thus side-step skin-colour issues.

Setting the text

Presenting your picture book to the publisher

To remind you, a picture book is not the same as a storybook. A picture book has narrative illustrations; a storybook has an illustrated text and is intended for older readers. Can you see the difference? A storybook story could be read and understood without the illustrations, whereas a picture book story would lose a lot from the absence of the pictures. However, the chances are that with both these examples the text will need to have 'read-aloud' qualities: meaning that the style and rhythm and patterns of the text will have to work when read *to* a child as well as read *by* a child. The easiest way to check on this is to read your script out loud – and maybe make a recording of it so you can listen to it over and over and check which bits work and which don't.

Picture books

As far as illustrations are concerned, unless you are a very talented professional with experience of illustrating children's books, the best advice we can give you is to *leave illustrations well alone*. There are various ways to present the text of a picture book story. Some authors merely type out 'Page 1', followed by the line(s) of text, and then use a fresh sheet of paper for page 2. Others will present as follows:

Page 1

Mum was late!

(Illustration of harassed-looking mum ... and so on)

By all means include a pictorial (stick-people) reference or a separate layout to help explain some complex visual requirement. You can even suggest perspectives and other potential ideas. However, the editor, art director, design department and/or publisher may have other ideas.

Often, when an editor reads a submission, they may be looking for a story to suit artists they already have in mind to use. In this case, a particular visual style will already be established into which your story might fit. At other times, an editor will seek an appropriate illustrator and may consult you for your opinion as to the final choice. It is fairly unlikely that you would enter an editor's office with your picture book idea fully formed and be allowed to say, 'I want it exactly like this, thanks.'

Many illustrators and artists have their own agents with a wealth of talent on their books for an editor to view. As in all things, publishers will generally prefer to use an illustrator whose work has proved popular, rather than use an unknown. Back to that old catch-22 situation.

One prospect more disturbing than having your own picture book illustrations discarded is if you have asked a friend to illustrate your book only to have your story accepted and their hard work rejected. You will then be in the awkward position of having to suppress your own euphoria while you break it to your friend that their labours were in vain.

Even an excellent draughtsman with a lot of talent may well fall into some of the more obvious traps when they try to illustrate a book. For instance: a face drawn across a double-page spread will look very odd when the nose vanishes into the cleft between the pages. There are other important techniques and limitations, ranging from colour processes to text overlays which an illustrator should know about when working on picture books. Leave the artwork to the professionals, unless you are one of a rare and fortunate breed of author–illustrators. In general, do–not take advantage of friends who *you* think can draw, nor submit your own work unless you really know the business of illustrating children's books.

Storybooks

Whereas picture books spread the workload equally between words and pictures, storybooks have more than twice the text, are usually smaller in size, and rely much less heavily on the artist's input. An average storybook text length starts at around 2,500 words. The story will be split into several chapters and spaced out with plenty of illustrations.

As with picture books, the story should be well balanced and full of interest and movement, but the balancing act between words and pictures need not be quite so precise. The 2,500 plus word-length allows much more room for dialogue and for brief descriptions of things which the illustrator will be depicting.

Some storybooks are illustrated in colour throughout; some are part-colour, part-black-and-white line illustration; and others are black-and-white line only. Check 'beginner reader's' series for styles. This is one time when you really do need to leave the Internet and go out into the real world. A brief trawl through your library will show you the range of illustrations used in storybooks, from the meticulously detailed and highly realistic full-colour works to the kind of cartoons that are so fluent that they look really easy – until you try it.

Let's say you have submitted a beginner reader storybook text. The editor is interested but wants you to make alterations before acceptance. These alterations may be intended to clarify or brighten the plot, or to spread the action out a little (especially if your story takes a little while to get off the ground and then ends all in a rush on the last page). Or the editor may think you have included some piece of grammar which is too complex for the intended readership, or a word or two which needs to be exchanged with something more simple.

By now you will understand the style and the sort of words you must fit into the scope of the target readership, but an editor may still make suggested alterations which change your original phrase 'inharmonious discord' to 'terrible noise' without losing its sense.

Once a text has been accepted, the publisher will work on marrying your story to an artist. As we have said, generally the publisher will choose the illustrator and an in-house design team will work on the layout. You may well not have much of an input at this stage, save to be informed of which artist the publisher has chosen and being sent examples of their work.

Next you will be sent proofs of the text set out as it will appear in the finished book, with gaps left for the illustrations. Then you should get to see some roughs (usually loosely sketched drawings) of the artwork. Sometimes the first thing you will see are colour photocopies of the finished pictures. Hopefully (but sadly not always the case), you will be asked for your input at the rough artwork stage, so that you can add your ideas, or point out any errors. We have seen picture books where one character had a moustache which appeared and disappeared, and another where a character's sweatshirt changed colour and style throughout the book.

Detailed illustrations could take an artist weeks or months to complete, so this process will take some time.

Moving on up the age-range from story books, you will discover middle fiction books with, say, ten or so line drawings and maybe small vignettes at the beginnings or endings of chapters. As with picture and storybooks, you will be kept informed of what is happening with the illustrations, but on the whole, scenes to be illustrated and the placing of illustrations will be out of your hands.

As you can see, the older the reader, the fewer pictures their books generally have. Of course, there are exceptions to this, one of which is the graphic novel style, intended to attract an older readership. Text for graphic novels has to follow the same style as that for photo-stories in teen magazines. It is almost a cartoon format and written mostly in dialogue with only very brief explanations. If this area appeals, do your research, study the layouts, and write and ask publishers for any briefs they may have for their series.

Book covers

A lot of your publisher's time, thought and effort ought to go into deciding what should appear on the cover of a book. The audience for which the book is intended ought to be considered carefully and the cover design aimed specifically at grabbing their attention. In a perfect world, your book should shout out from the shelves to be picked up and bought – but alas, in the real world, constraints of both time and finances can intrude detrimentally on this process and unfortunately you will really only be a bystander as this takes place.

The look of a book cover is created from several elements. If it is part of a series, then there has to be a series title somewhere. Then the title of the individual book and the author's name, followed by a picture, photograph, or montage intended to sell the books to the target audience.

If you have specific ideas for the cover of your book, then by all means let your editor or publisher know, but keep in mind that there are design and marketing teams whom you would hope know a lot more about the intended market than you do. Your opinion should be sought and hopefully you will be kept informed at every step but, to be honest, as one editor told us in a moment of weakness, if you were to express disapproval of a cover at a late stage, the chances of you being able to make any changes at that point are limited, not least because the artist will already be under commission and money will have been spent.

Nevertheless, as an author to whom we spoke testified, it is possible to effect changes. He was shown a 'finished' cover painting for one of his books, only to spot that the cat in the picture was an entirely different colour from the one described in the book. The next time he saw the picture, the cat had been repainted.

In other words, if your comments are concerned with inaccuracies, you may be able to effect changes, but if you just plain don't like the design or the pictures chosen for the cover of your book, you may well simply have to live with it.

If you are lucky enough to have written a book with crossover potential, then it may be published in two editions – one for the children's market and one for the adult market – and the jacket designs of these two editions will naturally reflect the different age-groups being targeted.

Illustrated non-fiction

Most of the same rules apply to illustrated non-fiction as they do for illustrated fiction. However, non-fiction books are far more design-led than fiction, as the text and illustrations are integrated across the pages. It is terribly important that you, as the author, see the rough artwork before it is approved for completion.

Presumably you will have researched your subject and be knowledgeable about what is correct. If your topic is the internal combustion engine, then obviously any drawn illustrations (as opposed to photographs) have to be absolutely technically correct.

Photographs, too, must be of the right subject and taken from the appropriate angle. A non-fiction work will probably have a great deal more editorial input and author guidance than a work of fiction. You may also have much more control over the suggested kind of illustrations and/or photographs to be used, unless you are writing for a series which already has a clearly defined style.

07

markets for fiction

In this chapter you will learn:
- about the breadth and diversity of the fiction market
- how your work should fit into that market.

Who writes?

People who seek to write for a living, or for part of their living, fall into four main categories. They are:

- *Ink junkies*: the obsessives, who write because they cannot help it; putting words onto paper is the way they best interact with the outside world. They can be prolific letter and e-mail writers and can also be found creating writing websites on the Internet and submitting fan fiction to pre-existing sites.
- *Light-bulb people*: these are people with *ideas*; they want to get these ideas out into the world and the only obvious way of doing that is by writing them down. Sometimes this character type will flit from good idea to good idea without ever actually researching or completing anything.
- *Drifters*: these are people who already have contact on some level with the publishing world or with the media and who slip into writing for children because it seems like a good career move. These types are often in for a rude awakening.
- *I can do that*: these are people who think that writing for children is easy, and that they can do better than the material they have seen on sale. They also think there is a crock of gold at the end of their writing rainbow.

The work you have produced, or intend to produce, will probably be driven to some extent by the fact that you fit into one of the listed categories. All of these category types have an equal chance of success as long as they take off their rose-tinted spectacles and co-ordinate their efforts professionally.

Assessing yourself

As this chapter covers how you are going to try and sell your work, this is the time for you to take a good look at what you have done so far.

You are over halfway through this book; by now you should have done a number of things. You should have your 'Ideas File' up and running. You should have done plenty of research, both on the Internet and in bookshops and libraries. You should have gone out into the world for first-hand inspiration. You may even have visited schools and/or book fairs.

The time has come for you to assess whether there is a market out there for your work. Hopefully, that raw piece of writing, or that unformed idea which first set you reading this book, has been honed and shaped by what you have read and learnt so far.

Now take a good, long, hard look at your work. Does it seem to you to be close to the mark, but not quite there yet? Perhaps it just needs tidying up, shortening, lengthening or better audience-targeting. The research you have undertaken should help you to address any or all of these areas.

Perhaps you have discovered that your big idea is already sitting on the shelves in a bookshop. Do not despair. Can you tackle the same idea with an entirely fresh, new approach? One famous author said that there is nothing *new* to be written, but that the job of an author was to add their own colours to an existing picture. A very successful playwright said that a person endlessly ploughs the same furrow but is always turning up fresh material.

Your idea may still be viable even though someone else has used it before, if you can view it with your individual eye and mind and add an unusual aspect to it.

Your research will also have given you an insight into the publishing world. Which publishers seem to you most likely to be interested in the piece of work you have produced? You will save yourself an enormous amount of wasted time, effort and postage by making your initial approaches to publishers who are at least in the market for the book you have written (or are planning on writing).

The practicalities of submitting work will be dealt with in detail in Chapter 9, so we need not discuss that here. What we will discuss are the types of publishers that exist in the world of children's books.

Who publishes?

There is a great variety of publishers on the look-out for picture books, illustrated books, and longer, text-only fiction. At the top end of the market are the major trade publishers whose products are distributed far and wide in bookshops, libraries, school book clubs, supermarkets, mail-order clubs, online booksellers, overseas and so on. These are mostly large corporations with their main offices in capital cities.

These large publishers are not the whole story. There are also many, many smaller trade publishers (who often specialize in niche markets), which include family concerns and regional publishers who concentrate on producing a small number of high-quality books. In these days of desktop publishing and freelancers, such small companies can literally be run from home and are well worth investigating. Both types of companies have points for and against. The big corporations have plenty of clout in the marketplace, and thus the ability to ensure your work is available on shelves throughout the world. However, a smaller company may be able to give you more personal attention. With these publishers you are less likely to encounter the ponderous decision-making processes that typifies larger companies, where every commission has to go through several vetting procedures before anyone is able to spend any money.

Smaller, independent publishers are quite capable of achieving very high sales figures in a quiet, unassuming way, through diligent hard work on your behalf, and through being able to concentrate on selling a small list; not to mention gaining prize-winning attention simply because their small number of products are of such a high quality. Major publishers with their sales and distribution power could be easily shamed by some of the excellent sales figures these independents achieve.

Usually both of the above types of trade publisher will pay advances and royalties.

Packagers

Another type of publisher in the marketplace is the 'packager' or 'packager–publisher'. These companies will often develop an idea on their own and then approach one of the major trade publishers with the completed product, the aim being that all the major publisher has to do is pay the packager, add the book(s) to their list and set about the distribution. Packagers might approach a 'major' with anything from a single picture book to a series of books. These are also the people who may design technically complicated products which have glossy artwork, holograms, cut-outs, and so forth. They may even present the publisher with merchandising spin-offs such as boxed sets of books which may include mugs, t-shirts, cuddly toys, bookmarks or an interactive computer game.

Such products are often seen in the bargain or remainder bookshops, toy shops, high street chain stores as well as the more usual outlets. To get an idea of how spin-off merchandising works, wait for the next Hollywood animated feature film to come out and then observe how rapidly the stores fill with a diverse range of merchandize.

Packagers are not generally geared to accepting unsolicited projects (an original idea by *you*), but a good idea suited to a particular company's style is well worth submitting. Such well-thought-out proposals, targeted appropriately, do not waste anyone's time and, even if your idea is not picked up this time, the company may well add your name to their author files and come back to you when they need someone for a particular project suited to your talents.

Packagers often only pay originators or contributors a flat fee or one-off payment, and also claim the copyright. We will go into this later, but here point out that your flat fee may look a little sick if the product you helped develop shoots off to become a major financial success.

Overseas publishers

Our shops are filled these days with cheap products of varying quality from far-flung countries. Children's books are no exception, and the material from such sources is often not of the trade publishers' mainly high standards. Author payment, if you should succeed in gaining a response and acceptance for your submission, is not usually very high. It is also difficult to monitor the accounting and sales procedures of these publishers.

First contact

Aim for the top

When selecting publishers for your work, the best bet is to aim initially for the top: the major publishers. Ensure that the work you want to submit to them falls within the boundaries of their 'list'. (A publisher's catalogue will give you easy access to the kind of material they are producing.)

Be prepared to adapt your work to fit the requirements of an individual publisher. Your chances of getting published are increased if, as a new author, you submit work exactly suited to their needs or for an existing series. A busy editor may well choose a work that fits their needs precisely and, therefore, does not require time-consuming editorial input, over a story of equal merit which is the wrong length.

Tip-sheets

Many publishers are willing to supply 'tip-sheets' or 'briefs' which will give you an idea of their specific requirements, especially where a series is concerned. These are usually single-page outlines which detail word-count, style and content specifications. After all, if you are submitting a young adult romance, it is handy to know in advance whether kissing is allowed, whether the courting characters are permitted beyond the bedroom door, or whether they are only allowed to hold hands.

A letter of enquiry to a publishing house accompanied by a stamped, self-addressed envelope, sent to the editor in charge of the series in which you are interested should produce a reply. You may think that a telephone call will shorten your waiting time, but this may not be the case. A busy editor may not relish the interruption of an unsolicited telephone call and you should remember that part of your task as a budding author is to keep on the good side of editors. *Letters, good; phone calls, bad.* And do *not* forget the self-addressed envelope: you may never hear from the publisher otherwise. One stamp may not seem to you much of a financial outlay for a company, but for a large publishing house one stamp multiplied by several hundred over the course of a year is a considerable cost for any company.

Editors do not like submissions by e-mail. Write a letter first – before you fax or e-mail; it is the professional way to behave: it shows you have taken care and time over your enquiry and it saves your e-mail from being instantly deleted along with a lot of other spam and unsolicited mails. Check the publisher's website – most likely they will have a section outlining their particular requirements on the submission of work.

Longer fiction

If your first piece of work is a young-adult novel, a trilogy or a sequence of linked novels, you will find that the number of publishers willing to consider your book(s) is considerably smaller. There are various reasons for this. A single book needs to be given a very high profile and a large amount of expensive publicity if it is going to be successful. Publishers are well aware of this and are nearly always going to go for work that they think will make money. Publicity budgets, especially in the UK, are very tight, and, unfortunately for the aspiring author, this money is invariably spent most freely on books that the publisher already knows will sell in high numbers. As a new writer, your book is unlikely to have a great deal of publicity money spent on it, and you may find that wonderful promotional ideas floated early on never actually materialize.

Young-adult fiction is taken on by a limited number of publishers, especially with one-off books, and these form only a small percentage of a market that is dominated by books for the younger age-ranges. This is partly because 'young adult' is quite a woolly term; and people in their early teens are as likely to be reading Jane Austen or Stephen King as they are to choose anything specifically targeted at their age-group.

Crossover fiction

As has been the case with the recent Harry Potter phenomenon, some books which were written and initially published with the specific aim of capturing the children's market, have been known to make the leap into the adult world. This is called 'crossover', and if you are lucky enough to experience it, you will quickly see the benefits of its money-spinning and fame-garnering potential.

The crossover is, of course, no new occurrence: adults have been buying children's books for their own entertainment for a long, long time – think of *Alice in Wonderland*, *The Wind in the Willows* and the *Winnie the Pooh* books as classic instances of crossover. And in the late 1960s and early 70s, it became quite the fashion accessory to be seen carrying Tolkien's *The Hobbit* around with you. (*The Lord of the Rings* is, of course, a crossover *sans pareil* – to the point now where it is hardly possible to tell whether it really 'belongs' in the children's market or in the adult market.)

Many books aimed at young adults now carry quite sophisticated jacket designs, which are indistinguishable from the look of modern adult fiction. These may appear in both the children's and the adult sales sections of bookshops.

Publishers will also repackage older children's books with an eye to attracting adults. Books read and loved by a child will still retain their magic when that child is grown up – and parents will often buy books that were their favourite childhood reads, not only for their own children, but also to allow themselves briefly to bring back more innocent times. The William books by Richmal Crompton are a prime example of this – having been repackaged in their original 1940s' covers – as are modern hardback editions of many Enid Blyton books and facsimile reproductions of several Billy Bunter volumes, the originals of which now command significant prices on the second-hand circuit. The retro look of these revisited covers is aimed very much at the nostalgia market.

More recently, books by Terry Pratchett and Philip Pullman have bridged the gulf between children and adults. Publishers have been quick to see the potential fully to exploit the crossover market, and will now simultaneously publish books in two distinct packages – one with a cover aimed at the children's market, and another geared towards drawing in as large an adult readership as possible. Also, the more sophisticated book jackets and covers will appeal to age-conscious teens who, while they would not be seen dead reading a kid's book, are very happy to have the adult version on display.

And, of course, many adults, wishing to take a breather from the more worthy tomes that they feel they are obliged to read, will take up a children's book as relief from the often grim and sombre vision offered by modern adult fiction, and bask for a while in the more simple and light-hearted pleasures that these books afford.

Another kind of crossover is provided by authors whose work is generally aimed at adults, but who are able to step across into the children's market. On rare occasions this can be done by someone from an entirely different branch of the entertainment industry – the pop singer Madonna, for instance – who is famous enough to get their children's book published because it is hoped that they will carry with them a potentially large crossover market.

However, the unfortunate truth is that no one in the publishing world is in possession of a crystal ball that might allow them to know in advance exactly what book or series of books might have the potential to be a crossover hit. All we can suggest is that you write the book you want to write – and keep your fingers firmly crossed.

Series fiction

There is a great demand for paperback series fiction for the simple fact that it is much easier to sell a book in a successful series or imprint than it is to sell a one-off title. By 'imprint' we mean books with a recognizable collective logo or jacket design with an identity within a larger publishing group – as opposed to 'series' books which will usually follow the adventures of a particular set of characters, or contain stories of a specific nature – say, horror or crime.

Before you decide to write for an existing series, do make sure that more titles are being commissioned and that you have a copy of the publisher's brief. Then you should submit a proposal or synopsis and three sample chapters.

For a series outline of your own, you would also need to submit further plots, so that the publisher is able to see that the idea has 'legs'. And if it is a school-based series or a series concerning a gang of friends, bear in mind that there are already very many such series out there, so you will have to come up with a very compelling angle or gimmick to attract a commissioning editor's attention.

Educational fiction

There are publishers who specialize in producing fiction for the educational market. Their activities range from buying titles from trade publishers and producing their own editions mainly for schools and libraries, to creating 'in-house' reading schemes.

Educational publishers also produce a wide variety of original fiction material to suit many special needs. This can range from picture books to longer fiction introducing such themes as bereavement and divorce, as well as issues for people of differing ability.

For children who find reading more of a challenge, high-interest but lower reading ability books, known as 'Hi-Lo readers' are produced. These books are for children and adults who may be learning to read but who are too old to be interested in 'Perry the Parrot' picture books. Hi-Lo readers are not easy to write, and you shouldn't attempt this without a very good idea of what you are doing.

Publishers' reading schemes will have been thoroughly researched and planned as well as having been tested in schools and focus groups. Your enquiry about writing for such schemes will probably result in the arrival of a very long and detailed outline, and sometimes even a word-list from which your text must be constructed. This is writing within very precise parameters and is not really intended for people without experience or apposite skills.

Educational publishers often approach authors and illustrators directly, or commission teachers whom they know to be good writers, as they will have a working knowledge of the way children are taught to read. If you work in this area, you may already have the necessary expertise that educational publishers require, but bear in mind that a good teacher is not necessarily going to make a good author.

If you are interested in this area of publishing, then there may be a school or educational fair which you can attend. There you will find the appropriate publishers and you will be able to do some research before making your initial approach.

Dual-language books

Dual-language books are published for those children whose first language is not that of the country in which they are living and being educated, or for those families who are or wish to be bilingual. These books are most often seen in picture book format, in which the text appears in two languages, and are most likely to have been bestsellers in their originating language. A few publishers seek original works in this area; if you are fluent and competent in other languages, then you may find this type of work of interest.

Religion

The religious publishing market has various publishers dedicated solely to the publication of religious or spiritual material. On the children's side, many religious publishers are on the lookout for work that fits their particular beliefs, but conveys the message in a subtle way without being didactic or 'preachy', particularly where the fiction area is concerned.

Graphic novels/comic books

When we use the term 'comic book' we are not talking about the *Beano* or *Fun-Time with Mickey Mouse*; comic books are the same as graphic novels, except that they are generally slimmer and are usually issued monthly – as with *The X-Men* or *The Fantastic Four*. Graphic novels or comic books are stories that are told in words and pictures in comic-strip form – typically Spiderman and similar super-hero characters. But this art form has come a long way since Batman first donned his cape and Spiderman got bitten by that radioactive arachnid. Nowadays the graphic novel is also frequently used to tell very stark and harrowing tales, and although many are read by children, a lot are certainly not intended for a young market.

In many countries, the fashion and passion for graphic novels has been growing steadily and continually, both with a children's and an adult audience – and frequently with both at the same time.

It is a visual and fast-paced way of telling a story, and you'll need to be able to write succinctly and with the artist in mind at all times. Many graphic novels or comic characters form the basis for children's (e.g. *Spiderman*) and adult (e.g. *A History of Violence*) films, television, computer games, merchandizing and so forth.

There is a great deal of crossover in the world of graphic novels, notably with titles such as *Tank Girl* by Hewlett and Martin (which also became a film, t-shirt etc.), Neil Gaiman's *Sandman* series, *Peacemaker* by Ennis and Dillon and *Aria* by Holguin and Haberlin. And this is not to mention the Japanese Anima and Manga graphic novels – many of which are startlingly graphic in their visuals and most definitely not for the children's market. As you will see from the above examples, these graphic novels are often co-written by the person who tells the story and the person who illustrates it.

In the adult world a notable graphic novel would be *King Lear* illustrated by Ian Pollock, although there are many other examples, including a graphic novel version of the movie *Serenity* by *Buffy The Vampire Slayer* creator Joss Whedon, as well as 'serious issue' works such as *Palestine* by Joe Sacco which uses the 'comic-strip' genre to explore the weighty problems of that region in the early 1990s, and of course Frank Miller's renowned *Sin City* novels, which now also exist as a movie – or possibly two or three by the time you read this.

As with all specialist fields, you would need to have a good working knowledge of the mechanics of the genre before you attempted to produce work of this type, and anything beyond an initial storyline would need to be seen by and discussed with an illustrator before there was any point in you taking it further.

Film, television, radio and theatre

If you are thinking of writing for film, television, radio and theatre, you need to understand that each of these is a highly specialized market area which requires its own very specific and distinct skills.

Writers are frequently commissioned to write to order a script based on an idea or within a framework already chosen by a producer or director or script-editor. For instance, writers approached to write a story for the TV series *Dr Who* will obviously be expected to take on board all the established characters and characteristics of the series. Similarly, if you are asked to script the next James Bond movie, your work will need to conform to all the expectations of the genre.

Alternatively, a writer may be approached to adapt an existing novel or TV series for radio, or a classic novel for television. Most work will come in this form, and it is very rare for an unknown writer successfully to place a brand new piece of work. Recycling is all the rage at the moment, and many films and TV series and radio plays are based on pre-existing books or comic books, rather than on new and original material.

This is a very tough arena for a newcomer to fight their way into – not least because the media world likes to bet on winners and winners are those with an established track record and proof of successful experience in the field. It's the old catch-22 situation again for anyone seeking employment in this world: commissions to write for broadcasting are rarely handed out to people who have not got a proven expertise in writing for broadcast.

As we said, different media require different skills. For instance, the plot of a film would need to be succinctly described in such a way as to make it clear that the entire story could be encapsulated in one-and-a-half to two hours of screen-time. In the heyday of the Simpson/Bruckheimer action blockbusters, a movie would have to be sold in two sentences, meaning you'd have to be able to say up-front: this is *Titanic* meets *King Kong* in order to get enough attention to have someone even glance at your script.

On the other hand, television may require a story to be broken into two parts, or four, or six or even more. And even a single-episode story will probably have to be divided into two distinct chunks with a cliff-hanger in the middle to help viewers jump the commercial break without changing channels. The original 25-minute episodes of *Dr Who* from the 1970s were broadcast by the BBC, and consequently without a commercial break, but the length of the episodes allowed for five minutes of adverts to be inserted when the series was sold abroad – and were written with a cliff-hanger at about 12 minutes in for this very purpose.

On radio, everything you want to convey to the listener will need to be in the dialogue that the actors speak, or in sound effects, or, as in the case of the radio dramatization of the *Gormenghast* books by Mervyn Peake, by a separate narrator or storyteller.

Theatre will again have differing requirements to suit the limitations of a flat stage and scenery changes. Many scriptwriters and playwrights have previous, published book-writing experience, but writing for these areas calls for entirely different abilities. The jargon differs from the book world, too. What we have been calling a synopsis would be called a 'treatment' in the film and visual arts world. There will be a cast list which may include descriptions of un-named characters, such as: THIN SPOTTY TEENAGER. There are technical terms of direction, for example 'FX' for sound effects, or 'beat' for a pause in the dialogue. Can you guess what 'POV', 'Fade In' and 'Int' mean? (OK, 'POV' means 'point of view' meaning the angle from which a shot is taken; 'Fade In' is probably fairly obvious, and as for 'Int' – well, if you really want to know, do some research.)

You would also need to learn a quite different way of dealing with dialogue, punctuating a spoken piece with adjectival explanations. For instance:

BOY (Terrified) *No way! No* (beat) *way!*

The 'slot-time' of a TV programme may be one hour, but with opening and end credits, as well as advertisement breaks, the actual dialogue of your script may run for less than 40 minutes of that hour – and that's without taking the big dialogue-free car-chase scene into account! These days an American TV series such as *24*, is often under 40 minutes long all-in, and the length is gradually being eroded as time is sliced out of programmes to make room for more advertising revenue.

Thus, part of the required skill lies in understanding how to lay out a script and how much time the dialogue takes on a 'read through'. If your script for a TV show over-runs, things *will* be taken out whether you like it or not, so you need to time this virtually to the second or risk losing something important in the 'cut'.

You will also need to be able to think visually, and to describe coherently whole scenes of action where nothing is said. In other scenes, you might be able to set the scene very quickly: (Int. Kitchen. Day), but even then the subsequent dialogue will need to be full of physical and emotional pointers – as with the terrified boy above.

There are many specialist books on the market for these writing areas (e.g. *Teach Yourself: Screenwriting* by Ray Frensham) and there are courses on scriptwriting which will teach you how to set out a screenplay and point you towards finding work for film, television, radio and theatre. You should definitely seek out some kind of professional advice or tuition if you wish to attempt writing for these areas. Even a seasoned writer such as John Cleese attended a scriptwriting and film-plotting course before embarking on *A Fish Called Wanda*.

You also need to realize that the children's slice of these markets is very small, but it is expanding healthily on television as the number of channels increases. However, at the moment, a lot of children's broadcasting air-time is made up of foreign series imports, so before you decide to adapt your young-adult novel for a television two-parter, you need to have some understanding of time-slots and the type of programmes being put out by whichever channel you choose to approach. Bear in mind that TV executives are not going to change things to suit you – it is you who must adapt your work in order to present them with something they might want.

Once you have gained the necessary scriptwriting skills, research will be your key. Unlike with publishing, in the media world *who* you know is as important as *what* you know. You can research the television and radio listings market for details of the programme producers to whom your work could be submitted, but it will be even more helpful if you know someone who knows that producer, or you have met them at a course, industry function or via a professional organization such as the Writer's Guild, or Radio Independents Group.

Media listings books are published annually, and these will give you a good idea of who's who in the media world, and where to approach them. There are also media magazines and annual festivals, although it would be a mistake to travel to Cannes or Sundance with a script under your arm. As with our advice for attending book fairs, a producer having a chat with friends at a party is unlikely to want to hear a half-hour 'pitch' from you detailing which A-list celebrities you think should star in your movie, and what CGI effects would work really well in scene 54!

Most films, television and radio programmes are produced independently of the broadcasting companies and they are often on the lookout for good ideas and new material. However, these independent companies have to research and raise interest, find a broadcaster or distribution, organize complex financing, clear rights, and get a draft screenplay written way before they can even begin to think of going into production. It's a deeply detailed area, with many different professions involved. Next time you are at the cinema or rent a DVD, take time to read the end credits and marvel at the range of people involved – from greensman, to completion bond companies, to insect wranglers, to script advisors – all of whom have played a part in making the movie you have just watched.

This massive and complex procedure can easily take a couple of years for a television drama, and often much longer for films. For radio broadcasts, programming can be decided up to six or even twelve months in advance, and for stage plays, well, a theatre that has a slot to take your play, and one that the production can afford, will need to be pre-booked.

Some publishers do produce fiction plays and playlets for schools and religious markets, both for trade and non-trade outlets. Long-running series, children's soap operas and educational broadcasts frequently use different storyline writers, but you will need tenacity and luck to break into this market.

The market for live theatre, ballet and dance is very small, and tends to be confined to previously published or other well-known works. Fame can follow the success of small local productions, fringe or festival successes, but short of finding a wealthy producer who likes your work, your best approach may be to find a theatrical agent who specializes in selling to these markets.

Payments for television and radio work generally adhere to specific guidelines, but are extremely complex to the untrained eye, and include repeat fees, overseas sales and so on. Payment can also be based on the experience of the writer – so a new writer for television will usually be paid less than an experienced writer, even though you may think you have done the better job! Guidelines can be obtained from screenwriting societies, but if you get a job, you may want to get professional advice on your contract so that you don't lose out if your work is widely sold. If you are particularly interested in these areas then joining one of the appropriate organizations will provide you with plenty of regular information, guidance and news of the latest market developments and legal complexities via their magazines.

Payment in all of these media areas is not the phenomenal amount that the movie-type industry hype and extravagance might lead you to believe – not until you hit the big time, anyway. Few writers in these areas are given a profit percentage – however, if you wrote the original book for which rights have been bought and which has been turned into a blockbuster film, then enormous numbers of books may sell as a result.

Electronic communication

As the world of electronic communication expands and evolves, steady work can be found for computer-literate authors. This work tends to attract flat fees as you will probably be one of a large number of freelance writers and editors working on a particular project. Also, the copyright of the project will belong to the producer of the electronic work or other software being developed. Work in this area could include writing sections for encyclopaedias, embellishing a game based on a best-selling series of children's fiction books or writing for educational websites.

There are many conferences and shows you can attend, although some *are* expensive. Exhibitors tend to be hardware manufacturers and software developers, displaying their abilities and wares, with very few actual publishers in attendance. Check before you go as to what exactly you can expect from a conference or show before making any expeditions.

Tracking down the original producer/creator of a software package in order to present an idea to them may be a difficult process, as they are often bought in by the publisher or especially commissioned from an independent firm. Computing and gaming magazines, shops and special supplements in educational newspapers will help you to narrow down your search.

Magazines and comics

The UK comic market is very small these days and you would be hard-pressed to find much beyond the *Beano* and the *Dandy*, but there are many children's magazines on the market, from those aimed at tiny tots to weekly zines with titles such as *Sixteens Only!* – which are aimed at 13-year-old aspirational girls. Much of the material for these markets is produced in-house, or bought in from other countries, thereby limiting your publishing chances even further. As ever, study the market and submit appropriate material for short stories, photo-stories, cartoons and so on.

Many of the magazines for younger readers are based on cartoon or well-known picture book characters. The magazine publishers license the right to use these characters from the owner (licensor). Authors are then employed to adapt or write suitable material involving these characters. The licensor then usually approves the work before it can be published, and this can mean rewriting work several times until it is judged fit for publication. Material may fly back and forth, as the licensors can be very difficult to please. You will need patience.

If you are able to get into these markets, they can prove a steady source of income. Experience in these fields, the ability to work to tight schedules, and writing about characters not of your own creation can be valuable experience. Potential book publishers are impressed by an author who shows versatility. It is worthwhile developing a range of writing skills, especially if you aim to make a living.

Competitions

A lot of newspapers and magazines run competitions for short stories and poetry, and some even for plays and novels. A number of competitions are annual events from organizations, societies and arts councils so it is worth keeping your eyes and ears open. Submit material which fits the competition regulations exactly, even if that means adapting something to suit. Writing to a specific order will be a useful experience and, while you may not win the big prize, you may well get to see your name and possibly your work in print which could be spiritually as well as financially rewarding. Winning a competition or being published in almost any kind of format will help instill confidence in a potential publisher for your children's work, too.

Anthologies

Some publishers regularly compile seasonal or themed anthologies of short stories or poetry.

It is too difficult to second-guess what these publishers might be looking for next, so find out who they are, and then ask them for information as to what is currently being commissioned. Often an independent editor or author is chosen to compile the anthology and they will have prepared a brief for their requirements. Once again, remember to write and enclose a large stamped, self-addressed envelope with all such enquiries; do not telephone.

Condensations

Yet another specialist market is for 'condensed' books – that is, shortened versions of 'classics' such as *Alice in Wonderland* or *The Day of the Triffids* or of similar out-of-copyright books. These may be aimed at the educational market and writers with a teaching background often have the appropriate skills needed to turn a complexly written classic children's book from the 19th-century into something that a modern audience will lap up. Writing styles and social attitudes shift so quickly that even works from 50 years ago may need a modern make-over to appeal to today's children.

And, finally, filler markets

There is less call for filler items in the children's market, but they include jokes and letters, as well as humorous story and information slots in appropriate magazines and newspapers. Choose those publications which will actually pay for inclusion of your material.

There are newsletters to which you can subscribe that will provide details of such work. Often they include useful information on competitions and the world of children's publishing.

08 non-fiction books

In this chapter you will learn:
- the complexity of the non-fiction market
- the specific skills and knowledge you will need to enter the market.

What's the difference?

What is the difference between 'fiction' and 'non-fiction'? It's the same difference that you'll find between 'truth' and 'facts'.

Everything you write has to come across as being *true*; that is, having an internal order and sense, no matter how unusual or strange that truth may be. Even the wildest cartoon or the most surreal comedy has to conform to its own inner logic, otherwise it just becomes incoherent. It is this basic created structure that we refer to when we talk about truth. It is all to do with creating a *willing suspension of disbelief*.

For a werewolf story to function, it has to be accepted as 'true' that people become lycanthropes on the nights of the full moon. Similarly, it has to seem credible that a penniless street urchin can grow up to become president of the USA. Such a story need not be factual and will probably benefit greatly from *not* being factual, but it has to 'ring true'.

These are the 'truths' of fiction – but non-fiction relies far more heavily on facts.

Getting it right

Non-fiction calls for research on a much more rigorous level than fiction. Once you have your basics sorted in a fictional novel, you can embroider the story with as much invented detail as you feel inclined. Not so with non-fiction. Whatever subject or area you approach, you must do it with a stringent eye on thorough research.

If you take a glance at the back of almost any biography, you will spot at once that the author has used a lot of information from *other* books. How else would you research a biography, for the sake of argument, about Napoleon? You can hardly go around asking people what he was like. All the people who knew him are dead. The only sources of information are going to be books, archives and written materials.

A question to ask yourself first is why you think the world needs another biography of Napoleon. Maybe you have come up with a fresh angle on his life and loves? Maybe you want to explore the way in which Napoleon's conquest of Italy allowed for the emancipation of indigenous Jews from the oppression of the Roman Catholic Church. Investigating this requires you to plough your way through scores of factual books and contemporary documents, gathering information, noting anomalies, joining the dots, and then fitting all this into your own 'take' on Napoleon.

Such research will always be of fundamental importance for anything historical and, in a way, it can prove the least demanding. Realize, though, that the books that you choose for research purposes will all have their own bibliographies which may demand attention. Also bear in mind that first-hand sources are always the best, if they can be found.

What if you want to write a book about the Amazon rainforests? Certainly you'll be able to pick up written and online information, but you will also need to consider a visit to the Amazon Basin for 'field research'. If you are considering the effect of the modern industrial world on the rainforests, then you will need to ask a few local people for their opinions. It is no good just chatting to industrialists and government mouthpieces. You are going to have to head into the jungle and speak to the indigenous people, to see what they think of things. If you are planning to write about any country or culture, you need to have experienced it from all angles for it to be an accurate and objective piece of work.

Any non-fiction book is going to take time and money: your own time and the time of people you interview or observe; and your own money, unless you're lucky enough to get a bursary or sponsorship from an interested party.

Even though you may consider yourself to be an expert in whatever field you are intending to write about, there are probably plenty of other 'experts' out there too. Though you may disagree wildly with their opinions, you will have to know what they are in order to refute them. The only way of finding out about their opinions is either to lay hands on these experts' writings, or to go and talk to the people themselves.

Faction

Previously we mentioned 'faction', and this is a good time to mention it again. Faction is *dramatized* fact and there is a lot of it about. It can be something like: ' I was a drummer-boy at The Battle of Gettysburg' or 'My Diary as a Royalist child in the English Civil War' or even 'I, Clytemnestra – a child in the Court of Ancient Rome'.

Or it can take the form of a school play depicting important historical events:

The scene: *the Atlantic Ocean in 1492*

J. Tar (a sailor): *Land ho!*

C. Columbus (an explorer): *Coo, look everyone! America!*

Full Ship's Company: *And about time, too!*

One of the purposes behind faction is that it can make facts more digestible for a young audience. To make the facts even sweeter, a lot of faction these days is couched in humorous terms. Writing a 'comic' faction version of a famous historical event or time period is very popular. Take a look around the bookshops to see what is fashionable in non-fiction.

Another example of faction would be the sort of picture book where a young child is taken for a tour of flora and fauna to be found on the seabed by a friendly and informative seahorse, crab or other character.

With children's non-fiction, the aim is always to find a new way of infiltrating information into a child's head, be it a simple *What are Insects?* guide for very small readers or a *Sex and Contraception* book for young adults.

In the realms of trade fiction a factual book that looks informative but light-hearted is more likely to be picked from the shelves than a dull-looking, school-like tome. Which would you choose? *Extra Maths for Beginners* or *Let's Have SUM Fun!*

A good non-fiction author has to embrace diligent research. You need to be accurate. Your publisher may not be an astronomy expert and needs to be able to trust that your inventive astronomical book is correct. Reviewers delight in finding errors in non-fiction books, and an authoritative attack on your work may kill the book's credibility and possibly damage your reputation. Your editor will also be less than amused if your location of Alpha Centauri or your certainty about the size of the sun turn out to be grossly inaccurate.

Journalists or people with a background in research often make good non-fiction authors. Interestingly enough, we have also found that very good non-fiction authors do not always make good creative fiction authors and vice versa.

Laugh and learn

In children's non-fiction, as we have said, the important element is that you present your facts in an appealing way. 'Appealing' in this case has to cover several bases. A piece of work will have to appeal to teachers, librarians and parents or guardians, as well as to the child itself. It will need to be targeted accurately to the intended age-group, with suitable language, interest and understanding levels, and it will need to deliver all the necessary information in as few pages as possible. It is a particular skill to impart information in a succinct and entertaining manner.

All authors should make sure that their book is a children's book, not a simple adult book in disguise. The text should also be carefully aimed at the publisher's needs.

[UK trade non-fiction publisher]

Writing in a high-level, technical way is not appropriate. The experienced, perfect author writes few words with clarity and style – appropriate for what is required, not to impress.

[UK educational non-fiction publisher]

Serious, studious, sleep-inducing books are out, particularly for the trade market. 'Force-feeding' with fun is in.

Illustrations

Most modern non-fiction books will overflow with illustrations. Information goes down better with photographs, pictures, cartoons or diagrams. Illustrators and designers are going to be deeply involved in the evolution of your non-fiction book right from the outset.

Your book may require photographs. There are picture libraries that keep vast collections and can probably provide a picture to go along with almost anything you might write.

Newspapers, magazines and websites will have their own pictorial archives which you may be able to plunder. Similarly, you may need to approach museums, art galleries and private collections to gather the exact source material you seek. A designer will usually locate the appropriate pictures, but there may be occasions where this time-consuming task falls to the author. You will need to know at the outset who is bearing the cost of these, whether they need any copyright clearance, and will the photos you have chosen quickly date?

Getting permissions

Before you can reproduce any work (be it written, photographic, electronic or otherwise) permission will need to be obtained in writing from the copyright holder, payment will almost always need to be made and an acknowledgement included in the work. Before agreeing to write any commissioned, illustrated non-fiction work, check your contractual obligations with your publisher to define whose responsibility it is to obtain and pay for permissions. It is *imperative* that enough time is allowed *prior* to your book going into production for permissions to be sought and granted. Tracing the actual copyright holder of a work can be difficult and very time-consuming. However, if you do not have permission to use another's work, an expensive legal action could ensue.

A letter of enquiry (and as a courtesy, a self-addressed envelope) to the copyright holder should include the information about what exactly you wish to reproduce, be it text or images. You should also include details of your proposed work, its format and publication details (if you already have them). Publishers who are the holders of copyright may reply with a form for you to complete; others may ask for further, selected details.

Sometimes, despite all your best efforts, it proves impossible to track down the copyright holder. You will sometimes see, included in the acknowledgements section of a book, wording similar to:

> *Every effort has been made to trace the owners of the copyright to XXXX. It has been impossible to trace the owner and the author and publisher would be glad to hear from them.*

Copyright law, particularly in regard to photographs and artworks, is a complex area. Seek advice from your publisher if you are in any doubt, or from a media copyright expert.

Checklist

Before you fling yourself into the world of non-fiction, ask yourself the following questions:

- How good are my research skills?
- How methodical am I?
- How tenacious am I?
- How accurate am I?
- Can I make seemingly dull facts fun or interesting?

Non-fiction authors who are primarily researchers by profession or by nature can be given a theme or topic and will be able to produce an authoritative book on a subject in which they previously had little interest or knowledge.

Exercise 15

Make a list of non-fiction subjects in which you have a particular interest.

Do you have any qualifications or experience relevant to the subject which will impress a publisher?

On how many of these subjects would you be willing to inject a good deal more research? Your project is going to fail if it turns out you have omitted an entire branch of alternative wisdom.

If you have knowledge of a particular subject, how up to date is that knowledge? In the field of computers, cutting-edge knowledge from a year ago will be blunt by now. You will also need to know what technology is under development if your work is to be as current as possible by the time it reaches the bookshops.

Difficulties

We asked a number of trade and educational non-fiction publishers to answer the question, 'What percentage of your list is author inspired or editorially/in-house inspired?' Their replies are worth noting.

Most of the list is planned here and then developed with chosen authors! Publication of unsolicited material is rare. Once authors are contracted to a project, much of the inspiration comes from them.

Over 80 per cent of our list is in-house inspired.

In-house 80 per cent.

Up to 90–95 per cent of our non-fiction list is conceived in-house.

Less than 5 per cent is author inspired. Our staff editors – or freelance packaging companies – come up with most of our titles.

Almost 100 per cent in-house.

Our next question was 'How do you find authors or contributors?' Almost every reply was similar and along these lines:

Agents.

Directories, academic bodies, agents, colleagues.

Word of mouth and personal contacts; institutions such as universities, colleges, museums, agents, occasionally unsolicited applications.

From previous projects, by putting requests to agents, and from rejected proposals that showed ability but were rejected on the grounds of unsuitability.

The marketplace

You will see from the publishers' comments that the non-fiction market is even more difficult to break into than the fiction market. To do so you will need skill, practice, perseverance and a certain amount of talent.

We next asked the same publishers if they had any words of wisdom for new authors. Every single one said the same thing: research the market and study your selected publisher's list before commencing work on a proposal. The following replies sum up the situation and offer a little more hope:

Do not be put off by rejection. Ninety per cent of the proposals that show some flair and ability are rejected because they are unsuitable for our list and not because they are simply awful! Study the market and think about what you are proposing. If you can show that you have thought through your ideas and investigated the market you may well be approached for some other project in the future.

While many of our authors come from the usual sources we also take on many authors/contributors who have written quite modest pieces/parts of books/edited etc. – and are ready to develop on from there, based on past records!

If you are an acknowledged expert in a particular field, publishers may approach you to write something or to endorse the work of others. If you already have had articles published in magazines and newspapers, this will certainly help open doors. Newspapers and magazines are good areas to consider. Periodicals are always on the look-out for new material; like television, they are great devourers of work and there is an enormous range of specialist magazines constantly needing their pages filled with new articles.

Even if these are articles aimed at the adult reader, publishers will be impressed by the credibility attached to actually having been in print. It may be that the article could be expanded to become a children's book. This is not so unlikely as it may sound. As an expert ornithologist, you may be able to write a children's guide to birds by judiciously rethinking a published adult article.

The in-house method of creating books means that commissioning editors are always looking for authors. If you have presented a professional proposal to a suitable publisher, the editor will have your name on file. There are many reasons why your work may have been rejected, including the possibility that the publisher had already commissioned a similar project at the time yours arrived.

Presentation

Because of the nature of non-fiction works, it is not usually appropriate for an author to present a publisher with a complete, unsolicited work. The best way to present your idea is in outline form. A proposal, sample chapter and rough page-layout guide will be enough, accompanied by a polite letter of enquiry. (See Chapter 9 for details of submitting work.) We asked our non-fiction publishers whether they preferred to see proposals or completed scripts, and what they appreciated in a covering letter. The replies were yet again similar and the following are typical:

> *I prefer proposals and sample text – that way I have an influence over the finished ms [manuscript]. Complete scripts are usually too wide of the mark – they usually aren't tailored to the company's needs or the needs of the marketplace. Scripts should be accurately typed and come with a CV and covering letter which gives me something about background and personality. An unmemorable letter gets forgotten!*

> *Proposals which include full contents outline and some sample text. Always helpful if author indicates what he/she considers the appropriate age-level, readership, sector of the market, rough extent and treatment of illustrations to be. And supplies a brief biography.*

> *Proposal – stating clearly and concisely the aim, market and main strengths of the book. A sample chapter to show style and approach is useful. Personal details and relative experience is useful. Covering letter – concise, with main points only.*

The wide range of non-fiction

The markets for non-fiction break down in a similar way to those for fiction: trade non-fiction books are primarily sold through traditional outlets direct to children, parents or whomever, while non-trade non-fiction finds its way into libraries, schools and other institutions.

The trade non-fiction market covers everything which is not fiction. This is broader in range than you might at first imagine: it includes puzzle books, joke books, books on how to create your own theatre, books on how to become a racing driver, and books on how to make a working origami submarine, kite-making, knot-tying, juggling, bike maintenance, how to look after a cat and a gerbil, how to extract your gerbil from your cat's mouth, first aid for cat-scratches, living with a neurotic gerbil and a homicidal feline.

While the age-groupings are similar to those for the fiction market, non-fiction books may have a much broader age-range appeal. For example, a book on fly-fishing may well be bought by a 7-year-old and a 13-year-old, as long as it is written so that it appeals to and can be understood by children of either age.

Such books have to appeal instantly to a fast-food generation, and this includes dishing out the information in easily digestible chunks as well as making it attractive to the eye. Thus, modern non-fiction books will be scattered with cartoons, jokes, information boxes, bullet points, interesting design layouts and so on. Anything, in fact, to catch the eye and interest.

Many non-fiction books are presented nowadays as being fun first and knowledge second. If a book can convey useful information without the child even knowing there is a learning process in action, so much the better. Such books can deal with topics as disparate as sport, art, the lives of famous people, 'true' ghost stories, 'real-life' mysteries, interesting historical events, and so on, with so light a touch that even the most wilful underachiever can be hooked and reeled in.

For the older ages, say, 8+, there is also a wide variety of more text-based books with little or no illustration, covering social issues all the way from coping with grief to growing through puberty. A multitude of serious issues can be approached this way, including peer pressure, problems encountered by stepchildren, how to survive divorce or how best to approach the job market. These books often include 'true-life' stories gleaned from research with children who have encountered these things first-hand. (Research for such a book would, of course, include many interviews with these children.)

Other non-fiction is largely illustration-led. A bath-time book on pond creatures may have a picture of a fish with the single word, 'fish', underneath. Or a backyard book could have a picture of a wriggly worm accompanied by the word 'worm', and similar pages for spiders, centipedes, beetles, etc.

Cookery books for children can form the other end of this illustrated genre. The book may explain the ingredients, recipe and cooking methods with simple text accompanied by large, colour photographs showing each stage of the process.

You could even write an illustrated book on how to make your own illustrated book.

As with illustrated fiction books, these illustrated non-fiction works are very costly to produce and a lot of the comments included in Chapter 6 are pertinent here. Publishers will be very selective about what they produce because of the cost of commissioning artwork, photographs, picture research and designers. Trade publishers in particular will be on the lookout for something with an international appeal, something that will suit as many different countries and cultures as possible, so it may be as well not to be too parochial when you present your proposal.

This is not to say that a publisher would automatically dismiss a book exploring the flora and fauna of a particular country or region, or a book which explores that country or region's traditions or politics. Such books have a place in the non-fiction market – they may just be a little harder to sell in large quantities. On the other hand, a well-produced book on the Sahara Desert or the Florida Everglades is likely to find a worldwide audience and sell in good numbers.

Payment

Many non-fiction authors are paid a flat fee or a one-off payment for their text work. This is because their input is seen as just one element in a complex production process. They are not generally viewed as the 'author' of the work but as a single contributor.

Hence, advances and royalties are less forthcoming from non-fiction publishers than they would be in the fiction world because of the extra preparation and production costs involved – which is something else to bear in mind before you head off for a six-month research trek across Siberia.

Educational publishers

Specialist educational publishers produce books mainly for the school and library markets, so they will be seeking projects which are educationally linked. If you are interested in this field, you will need to know what children are studying and at what age, so that books can be pitched appropriately. For instance, if children study ancient China only between the ages of 7 and 8 in your country, there is little purpose in preparing an educationally based proposal on this subject for 13-year-olds. No-one will want it.

Books produced by educational publishers range from history to art, from science to social issues, from mathematics to special needs, from drama to literature, and all points in between. They will include books providing interesting information: technical know-how from photography to mechanics to quantum physics.

These books can include companion websites, photocopiable teaching aids, beginner readers, dictionaries, study books, encyclopaedias and DVD and computer disks.

Non-fiction multimedia ranges from learning a foreign language to 'how-to-draw' packages, from encyclopaedias to interactive games, and so on.

Essentially, you must take a long look at your skills and carefully consider how best to use them. Those of you with teaching experience will find that this scores highly with a commissioning editor, assuming your projected book falls within the parameters of your expertise.

How to annoy publishers, part two

We asked the non-fiction publishers what their pet hates were. These included:

> *Ill-considered proposals, people who 'cold-call' wanting to discuss their project at length over the phone.*

> *Writing in a high-level, technical way when not appropriate. Writing too many words, even after an editorial briefing! Unreliability. Lack of clarity. We also never bring together authors who don't know each other and automatically expect them to work well together. So – if the author of a submission can work well with a co-author, suggest it.*

> *Authors who draw their own pictures, or naively think they have to do all the artwork and take all the photos themselves.*

And if you still have not received and understood our main message, take heed from this publisher:

> I will give a lot more attention to letters from people who have bothered to find out what we publish. I get irritated by people who haven't done the slightest bit of research before they write. Unrealistic proposals are a complete waste of time.
>
> I received a two-line letter from someone who was proposing to write a history of Britain. The two lines contained four spelling mistakes (including the writer's address). The accompanying proposal comprised a box (in which I was supposed to imagine a picture of George III) and four bullet points of four or five words each about George IV. There was no CV, and no other clue to the author's identity. Nothing. Would I give any time to someone who treated such a huge project so feebly? Of course not!

Schedules are often very rigid in children's non-fiction, with very heavy initial investment costs. When an author doesn't deliver the goods, it's extremely painful. Most editors will therefore tend to turn to the authors they know and trust rather than try out new names who might not deliver what's wanted on time. What this means is that unsolicited material gets a lot less attention than it does in other areas of publishing. It doesn't take much to consign a proposal to the dustbin.

Co-writers

You may be asked to co-author a work of non-fiction with one or more other authors. But when it comes to dividing up the writing duties and the subsequent money, authors can fall out with each other permanently unless boundaries and percentages are agreed in advance. Your editor may be able to mediate. The same applies if you are asked to 'ghost write' a work – perhaps for a blind author who cannot key in text, or for a famous person who created a storyline idea but who cannot actually write children's books (in which case, their name is really being used on the cover as a selling feature).

Checklist

Before beginning work, and before you submit that non-fiction proposal you should follow these steps towards success:

1 Find a theme, topic, or original or unusual subject.
2 Approach it from an interesting angle.
3 Decide upon your style, be it humorous, serious or whatever.
4 Get the whole thing onto paper: outline, sample chapter or suggested layout.
5 Seek out an appropriate publisher.
6 Send the proposal off along with a polite, brief yet informative letter of enquiry, and your biographical details.
7 While you are waiting for a response, work on another idea.

09
presentation and submission

In this chapter you will learn:
- the importance of presentation
- guidelines to help you with your approach to publishers and agents.

Luck or judgement?

It is not *what* you know, but *who* you know that counts. Well, that's true enough. Knowing the right people can be very helpful in opening life's more securely fastened doors. But even if your grandparents own a publishing house (which these days they probably wouldn't – it's more likely to be owned by Global-Mediagobbler-Intl.) it does not automatically follow that *you* are going to become a published author. Getting into the business involves a little more than a fortunate birth; you cannot leave it all to luck. Within acceptable bounds, you're going to need to know how to sell yourself.

So, you are desperate to get your work published. You are invited to a party and happen to bump into someone who is involved in the world of publishing and who seems to you likely to be a useful contact. Do you accost this individual and force your ideas on them for the rest of the evening?

No, you don't!

Heed this advice from a weary publisher:

> Don't *talk about projects at social occasions; ask for a name and address/card.*

> Don't *then ring up the office – write.*

A dialogue

> The scene: *A supermarket checkout. A person with many years' experience in children's publishing is waiting in line to pay for their week's shopping. A hopeful author happens to have found out what this person does for a living, and sees the chance to advance their cause!*

> The characters: *Anne Eddittorre and Hope ffulle-Author.*

> (Hope ffulle-Author shoves her way through the line of shoppers)

> HffA: *Hello, there. My name is Hope ffulle-Author. This is your lucky day – I've written a brilliant book that will make us all rich.*

> AE: *Ye-es ... uh, is it a book for children?*

> HffA: *Well, it's got a message for everyone, really. Everyone from 8 to 80. Ninety, even!*

AE: *I take it it's fiction. How long is the story?*

HffA: *It's sort of fiction, and non-fiction, really. The story revolves around my lovely old dog Bozo who sadly died a couple of months ago. We've had him stuffed and mounted in the hall if you'd like to come around and see him some time. Anyway the really brilliant thing is that I've come up with this stunningly original concept where Bozo can speak!*

Fantastic, huh? And he can fly and do just about everything. In Chapter 6 he single-pawedly solves all the ecological problems of the entire planet and discovers how to make sure everyone loves everyone else. In the nicest way, of course. No smut, you know. And then he flies off into outer space in search of the almigh …

AE (politely but firmly interrupting): *I see. Sounds interesting. How long would you say the script was?*

HffA: *Uh, I don't know. I haven't actually finished typing it out yet or anything. But my writing is really easy to read. I mean, take no notice of my friends – they say I write like a dyslexic spider in boxing gloves. It's just not true. My next door neighbour is a doctor, and she says she can read nearly every word. And she thinks it's brilliant. Anyway, the book is about 234 pages long so far and still going strong. Would you like to read some of it? As it's the weekend, I don't suppose you'll have much on, so I could get the first 12 notebooks over to you later this afternoon, if you like. No problem.*

(Sound of Anne slumping to the floor)

HffA: *Oh dear, she seems to have fainted. It must be the excitement! Help! Call an ambulance, somebody!*

This scene could also take place in line for the drinks at a party, in a crowded lift or in the office of an editor who forgets to put his voicemail answering machine on, and unsuspectingly picks up the ringing telephone. It need not be an editor on the receiving end, either. It could be anyone whom Hope ffulle-Author happens to know is involved in some way in children's books. In 10 years' time it could be you.

A letter

The following is a hypothetical letter sent to a publishing house from another eager author. This time, a Mr Ivan E. Normusego writes:

> *Dear Sir or MAdam*
>
> *I have looked at all the meterial avaliable for chidlren and a lot of i'ts at the best unsuitable and at wort itter grabage, I no i can do much better ans so i wrote a series of books about a little school bu called Mister Toot-Sweet dn all the fantastical going on he comes acorss in his erevyday journies. I have reed it to my next door neigfhbour who is a supermarket manger and nobodies' fool, and he says its a sur-fire woinner and I going to get Mister_Toot sweat trademarked and the quartersize salt-dough model I have made also patented,*
>
> *I also see Mister Toot-Sweet as a cartoon which Dizney could animate and also it has a million marketting and merchandising pissibilities!!!*
>
> *This idea miust be treated in the strictest confidense and i await your reply by return of post otherwise i shall take it to someone else and then youl'l be sorry..*
>
> *Your sincerey*
>
> *Ivan E. Normusego*

Exaggerations? Unfortunately not: the above are fairly realistic examples of the sort of incompetent approaches that the worst would-be authors make to people in the world of children's books all the time. Sadly, the chances of Hope or Ivan ever getting their work into print are very slim unless they mend their ways.

In a competitive market like children's publishing, you have to give thought to *presentation*. You cannot wrap a bad idea up in pretty paper and get it through the net – but you can make a good idea *better* if you take the right approach.

Let us go back and take a look at exactly what those two would-be authors did wrong.

Hope ffulle-Author – how to crash and burn

Timing

Everyone knows the story of the professional comedian approached by someone at a party and asked to tell a joke. 'What do you do for a living?' retorts the comedian. 'I'm a plumber,' comes the reply. 'Okay, then,' says the comedian. 'Let's see you fix a ball-cock.'

Hope ffulle-Author has done something similar by assaulting Anne Eddittorre out of working hours. You should only ever approach professional people at their place of work, and in an appropriate way. The alternative is simply rude.

What's wrong with Hope's 'book'?

Age-range

Not many books are read by people of all ages. As you are now aware, children's books are fitted into specific age-range categories. The fact that Hope imagines that her book will be read universally shows that she doesn't understand the market.

She has not even finished her book, let alone typed it up. In fact, she has no clear idea of how long her book is or how long it will end up being.

She also makes another big mistake. Suppose she really does have a good idea, a totally brilliant idea – something that doesn't involve a talking dead dog flying around and saving the universe. The very last thing she should be doing is telling all and sundry before her idea is in a finished and presentable form.

There are several reasons for keeping a good idea to yourself. 'Ideas' once they have been aired have the strange tendency to resurface elsewhere – written by someone else. Ideas are not intentionally stolen, but such things can lie dormant in someone else's brain and then emerge from the subconscious as if from nowhere. There is a familiar phenomenon in the publishing world whereby several stories or proposals on virtually the same subject, by authors who have never met, will land on an editor's desk in the same week.

If you have a good idea, just jot it down, keep it private, and only discuss it with people you trust. Hope ffulle-Author would be very put out if her doctor neighbour had a book published called *Bozo the Superdog*, but she might not be able to do anything about it. (We will cover safeguarding your work later.)

Ivan E. Normusego – the idiot's guide to letter-writing

Addressee

Ivan has not taken the trouble to find out to whom he should be addressing his letter. In fact, for all Ivan knows, he could have made contact with a publisher who deals solely with Russian-to-English translations of sewage plant equipment manuals.

Spelling and typing

Ivan cannot spell. Not all writers can spell, but there are dictionaries, spell-checkers on computers and even dinky little electronic gizmos to help you out, as well as literate friends or colleagues. Nor can Ivan type. Everyone allows the odd 'typo' (typing or typographical error) to slip through, but there is no excuse for anyone to send a letter that looks like someone has spilt a can of alphabet spaghetti onto a sheet of paper and then sealed it in an envelope.

It would be very clear to whoever receives this 'communication' from Ivan that he has not even bothered to reread his own letter and, even though these days his spelling and grammar may well have been cleaned up by a computer, his attitude is still way off the mark. As we said before, presentation is vitally important. It is part of your professional approach.

The market

Ivan says he has taken a good look at the market for which the book is intended, but his observations are made clearly from a very biased point of view. Anyone who announces that everything available to children is 'garbage' does not have a very objective view of things.

He should also bear in mind that the opinions of family, friends and neighbours are usually of limited value. The supermarket manager, in thinking Mister Toot-Sweet would be a money-spinner, might be right. Then again, he is just as likely to be wrong. The fact is that unless your family, friends and neighbours are involved in publishing, their opinion has no real weight. You should also bear in mind that people from whom you seek opinions are unlikely to tell you that your beloved project is utterly ghastly. These people are more likely to be polite to you, and will usually tell you what they think you want to hear:

A very common statement in submission letters is '... I've shown it to all my friends and they think it's great.' Well they would, wouldn't they? My boss once said that he would love to get a proposal from someone which started 'I've shown it to all my friends and they all think it's a load of rubbish, but I still think it's a good idea.' At least then you'd feel you were getting something original, something the author really believed in.

[Publisher of children's trade non-fiction]

Expectations

Maybe Ivan's idea *would* make an amazing special-effects movie; and possibly children throughout the world would stampede over their own grandparents to get at a Mister Toot-Sweet pencil case. First and foremost, however, Hope's and Ivan's ideas should be seen as *books*. The spin-offs would come later on, if at all, and a prospective publisher is unlikely to be swayed by the grandiose merchandizing concepts of either budding author.

Know the publishing style and philosophy of a house before you submit your work; you can get a sense of this by requesting a publisher's catalogues and by reading the books they publish. If your work doesn't suit a particular house, don't submit it; find a publisher that's compatible with your style. Be selective and target your submissions carefully.

[US publisher]

Research publishers' lists through bookshops, libraries, catalogues, to discover if the project is likely to be suitable for them before sending it off. Also research the competition and consider how your project would/could stand up to it. With non-fiction, try to understand the difference between an educational list and a non-fiction trade list.

[English/French publisher]

I hate unsolicited e-mail submissions addressed to info@ which begin 'Hi' and go on to suggest that if I want to read some of their work, I'm to check out their website. You just know every publisher and agent in town, if not the world has received the same round robin untargeted, lazy e-mail, and it's the fastest way to get me to hit the delete key!

[UK agent]

Your aim is to get your work published. You should be nearly ready to draft your submission letter. Before doing that, consider the following:

The scene: *an interview room for a Very Important Merchant Bank. Three Very Important People sit behind a long desk looking Very Important. In front of the desk is a solitary chair.*

(Knock on door)

Chief interviewer (to his colleagues): *Ah, that will be Miss Burglebrain, who seemed from her written responses to be the ideal candidate for the job we have on offer. She is charismatic, charming, intelligent, go-getting, capable, painstaking and a leading member of Mensa.* (Aloud) *Enter!* (Enter Miss Burglebrain)

(She is wearing a tutu, wellington boots, a fireman's helmet and a half-metre-long hose which revolves and sprays cocoa)

Miss Burglebrain: *Hiya, folks! Is it okay to bring my pet skunk in?*

Chief interviewer: *NEXT APPLICANT!*

What did Miss Burglebrain do wrong? She packaged herself very badly. She gave herself no chance to prove whether she would have been any good in the job or not. Do not put yourself into the same position. When your work lands on a publisher's desk, make sure that you have given it the best chance possible. Good presentation of your material is absolutely vital.

You want, via your presented work, to be seen as a professional author.

The finished product

Example

SHADOWBACK

Chapter One: The Voice From Nowhere

'Are you all right?'

Dominic Carroll almost jumped clear of his chair as that faint, hissing voice broke the silence. A girl's voice. A projected, urgent whisper, like someone trying secretly to get his attention without being overheard by anyone else.

Except that Dominic was alone in the room. There wasn't anyone else.

He listened intently for a few seconds, turning his head this way and that: trying to home in on the source of the uncanny voice.

Maybe it had been someone passing by out in the street. Maybe it had been a voice on the television down in the living room. Maybe he was just hearing things.

He shook his head and went back to his impossible maths homework. The strain of an hour with numbers that simply would not add up or divide or multiply the way they should was enough to make anyone start hearing things. It was as if those numbers had taken on a mischievous life of their own.

He grabbed a pencil and wrote: 10 + 10 = 92.4.

He gazed down at the paper. Ninety-two point four?

> He tried again. But this time, although he <u>thought</u> 10, his pencil wrote 66.
>
> He threw the pencil down with a snort of annoyance.
>
> He decided to give up on his homework. Maybe all those disobedient numbers were beginning to damage his brain? Whatever was going on, he needed a rest from maths: that much was certain.
>
> He slipped off his chair and sprawled out on his bed, staring up at the sinister trapdoor in his ceiling. Dominic's room was small, its walls pushed inwards under the roof. There was only a narrow stretch of flat ceiling, and it was dominated by that trapdoor. He had never felt entirely at ease with it. He knew that it led only to the dark and dusty roof-space, but he couldn't help the fact that his imagination believed otherwise. His dreams were often darkened by images of the trapdoor opening silently in the deeps of the night, and of the crouched hulks of the things that would come slithering down to get him.

Your typescript (which is still often called a 'manuscript' in the publishing world) must be presented professionally. The actual layout is acceptable in slightly varying formats, but the sample page here shows you the basic idea.

White paper

Despite everything we've said about the electronic age in which we are now living, your manuscript must initially be presented to a publisher on paper: preferable on good-quality white A4 paper. Thin paper, which is easily torn or damaged, will start to look scruffy after one or two read-throughs. But avoid expensive, heavyweight paper: it will cost a fortune to send through the mail and will be wasted if the manuscript needs to be rewritten – which it probably will. Standard photocopying paper does the job perfectly well.

Black print

Your manuscript must be printed in black ink. This photocopies better than any other colour, as well as generally being easier on the eye. Choose a typeface of a size and style which is easy to read, such as Times New Roman, Helvetica, Arial or similar; 12pt is the best size to use. If you are working on a computer, be sure not to use draft printouts for your final presentation copy. Ensure that your printer is working properly and that every line of every page is clean and legible.

Layout

The layout of a page is all-important and pretty much standard throughout the publishing world. Use double-spacing: this means you must leave a full line gap between every line of print. Also be sure to leave wide margins on either side of the text and at the top and the bottom of the page.

Wide margins and double-spacing are there to allow a copy-editor enough room to make notes and alterations and to write down instructions to the typesetter/printer, which usually will be done in red or sometimes blue ink, which will stand out from the black type.

Also note that italics are not used in the example above; the words which you would wish to be italicized in the final version are for now simply underlined – the editors will know what you mean. Similarly, you would not want to use bold print in the text of the manuscript – the general rule is to keep any kind of fancy formatting to a minimum.

The copy-editor, by the way, is the person who makes all the alterations and corrections in the code understood by typesetters. We have included opposite a page of our second draft script, from this chapter, which was patiently edited by our long-suffering friend, and freelance editor, Iain Brown.

If you compare this page with the final printed one in this chapter (on page 182), you will see how a copy-editor will work on your script, making suggestions for improving the text and drawing the author's attention to anything that may be confusing or unclear to a reader.

The title page of your manuscript should include the title of the work and your name or the pseudonym under which you would like the work to be published. It should also include your address, telephone and fax numbers, and e-mail address.

In general, the text should have a straight margin on the left (ranged left (this is called]). It should not be "justified". A "justified" script is one where there ~~is~~ are straight ~~line~~ edges down both the left-hand and right-hand sides of the script, as in a book. ~~An unjustified script looks much like a more widely-spaced business letter.~~ If you are working on computer, do not "justify" your script as this may cause ~~spacing~~ confusion for the typesetters ~~later on~~.

You should leave one blank space after ~~the~~ a full stop, ~~of~~ START ~~comma, semi-colon or colon~~ ~~one sentence and the beginning of the next.~~ Don't use "bold" print for emphasis or italics, but simply underline words you wish stressed ~~or put them into CAPITALS.~~

You may have been taught to /indent/ new paragraphs and dialogue ((i.e.), leave five letter spaces before starting a fresh paragraph or piece of dialogue.) This is no longer strictly necessary as a copy-editor will alter the layout to suit their requirements / Publishers prefer a one-line gap between paragraphs.

Likewise, ~~However,~~ each new piece of dialogue in a conversation should be given a fresh line. It looks better (on the page) AU: Pls clarity and makes it easier to follow the conversation than would be the case if ~~it~~ was all strung together in a single paragraph. dialogue

Every new chapter should be started on a fresh page. [LESLEY: CRIKEY! REALLY? YOU NEVER TOLD ME THAT.] This

Delete!

If you are represented by an agent, then their name and address should be included on the title page in place of your address. Also provide the word-count of the script; that is, how long it is.

One thing you should *never* do is to date the manuscript, as it may have to pass through the hands of several publishers before it finds a home. Each stopping-off point could mean a gap of several weeks (or even months), and any printed date will make it clear to a publisher that they are not the first to have seen it. This is not a good idea if you want a positive response.

The moment your script starts to show its age, it will lose a good deal of its initial appeal. Hence the use of reasonable quality paper that will survive a few readings, and your avoidance of anything that will show it has 'done the rounds'.

Text for typescripts and disks

These days scripts can be delivered in 'hard copy' (printed on paper) or on disk or as an e-mail attachment. (Remember! E-mails are only to be used once initial contact has been made and an editor has shown interest.) Once your work has found a home you can check your contract or ask your editor for details of what they require. Many publishers have briefs on how to submit final work. In general, the text should have a straight margin on the left (this is called 'ranged left'). It should not be 'justified'. A 'justified' script is one where there are straight edges down both the left-hand and right-hand sides of the script, as in a book. If you are working on computer, do not 'justify' your script as this may cause confusion for the designer or the typesetters.

You should leave one blank character space after a full stop or any punctuation mark. As we mentioned above, do not use 'bold' print for emphasis or italics, but simply underline words you wish stressed. Avoid any fancy type (font) styles, too.

You may have been taught to indent new paragraphs and dialogue (that is, leave five character spaces before starting a fresh paragraph or piece of dialogue). This is no longer strictly necessary as a copy-editor will alter the layout to suit their requirements. Publishers prefer a one-line gap between paragraphs. Likewise, each new piece of dialogue in a conversation should be given a fresh line. It distinguishes it from the prose on the page and makes the conversation easier to follow.

Every new chapter should be started on a fresh page. This fresh page should include the chapter number and its title (if it has one).

Your computer will have a header and footer facility. It is a good idea to use it, to save loose pages getting entirely lost: all you need to do is include your name and the book title. In this way, pages that go astray can easily be returned to the fold.

Page numbering

Page numbering is absolutely *vital*. The pages of your manuscript must be numbered consecutively right through the book. In other words, the first page should be '1' and the one-hundred-and-thirtieth page should be '130'. Do not number new chapters afresh. Follow the numbering sequence right through. The page numbers should be located either centrally at the bottom of every manuscript page, or in the top right-hand corner. A computer will do this for you with ease – but only if you ask it to, and you don't want to have printed out your full manuscript only to realize when it is in hard-copy form that it has no page numbers. If you are three-quarters of the way through a typed script and have forgotten to add page numbers, do not despair. There is nothing wrong with adding them by hand, but do it soon. An open window and a stiff breeze could result in a full day spent sorting out an unnumbered script.

As well as typing services, there are also 'criticism' services available if you would like an 'in-the-know' outside eye to be run over your work before you present it to a publisher. It may be beneficial to have an objective viewpoint to edit, tidy up and make constructive or even detailed editorial suggestions on your work. This service, as well as that of typists, can be found through various author associations, magazines, and websites, but compare prices and use a recommended service if possible. It is not necessary to sign up to a proofreading course, or any other kind of suspiciously expensive service if you have followed the basic advice in this book.

Fiction synopses

Once you have made contact with an interested editor, you will most likely be asked to send in a synopsis of your work, along with the first three chapters, especially if it is a work of 8,000 words or more. You may well think your book deserves to be read as a whole, but there is a practical reason for this limited initial approach – an editor whose interest you have piqued will seldom have time at this stage to read a full manuscript, but they will want to know what the story is about and how well you write – hence the synopsis and opening chapters. If the editor likes what they see, you will then be asked to submit the full manuscript. The synopsis, incidentally, should not be shorter than half a page, and could be considerably longer in a complex novel – but do not get carried away: the job of the synopsis is to present the story in as brief a way as the weight of the plot will allow, and it will do you no favours if your carefully crafted plot gets lost in amongst a lot of unnecessary details.

Non-fiction products

The title page for a non-fiction manuscript should be the same as outlined above, but you should also give an idea of the type of material contained in the manuscript. Explain what it is that you are proposing to convey and to whom it is targeted. For example:

> Edible Bookmarks for Beginners *(working title), a proposal aimed at the 5–7 year age-group on how to make, bake and create bookmarks which can be eaten.*

You can decide exactly how to lay out your title page, but if you have a computer then you can use a large typeface for the main title, and centre it on the page.

What to include

A contents page would help to give a quick impression of your book. Include chapter headings with perhaps a sentence or two about the material contained in each chapter. Remember that it is not a good idea to submit completed material. It may turn out to be the same as another recently published work, or possibly your ideas may suit a publisher while your style does not. Thus a synopsis will give you the opportunity to present your ideas and allow a prospective publisher to guide you in the actual writing of the book so that it fits in with the house style. This could save you having to write the book twice.

Your proposal or synopsis outline could also include any marketing ideas you may have for selling your book. Potential sales areas for *Edible Bookmarks for Beginners* would include the usual trade and non-trade markets, but might appeal to foodstores, with a promotional link to a particular product or range of products. The more innovative yet practical ideas you can suggest, the more your publisher will know that you have done your homework, and the more they may be convinced that yours is a viable project. (We shall expand on marketing and promotion in Chapter 12.) You will also need to include a sample chapter, or some example page layouts of your proposed work.

Illustrations

If photographs or illustrations are integral to the book, then send photocopies or scanned images, preferably on A4 paper, to give the script a well-packaged look. Colour copies or printouts can be produced easily and cheaply these days. Remember to get permission to use photographs and art and to send in copies of the permission documentation along with your submission. Only send your images on disk if your editor has requested that you do so.

Should you have a very specific idea for the layout of your work (if it is to be highly illustrated, for example), then send in a design plan to the publisher. This can be done by using some A3 paper (420 mm × 297 mm, the size of two A4 sheets placed side by side), folding it in two and then showing the proposed design for a typical spread. In this case, text could be typed or *neatly* handwritten with copies or hand-drawn illustration layout suggestions ('roughs'). It does not matter if you are not an artist, or are not planning to illustrate the book yourself, simple drawings may well be enough to convey your meaning.

Think very carefully before submitting unsolicited original illustrations. At the very least, they may well be out of your hands for several months; at worst, they could get lost in transit. Even if they arrive safely at their destination, your illustrations could still get battered, knocked about and trodden on, and have coffee spilled on them, or simply disappear forever between publisher's offices. Colour photocopying or the purchase of a computer scanner may seem expensive, but in this case, the financial outlay will at least ensure that your original work survives intact and in pristine condition.

Author/illustrators of all work

If you are an author/illustrator familiar with the technicalities of producing an illustrated children's book (as explained in Chapter 6), then you can go about presenting your work in one of several ways. If you have completed the artwork, then you could submit colour photocopies or scans, numbered to correspond to the script. If you do not possess or have access to a scanner, and colour photocopying the entire book proves prohibitively expensive, a better option may be to submit one or two colour copies of those illustrations in which you have the greatest faith, and the rest could then be copied in black-and-white. (Publishers' abbreviation for black and white is 'B/W' or 'B&W', by the way.)

You may wish possibly to present a 'dummy' book, by which we mean a mock-up of your book showing the page layouts, style, size and even examples of any paper engineering if the book is intended to include cut-outs or additions. Such a dummy book can range from a stapled-together booklet executed in pencil, to an A4 page of simple sketches or a 'zig-zag', which is a length of paper folded concertina-like. We won't go into any more detail here, because if you do not know what we mean, you probably should not be submitting your own artwork!

Presenting your work

You have a completed manuscript in front of you and you have been asked to send it in. What do you do next? Firstly, do not hole-punch it, ring-bind it, staple it chapter by chapter, paperclip parts of it together or do anything else to it at all. The same rule applies to your synopsis and initial three chapters, as mentioned above. Your manuscript must be left *loose-leaf*, no matter how uneasy that makes you feel. Your work is almost guaranteed to pass through several pairs of hands. Punched holes can easily tear; the paper will show creases, curls and scuffs from being folded over staples; and any kind of binding will speed the deterioration in the look of the script. They are also time-consuming for a busy editor to struggle with. Many editors can and will speed-read a submission. Clips and bindings slow that process down and can be annoying, and the last thing you want right now is an annoyed editor.

Simply put the manuscript or the synopsis and opening chapters in page order, give it a quick shuffle and thump to make it look neat and tidy, and slip a couple of elastic bands around it. Two elastic bands side to side and two top to bottom should do the trick and will ensure that the pages stay together in transit. Place your work in a simple cardboard folder of a snug size which will fit into, usually, an A4 padded envelope. (Illustrations can be sent in an A3 size package, but be very wary of sending a publisher anything too large: enormous great packages will not find easy accommodation on a desk, and who knows where it may be slipped temporarily so as to be out of the way, and then forgotten.) For additional security you could add card sleeves to either end of your work before placing it in the folder.

On the outside of the folder, write your name or pseudonym, your address, the title of the work and, this time, the date of submission. Why date it when we were so adamant that the work itself should have no date? It is simply that a date on the folder may well remind the recipient that it is high time they read it. If the work is returned, the folder can be replaced with a new one, or if it is in good condition the information can be covered with a label with a new date on it. Don't forget your stamped addressed envelope if you want your material returned.

The title

It is not vital for your work to have a definite title at this point: it could have a 'working title', which is a word or phrase by which you can identify it – *The Earwig that Flew to the Moon*, for instance. In this case, write on the folder: 'THE EARWIG THAT FLEW TO THE MOON (working title for 32pp children's story) by L. E. Fant'. In the case of non-fiction: 'PIRACY FOR BEGINNERS – proposal idea for 7–11-year-olds, by R. Jimlad'.

Before you settle on a final title, be sure to check that it is original. There is basically no copyright in titles (trademarking of original typography or titles is an exception), but it would be daft to select a famous published title or one very similar to something already in print. *The Earwig, The Witch and the Wardrobe* will not get very far. Neither will *Lord of the Earwigs*, or *Harriet Potter*. On the other hand, it is not worth agonizing over a title at this stage, especially as your publisher may have their own ideas as to what your work should be called.

Covering letters

Your proposal is prepared, packaged and ready to go in the post to your chosen publisher.

You may have found your publisher's address from an annual writer's reference book or website. This is as good a place to start as any, but the speed with which things change in the world of publishing could mean that an incumbent in the New Year may be gone by May. The safest thing, if you have any doubt about your information, is to telephone the publisher and ask the receptionist the name of the senior commissioning editor. Be certain to ask for the name of the editor in the particular field in which you are interested. Large publishing houses are split into many departments; make certain you have been given the name of the right person. 'Could you give me the name of the editor in charge of children's non-fiction, please?' will do the trick. If, for some reason, the receptionist is unable to help you, they may put you through to someone in the appropriate department.

Do not use this as an opportunity to buttonhole an editor: it will not go down well. Briefly, politely and professionally ask for the name you need, and check the spelling and title (Mr, Mrs or Ms) if you are at all unsure.

Of course, if someone asks you why you are enquiring, then by all means give a very brief outline, but do not treat this as a pre-interview, or you will become like Hope ffulle-Author!

The submission letter is possibly the most important item in your package. It can instantly enchant or antagonize the recipient. Thus, it must be well written; it must be professional.

All the publishers we contacted with our questionnaire, both fiction and non-fiction and from all over the world, said precisely the same: that they want to receive typescripts and proposals in hard copy, in the manner we have described, and never just as a computer disk or an e-mail attachment. *All* the publishers said they did not want telephone calls describing your work at length. *All* said that they did not wish to receive original or amateur artwork. *All* agreed on what they do and do not like to see in a submission letter. The following two responses are typical:

> *Badly written letters, or proposals containing poor spelling and punctuation get rejected. If a writer is incapable of checking an introductory letter then there's precious little chance that he/she is going to take care over a manuscript.*

> *[Non-fiction publisher]*

> *Covering letters should be kept as brief and to the point as possible. It's easier to say what I do* not *appreciate in them:*

> *a) I do not want the author's life history.*

> *b) I do not want to know that several kids next door/their son's class at school or whoever think this is the best book ever written.*

> *c) I certainly do not want emotional blackmail. It makes me uncomfortable and annoyed if I get letters telling me that the author has recently been made redundant/has multiple sclerosis/suffers from depression. I've had all these more than once.*

> *[Fiction publisher]*

> *I like to see a correctly addressed and decently laid out letter in the first instance, with a little bit about the writer, and a reasonable overview of the proposal – which could be told in a paragraph. A synopsis and first chapter will probably be enough for me to assess whether I can find the idea a home in the long run, but often I can make an educated guess on that first letter.*
>
> [UK agent]

Type or print your letter on good-quality white paper, preferably A4, and with a legible, standard typeface (avoid handwritten letters). The letter *must* include (at the top) your name, address, telephone and/or fax number, e-mail address and the date.

Start your letter by giving a very brief explanation of the material you are submitting, include its title (in capitals or italics so that it stands out) and a very small amount of relevant information about yourself. Include any previous successes you have had in getting into print, and any press or marketing angles you may have come up with. In the case of a non-fiction work, give appropriate background information about yourself to reinforce the recipient's understanding of why you have written the book. Endeavour to keep to one page (if it is more than one, paperclip it together), and if you are also submitting work, attach the letter to your folder with another elastic band.

Confidentiality

You can assume without concern that the publisher will treat your submitted work with complete confidentiality. But if you feel that your project is especially innovative, then it might be wise to reinforce this element: 'This typescript is submitted to you in confidence' will do, but only use it in very special circumstances.

On the other hand, if you truly believe that you have created the next world best-selling idea, then find a media copyright expert and ask them to draw up a letter of confidentiality. You will of course have to pay such experts; but the letter of confidentiality will be sent to, and signed by the prospective recipient before you deliver any material. These letters are more commonly submitted in connection with material which may be libellous or controversial, something we do not normally expect to see in connection with children's books.

Return postage

You must include sufficient stamps to cover the return postage of your package if the publisher rejects it. Mention in your letter that return postage has been included and then tuck the stamps securely under the paperclip. Better still, include a stamped, self-addressed label or envelope. Get yourself an up-to-date copy of postal rates and an accurate set of scales so that you can weigh your package at home and put the appropriate number of stamps inside. Should you have to go to the post office to find out what the postage will be, leave the package open and take some sticky tape with you so you can insert the stamps and seal the package there rather than having to take it all the way back home again.

You could also include a stamped, self-addressed acknowledgement card, which on one side has the name of the publisher and a line saying 'We acknowledge safe receipt of *A Bucket of Sludge* by Pete Bog, dated ...' Some publishers do not automatically send out such cards, and you do want to know that your package has arrived safely.

Keep a copy! Keep a copy!

Never, ever, under any circumstances send off your one and only original copy of a manuscript. Publishers cannot be held responsible for the disappearance of your work, and although the post office may be held liable for things that go astray in their hands (if proven), no compensation is going to make up for the absolute loss of many months' hard work. If you are working with a computer, you should make a second 'hard' copy and also save your work to a labelled floppy disk or CD disk to save you from the results of a serious hard-drive collapse, and then you should keep that copy in a safe place.

There is no need for you to go to the additional expense of insuring or registering your package. If you have addressed it clearly, put sufficient stamps on it, given a clear return address on the back of the parcel and sealed the package securely, then you should have no worries. Nor is there any need for hand-delivery, not unless you are passing by anyway. You will probably not be able to put it directly into your recipient's hands, and it may become detached from the normal internal mail system. Leave the parcel with the receptionist, ask for a receipt and leave. *Never* cold-call a publisher expecting to be welcomed in for a cup of coffee and a chat.

Two weeks later

If at the end of two weeks you have not yet heard anything from
the publisher, it is permissible to write a short, polite follow-up
letter to check your package has arrived safely. Try not to phone
or e-mail however anxious you may be at this stage. Your editor
may have been away from their desk on holiday, at a sales
conference or attending a book fair and has returned to a huge
pile of work demanding attention, and an even bigger pile of
unsolicited manuscripts. You do not want to sound like you are
nagging, or aggrandizing yourself.

Six weeks later

Assuming your initial follow-up letter proved that your
manuscript had arrived, you should then wait a further six
weeks before your next follow-up letter. In this case, there is
little point in telephoning. Write another polite enquiry about
your manuscript. A brief letter sent after an appropriate gap
may jog a busy editor's memory. But remember to leave at least
six weeks between letters. An editor who feels pressured into
making a decision will usually decide to reject.

> People who pester do not endear themselves to me. So
> please don't send me a manuscript and then phone up
> two days later to see what I think and try to discuss it
> with me. I will get around to looking at it, but my first
> responsibility is always to the books we are actually
> publishing and the authors already on the list.
>
> [UK publisher]

> I do not appreciate people phoning and demanding to see
> me that day because they happen to be nearby, with the
> idea that they can sit there whilst I assess their work. A
> good submission may be considered and discussed by
> several people and will need time. The author took time
> to produce it, so they don't really want a ten-minute
> pressurized consideration, do they?
>
> [UK agent]

Remember this: if you demand an immediate reaction from an
editor, that reaction will very likely be 'No!'. Editors are always
under pressure. If someone keeps sending them nagging letters
asking about their manuscript, what is the quickest way of
bringing this to a stop? Send the manuscript back. And what if
your editor felt they *almost* liked your book, but were not

entirely convinced and wanted to dwell on it for a while, or seek other opinions? Your complaining letters could put a stop to that by putting the editor under more pressure.

It may be that your project really does require that you meet the editor face to face to explain some computer innovation or distinctive new DVD animation showreel or laptop computer display. In this case, *send* as much information as you can and request an appointment to meet with the editor should they feel your project as explained on paper is one in which they may be interested. Do make sure that you give the editor some idea in advance of what you wish to discuss. It is a waste of everyone's time for you to arrive at a hard-won appointment only to find within the first few seconds that your idea does not fit in with that particular publisher's requirements or list. Do not expect a decision on the spot. Even if the editor with whom you have met is enthusiastic about your project, any purchasing decision will have to be made by a whole team of different people.

Timing of submissions

The last thing on your mind is likely to be an appropriate time of year for submitting your work. Nevertheless, it is as well to be aware that there are definite 'black holes' in the year. Editors are always busy, but some times are busier than others. For instance, the weeks surrounding major national or international book fairs are especially fraught. The main ones are the Bologna Children's Book Fair, the Frankfurt Book Fair and the London Book Fair; and in the USA, the BookExpo.

The summer is also a peak sales conference and holiday period which will take editors away from their desks. Some European publishers and agencies will actually close for two or three weeks completely. If you submit material in March/April or September/October, give it a little longer before you start to worry.

There is no perfect time to submit your manuscript; the best approach is to fill in the waiting time by getting to work on your next project. January: send off project number one. February: start on project number two. March: send off project two. April: start on project number three. May: get a publisher's response for project number one. It shouldn't take *that* long for your first project to get a response, but you can see what we're getting at: don't just sit around – keep working.

Make a submission index

To be extra efficient, you could make an index using a card, book or computer filing system to keep track of your submissions.

If you use a card index, it could look like this:

(Title) The Zany Zoo *(Storybook length)*   *(Year)* 2007

(Submitted to)

<u>Zaney Books</u>, *Anne Eddittorre, 14 January '07. Acknowledged 23 January '07. Reminder letter 1 March '07. Material returned 1 April '07, editor commented: 'It's too zany for us.'*

<u>Alfabetti Publishing</u>, *Fred Bear-Excuse, 2 April '07. Mat. retd. 11 April '07 with comment: 'We've decided to publish only picture books.'*

You can file your submission details in any way you find practical, in alphabetical or month order, and that way keep track of what is where and when a reminder letter could be reasonably sent. You could note the dates in a works diary on your computer, and set pop-up reminders to let you know when to make follow-up enquiries. Your submission file should also include any information which might be useful. For example, you now know that Fred Bear-Excuse is seeking only picture books. Could you write one?

If Fred Bear-Excuse moves to another publisher before you have sold *The Zany Zoo*, it will also remind you that he has seen it before. He might want to see it again if he is now commissioning books about zoos, but if *The Zany Zoo* is now a year unsold, he might think, 'Hmm, wonder why no one else has bought it?' in which case, send him something else.

Multiple submissions

Impatient? Want to cut corners? Want to cover all the bases? Here's our handy three-stage method.

Stage one: Write an all-purpose letter headed 'Dear Publisher'.

Stage two: Copy this letter and send or e-mail it off to a whole bunch of publishers at the same time, along with some poorly copied pages of your typescript.

Stage three: Enrol in an origami course so you have something constructive to do with all the rejection letters that will come flooding in or dig a hole and fill it with the resounding silence.

There is no way of cutting corners in publishing. Publishers like to feel special; they get all huffy and irked if they think you have sent your manuscript or project off to anyone else at the same time. They like to feel *chosen*. Never send a photocopied submission letter. Print or type a fresh one out for each publisher, no matter how time-consuming this may seem.

If you really cannot bear to wait, or if one publisher seems to be taking an unreasonable length of time considering your work, then send your work to no more than three publishers in total. If you do feel the need to do this, then make a careful note of who has what, and when they got it, in your index system. If you are not careful, you could end up in a terrible and potentially embarrassing and damaging muddle.

Copyrighting your work

There is obviously no way of copyrighting *ideas* or concepts (meaning an idea thought or spoken about) but as soon as you commit your idea to *paper* it is automatically a tangible thing which is now your own copyright. If you really feel the need additionally to protect the copyright in your work, then by far the simplest way is to post it to yourself. Seal your project in an envelope and take it off to the post office. Ask the staff to date stamp it across the sealed flap, and ask for a certificate of posting.

When you receive the package through the mail, *do not open it.* Store it away safely somewhere *unopened*. If you are feeling especially nervous, you could even store it with your bank or with your solicitor, although you will most likely have to pay for this additional security. If you think you have a potentially multimillion dollar idea, and are concerned that it could be stolen, the additional expense may seem worth it. Should it then ever become necessary to prove that you were the first person to write down this idea, then the unopened and date-stamped envelope should provide sufficient proof when opened, for instance, in court.

Things to remember

Before you finally submit your finished work, note the following.

Keeping ideas safe

Do not go around explaining all your best ideas to people. Get your ideas down onto paper first, and then keep them to yourself. Any other medium (a computer disk, for example) is easily alterable, could become corrupted or wiped, and therefore is not safe.

Plagiarism

Stealing other people's copyrighted ideas is called plagiarism. It means you have copied or used another person's work without permission. If you wish to quote other people, or emulate their artistic style, always seek permission first. Otherwise someone, somewhere, someday may knock on your door with a legal action.

Copyright is an involved and specialist branch of law, and becoming more so all the time. There are books available on the subject and experts in the field. If in doubt, *always* seek advice from an 'intellectual property' lawyer or copyright consultant.

Libel, doubtful taste and other things

Libel is another subject which we do not have the space to cover extensively. Children's books have been withdrawn from public bookshelves because they have become the subject of a libel action. The neighbour whom you hate and have included as a rather nasty character in your children's novel may well recognize themselves. They may also have little difficulty proving it to a court. Yes, your characters and situations will probably come from life if they are to be realistic, but use your common sense and imagination to mix them up into unrecognizable and untraceable people and events. Have you seen those disclaimers at the end of some fiction television programmes and films? The producers here are trying to protect themselves from anyone claiming to recognize themselves in a character.

You can also create expensive trouble for yourself, in terms of reputation as well as money, if you pretend to be someone or something you are not. Never claim to be a university professor in an attempt to impress a publisher. Nor pretend to be a child prodigy if you are eligible for a pension.

Your publisher will most likely edit out any unsuitable language, situations or views you may hold which could upset others. These days, book contracts contain extensive libel and other warranty clauses. Check your facts if you are going to be contentious, and be moderate and sensible in other areas, for example, cooking recipes and scientific experiments must include clear safety instructions and guidelines. You do not want to be confined to your home because there is an angry mob and a gang of reporters outside waiting to pounce.

Trademarks

If you come up with a great character or concept (or even in this case a title or name) which you want to protect more firmly than can be done by copyright, then you may wish to consider having it trademarked. There are specialist trademark agents who will do this for you, at a price, or you can do it yourself – in much the way that it is theoretically possible for you to negotiate your own house sale or purchase, if you have the time, diligence and patience. The best place to start your research into this subject may be the government trademark website on the Internet, or you could try a reference library or an up-to-date writers' reference book.

Agents

It may seem to you that to employ an agent as a go-between just adds a pointless layer of bureaucracy to the whole process of getting your work published. This is not actually the case, and you may find that an agent can be an invaluable asset in your attempts to see your work in print.

In the publishing world there are various go-betweens: literary or authors' agents, illustrators' agents, theatrical agents, merchandising agents and so on. These are specialists who know intimately the field in which they work.

Of course, they do not work for free. On average, an authors' agent will take between 10 and 25 per cent of basic commission as well as possibly asking you to sign a contract making them your sole representatives. An illustrators' agent may take 25 to 50 per cent, and a merchandizing agent from 40 to 60 per cent.

'No way!', you may think, but bear in mind that 80 per cent of *something* is a lot more than 100 per cent of *nothing*. And that may be the choice you are faced with, as many publishers these days do not even *look* at unsolicited work unless it has come to them via an agent. There is a practical reason for this: publishers do not have the time or finances to deal with the costly business of going through heaps of unsolicited material. At least when they agree to look at a manuscript or project recommended to them by an agent, they will know that a stringent grading process has already taken place. In other words, they are not going to be sent unsuitable and unpublishable, half-thought-out ideas. An agent will be too intent on maintaining their reputation and in securing the most advantageous deal they can on your behalf to do that.

The problem you may find is that it is really not much easier to have your work taken on by an agent than it is to find an interested publisher. The *big* difference is that an agent may see some spark of talent or originality in your work and be prepared to give you the necessary guidance so that the spark can ignite. Very often a large publishing house will be too busy with its own projects to afford you very much advice if yours is rejected.

If an agent agrees to take on the task of trying to sell a piece of work by you, then you can be sure that the agent is fairly convinced that they will be able to find a home for it. As with publishers, agents cannot afford to waste time and resources trying to sell unplaceable projects or services.

You will be able to find the names of the major players in the world of agents via the Internet, or a writer's reference book, or the Authors' Agents Association, or by meeting them at book talks, book societies or conferences. Another possible way of choosing an agent could be to write a brief, polite letter to a publisher who handles the kind of work you are producing, and asking them if they could recommend any agents to you. (If you do try this route, remember to supply a stamped, self-addressed reply envelope.)

You should submit your work to an agent in exactly the same way as you would to a publisher, but first of all ensure that the chosen agent is actually in the business of accepting unsolicited manuscripts. Many agents these days have a full client list and are unable to expand that list.

A few agents require a contribution towards their editorial costs for considering your material, so check on this in advance, as well as requesting a copy of their commission schedule. This will outline their commission percentages and detail any extra charges, say, for emergency delivery or copying. An agent will have to invest time, faith and money in you before they see a return for their efforts. Commission will be deducted only from work they sell or act for on your behalf.

An agent who likes your work should want to arrange a meeting with you, if at all feasible. At this meeting you should be able to get a clearer idea of what your agent is like, as well as this being an opportunity for the agent to get a look at you. You will be able to ask questions face-to-face – possibly for the very first time with a professional – and establish what is expected from both parties.

Remember, this may turn out to be a career-long relationship. Agents tend to stay in one place, unlike many publishing editors. Your agent may well end up as a friend, confidant, editor, accountant, security blanket, a shoulder to cry on and so on. It is as well to consider up-front whether this person is someone you would feel happy working with long term on many different projects.

Also, it is as well to find out what kind of an operation they are running. Is it a one-person show? Are they a well-established company? Do they have a client list of children's authors, or do they mainly represent other areas? Are they right in there with the day-to-day cut and thrust of the publishing world? Will you be asked to sign a contract with the agent? Last, but not least: are you prepared to accept their advice?

From your agent, you can expect editorial advice, representation, legal and contractual negotiations, invoicing and chasing of monies and royalties, mediation, as well as information on work required by publishers which may be suitable for your talents.

Incidentally, 'representation' means that the agent will endeavour to place your work with an appropriate publisher and for a good price. No one would suggest that publishers might try to underpay you for your work, but publishers are first and foremost business people and they are out for a good deal. An agent will know the going rate for your work and will ensure you get it.

An agent will also be able to go over the contract with a fine-tooth comb and wrinkle out any little oddities that may have crept in. It can happen, and you are unlikely to be so well up with the small print in publishers' contracts to spot the odd percentage point shaved off your royalties.

In essence, a good agent needs to be a Jack- or Jill-of-all-trades in the publishing world and should have the knowledge and contacts to be able to step in and help you at every stage of the publishing procedure.

So the question remains: do you need an agent? Well, maybe not if you're prepared to become an expert in the ever-changing world of publishing and contractual law. Not if you don't feel the need to have a knowledgeable professional in your corner when a publisher is causing you problems. Not if you're happy to keep detailed accounting records and are able to fully comprehend the complexities of royalty statements. In all these areas and more, a good agent should be an enormous asset, and you would be wise to investigate this possibility before deciding to go it alone.

One final word: you will need as much professionalism and persistence to find an agent as you would to find a publisher. In other words, everything we have already explained about how to approach a publisher, goes the same for how you should approach an agent.

A submission checklist

1 Proposal (synopsis, contents, chapters or complete script, of which you have kept a copy).
2 Folder for proposal.
3 Stamped, self-addressed envelope or return postage label (or voucher if you are submitting something overseas).
4 Stamped, self-addressed acknowledgement card.
5 Submission letter (plus curriculum vitae if you have one, and if it's relevant to your proposal).
6 Your name and address on everything.
7 Make a note of date on which the submission was posted.

Oh, and don't forget to post the package: as one author said to us,

> *The most useful piece of advice that anyone gave me was: 1. Finish the book, and 2. It won't get published lying in a drawer somewhere.*

10 dealing with rejection

In this chapter you will learn:
- how to cope when a publisher rejects your work
- the importance of addressing constructive criticism to improve your writing skills.

I had a meeting with a commissioning editor of a large and well-known publishing house to discuss my first book. I was told that they were interested in it but that they thought it needed a different title and a lot of rewriting. I agreed to make all the required changes – but a few weeks later, when I resubmitted the manuscript I found that the editor who had liked the book no longer worked there and no one else was interested in it. The book was rejected. It took approaches to a further six publishers before it found a home! You just have to accept that these things will happen.

All those hours locked away in your lonely garret. All that work, love, care and attention that you lavished on your project, and some ignorant publisher who would not know a bestseller if it marched up to them in the street wearing an 'I am a best-seller' t-shirt and punched them on the nose has sent it back! *Arrrrrgh*!

Of one thing you can be quite certain – your rejection letter will be couched in very well-mannered terms. Publishers are invariably polite in print, no matter what they may privately think of your work. The cut-throat nature of the publishing word is carefully concealed by a veil of courteous and respectful behaviour and of glib and gushing compliments – and it can be tricky sometimes to get behind the mask and work out exactly what is going on.

In order to get some idea of why your work has been rejected, you really need some basic understanding of the way that the world of publishing actually functions. For an in-depth view of this, we recommend you take a look at *Inside Book Publishing* (3rd edition) by Giles Clark and its companion website, www.insidebookpublishing.com. This will give you a broad understanding of the who, what, when, where and why in publishing, as well as furnishing you with an extended bibliography and a lot of useful addresses and links.

So, how come you've been rejected?

Let's follow the progress of your unsolicited manuscript as it passes from the hands of the postal service and enters the echoing marbled halls of the publisher of your choice.

The task of dealing with your manuscript will probably fall to a junior editor. Alternatively, your manuscript may be looked at by someone on unpaid work experience, or a freelancer brought in especially to help with a large backlog of work, or even just someone who happens to have a spare five minutes.

Face it, your unsolicited manuscript is not going to be prioritized. It may be read 'in-house' (that is, by someone on the publisher's pay roll), or it may be sent out to an outside 'reader' or possibly two, if you are lucky. This reader will be someone whose opinion is trusted by publishers and who will be given a set fee for their report on your manuscript. They may be a teacher with known experience on the subject about which you have written, or a freelance editor or some other well-read person whose views have some weight with the publisher. The idea is that this reader will give as objective an opinion of your work as is possible.

Naturally, there really is no such thing as absolute objectivity when you are addressing something as broad as children's literature. Even when it comes to prize-winners, some people are devoted fans and others would not have the books in the house. Despite this, a good reader should be able to give a fair assessment even if the book you have sent in is a fantasy, and that reader personally hates fantasy.

If your manuscript is to be read by such a person, then you need to bear in mind that it will have to be *sent* to that reader. This obviously adds to the time that you will have to wait before getting a response. And if the reader's report is a little undecided, then the editor may well seek a second opinion. See how six weeks can easily pass before you hear anything?

It may be that the commissioning editor who first received your book decides that they absolutely adore it – but you're still far from home and dry. That editor then has to present your book to the kind of committee we mentioned in Chapter 1 – and their deliberations are going to range across a whole spectrum of considerations before a final decision is made. Is it marketable? Does it fit our list? Does it 'ride the zeitgeist' (publisher's speak for 'jumping on the bandwagon'). Will it be relatively cheap and easy to produce? Will it make us a quick profit?

It may be that these meetings take place once a week – possibly only once a month. You're not going to hear back from your editor until after that meeting has taken place. Your script could be out of your sight for quite some time, but this is not a reason to worry. In fact, if your manuscript comes back to you very quickly, attached to what looks like a standard, impersonal letter, then the chances are that one of the following has happened: your manuscript has not been looked at; your manuscript has only been glanced at; you have chosen the wrong publisher; your material is way off-target; or the editor hated it and is simply being polite.

Such a letter will read:

> *Thank you for the submission of your script, but I am afraid it is not suitable for our list.*

Or:

> *I enjoyed reading your submission and found it rather sweet, however the storyline is not strong enough for our requirements.*

If you have submitted a non-fiction work concerned with capital punishment down the centuries, then the use of the word 'sweet' would strongly suggest that the person responding has not actually read your work. And 'strong' is a frequently used word which means whatever the publisher wants it to mean, usually not a lot, to be honest.

Other 'standard' rejection letters include the wording:

> *We are not looking for unsolicited scripts at the moment.*

Or:

> *We are not publishing new authors in the current economic climate.*

Your first reaction to such a rejection may be, 'The fools! I'm going to give them a piece of my mind! They need to understand the terrible mistake they have made by rejecting me!'

Seriously, folks: do not bother. If they are not interested at this time, then they are not interested. An irate letter demanding an explanation will only alienate you. Move on!

Perversely, a long rejection letter, *coupled* with a lengthy gap between submission and response, means the publisher liked your work. No, really – this may sound a little odd at first, but think about it. If all the publisher can be bothered to do is to write two lines, that's because they don't feel they have anything helpful to say. If you get two pages of criticism, apparently tearing your work to shreds, that means the editor in question was sufficiently impressed to spend time not only going through your manuscript in some detail, but also thought it worth while giving you the benefit of their experience and opinion.

For an author this can be a difficult thing to handle, but the more your work is criticized the better it is for you in the long run. One well-known children's author told us the following:

I once wrote a TV sitcom and sent it to the BBC. It came back accompanied by the following 'though there's the occasional good line, your dialogue, if literate, is too literary, and often in the form of a paperback novel. Situation comedy means what it says: comedy arising from and furthered by a strong situation. Here we have only endless conversation, mostly with the same subjects under discussion, resulting in some heavy-handed plotting of a feather-weight storyline.'

Did that author decide to become a train driver instead? No, he goes on to say this:

Useful advice? Definitely! I'd been told I could write good lines; that I had the style of a novelist (albeit minor); and that I was literate. My writing ambition switched overnight. There were still plenty of failures to come – but it was a turning-point for me.

Readers' reports

Just because an editor comments on your work constructively or critically, you should not assume that the editor has actually read your work. They may well be quoting from a reader's report or two. In fact, if your work is non-fiction, it is more than likely that your work will have been read by a third party with some expertise in the field in which you have written. If the report is constructive, the editor may send you a copy. This can be very helpful; just remember that it was not intended for your eyes and do not take any criticism too harshly.

A reader's report will include, in the case of a work of fiction, a brief summary of the plot. It will then detail strengths and weaknesses, outline particular points that need to be addressed by the author and then end with a 'verdict' as to whether, in the reader's opinion, the manuscript would benefit from being rewritten or if it is beyond hope, or if it is just what the publisher has been looking for.

If, in the letter of rejection, the editor comments that they liked your work, and that they would be interested in reading anything else you may write, then you can feel very pleased with yourself. This is a great step forward. It means that for one of several reasons the work you submitted was not quite right for them, but that they were sufficiently impressed by it to wish to consider something else by you.

This publisher is worth following up!

If you receive a helpful and reasonably lengthy rejection letter, some of which you may genuinely not understand, or you believe the editor has completely missed the point, then a brief, professional telephone call or e-mail to that editor is now permissible. Do not be surprised if you find that the editor has not actually read your script, but tried to save themselves some time because their readers firmly recommended a rejection. Be friendly, and be forgiving. Editors have been known to ask an author to resubmit their material.

Conversely, if you sense a certain dismissive tone between the lines of your brief rejection letter, and you decide to approach the same publisher again with your next offering, it may be wise to write to a different editor. It may be even wiser to choose a different publisher.

The returned manuscript

Beware! If you get a rejected manuscript back, make sure you check it thoroughly before sending it off elsewhere. Make sure it is all there. Make sure the pages are in order and all the right way up. Make sure there are not jammy fingerprints on it or coffee-cup stains or claret-glass rings. Cat paw-prints are also weirdly common. It is not unknown for editors to scribble uncomplimentary comments on the actual script (very rude and unprofessional, but it does happen), or accidentally leave a damning page of comments amidst the text. The last thing you need is for the next publisher to be privy to the musings of a publisher who has already rejected your work.

If you do encounter scribbles or accidentally enclosed notes, try to steel yourself for the experience. They may be both eye-opening and deeply wounding. Rejected authors who read the publisher's notes are unlikely to encounter anything they will enjoy. Try not to take it too much to heart. One agent we know scribbled a note to her editor, following the cold-calling of an overenthusiastic, scary and eccentric author. Her experienced eye glanced over the 200,000-word story for 5-year-olds and she wrote a note intended for her editor: 'This stuff's rubbish, the guy's bonkers, send it back at once for me with a nice thanks-but-no-thanks note.' It would seem that a well-meaning temporary member of staff returned the note, too, because a suicidal and somewhat unpleasant reply swiftly ensued from the recipient. Temporary members of staff who do not know the publishing system can be responsible for some classic mistakes, including returning only half of your material. Double-check your returned package.

The thing to do before you send your script off for a second, third or fourth attempt is to eradicate any sign that anyone else has ever seen it. If this means printing out a new copy or making another photocopy of the whole thing, then so be it.

We promised our editor we would never suggest that when submitting your typescript you should do things like putting in a couple of pages upside down or back to front. Nor any other little trick like a carefully placed thread, which might indicate to you that the reader never got beyond page 2 of your submission. The problem with these tricks is that many experienced editors realize they are being tested and will carefully replace the thread, or assiduously leave chapters out of order or back to front as received.

Another point: it is not always necessary for your manuscript to be read from start to finish. An editor may instinctively know within the first chapter or two that this project is not for them. This may seem unreasonable to you, but remember what we told you in Chapter 5: grab them by the lapels on page 1. Most experienced editors or agents admit they will have formed an opinion as to whether it is worth reading the whole script by the time they have read the submission or covering letter and the first chapter or two.

Let's say that your book has made its way successfully through the reader's report stage and has been presented to a committee at an 'acquisition meeting'. Let's say the committee votes in favour of your work. Time can still pass all too slowly for you. It may be that one or another committee member wants to go away and look at your work in more detail before making a decision. They may say they will report back at the next meeting – and so another month can drag by.

Even if your book is given the green light, more time will pass while your editor goes away to do some 'costings'. They will need to decide how much they can afford out of their annual budget for the initial printing, artwork, design, and editing. They will need to decide what grade paper to use and whether to print in hardback first or risk a trade paperback publication with all the additional publicity costs that it will engender in order to get the book on the shelves in enough numbers to warrant a large print-run. They will need to decide whether illustrations are required and, if so, who should be hired to do them and how much money they will demand for their work. They will need to take a look at their long-term publishing plans and find a suitable publishing date, invariably in the following year – maybe even the year after.

Even if you get a letter telling you your work was loved and cherished by the acquisition team, you could still be kept on tenterhooks for some weeks while all this unseen work goes on. Your formal acceptance letter could take weeks and weeks to arrive.

We shall stop there, because this chapter is not about what happens when your manuscript/project is accepted. This chapter is about coping with rejections, so let us carry on coping. The authors we consulted said the following:

> Don't take any notice of anyone. Just write.

> A degree does not mean one is automatically a writer. I had to do my apprenticeship, just like anyone else. It took me seven years to produce a saleable book.

> Don't give up if you have any signs of real encouragement from publishers. But if every returned manuscript is accompanied by a rejection slip, or a bland and vague letter, take a long hard look at your submissions.

> Keep at it! Writing is a craft as well as an art and needs to be practised assiduously if you want to get published.

> Write, write, and rewrite, however long it takes. Keep working at it until you make it.

> Nothing is ever wasted, because it helps build writing technique.

Responding to positive criticism

If you have received, say, three brief and impersonal letters of rejection, it is probably time for you to rethink your work. You might need to assume that you are going wrong somehow or somewhere. Perhaps you would be better off trying something new, writing for a different age-group or maybe approaching your chosen topic (should you still have faith in it) from a different angle or in a fresh way.

What, though, if you have three longer rejection letters from publishers? What if it is clear from the contents of these letters that people have actually read your work reasonably thoroughly? And what if the comments you are getting back seem to have some common theme? This is the time for you to give careful thought to the criticisms you have received.

You want to be published, don't you? That's the whole point. Therefore, it's a serious mistake for you not to take on board the opinions of professionals – whether you agree with them or not. Certainly editors can and do make errors of judgement, but on the whole they do have a pretty clear idea of what is going on in the market and whether your work, be it ever so well written, is going to actually sell.

Be aware that tastes and fashions change. You may have written a book that would have sold instantly 20 years ago, but no matter how brilliantly it is written, anything that comes across as dated or old-fashioned will be unlikely to find a home. A book written a year ago may no longer be fashionable, or topical. All the authors we spoke to said, 'Study the market.' All the authors said, 'Keep at it, keep on writing.' All the authors said, 'Revise and rewrite until you succeed.'

Assuming that three publishers have now seen your work and have made similar critical comments, the last thing you should do is to carry on stubbornly sending the unaltered manuscript/ project off in the hope that someone will have a better opinion of it. By doing this, all you will effect is to 'spoil' the market for your work. Three publishers have seen it and rejected it. You need to *revise* your work before submitting it again.

Unless one of the rejecting publishers has actually *asked* you to revise and resubmit, it is not worthwhile sending them a rewritten version. Send it to someone new and see what they say.

It is almost like engaging in a treasure hunt. The prize is publication, and along the way you will pick up various clues which allow you to move on to the next step. One publisher may tell you your work is far too long. You shorten it. The next publisher may tell you the language is inappropriate for the target age-group. You amend accordingly. The third publisher may point out redundant characters and confusions in the plot line. You attend to them. Do you see what is going on? By taking on board these constructive criticisms, you are honing your work for the market.

If you have patience, natural talent and the ability to take criticism on board and learn by it, then you are well on the way to getting your name in print.

In the past, it was possible that an editor who perceived some worthwhile spark in a rejected work would have the time to nurture you until you produced a polished and consummate manuscript. Sadly, that is seldom the case these days. Increasingly commissioning editors demand material of such high quality and presentation that it could almost be sent straight to the printers without the publisher even having to touch it. We did say *almost* – in much the same way that ant-eaters eat ants, so editors edit – they really can't help themselves, no matter how vocally they might protest otherwise.

If you find it hard to make coherent sense of all the criticisms of your rejected work, then maybe this is the time to present it to one of the criticism services we mentioned earlier. Or if you are in a writers' group, maybe you should take it along for general appraisal (if you are not in a writers' group or class, this may be the time to seek one out).

Just remember that the nearer you get to possible publication, the more the criticism will be stepped up as editors start fine-tuning and adjusting your work for the marketplace.

This may be the time to approach an agent. If you have several near-miss rejection letters from different publishers, these may help to gain an agent's attention, bearing in mind that an agent will usually be better able to give you long-term advice and encouragement than will a publisher. Therefore, send these letters off with your manuscript: agents understand only too well how hard it is for a new author to get a foot in the publishing door and can read between the lines of an editor's rejection letter. They are familiar with the good old catch-22 situation: 'Come back when you've made a name for yourself and we'll publish your stuff.'

One author we know had a middle fiction humorous novel submitted to a publisher via an agent. The story revolves around a girl who wants to be a secretary when she leaves school, marry a hunky super-hero and live happily ever after. Her mum, who is a boot-wearing, Green feminist building labourer, has other ideas, and her step-dad is no help in his house-management role. The first publisher who saw the script rejected it along with a two-page letter of disgust to the agent. That publisher missed the point: they took the plot seriously. The second publisher telephoned to say that he thought he ought to buy the story but had been unable to read it himself, and no work was being done in his department. His staff had hijacked the script and all he could hear were peals of laughter!

When you do, sooner or later, find someone who likes your style, or your humour, or your imagination, what happens next is only the beginning. Read on.

acceptance

In this chapter you will learn:
- how to react to an offer from a publisher
- about the complexities of contracts, royalties and rights
- about the publishing process
- about forming a relationship with an editor.

(Brring-brring. Brring-brring)

Hello?

Hello, there. Could I speak to Miss Hope ffulle-Author, please?

Speaking.

Hi! It's Anne Eddittorre, here. I have some wonderful news for you! I took your book to our acquisitions meeting this morning, and I'm thrilled to be able to tell you that everyone totally loved your work and we really want to publish it!

(Thud of Hope hitting the floor unconscious)

It will happen something like that. A telephone call out of the blue to tell you that all your hopes, desires and dreams have finally come true. Of course, it is not obligatory for you to collapse into a theatrical swoon on the carpet. But you are allowed to celebrate in one or more of the following ways: run around the room, screaming; run down the street, screaming; call all your friends and family and scream at them; just stand there clutching the phone and scream.

Once you've finished with the screaming there are several things you need to do.

First, and this is the really down-to-earth and gloomy bit, you must keep in the back of your mind the possibility that everything could still go pear-shaped. In other words, a telephone call telling you that your work has been accepted is a long way from a finished book landing on your doormat, and quite a distance from an *official* offer on paper. When you've finished screaming at Anne Eddittorre, you must tell her that you are looking forward to receiving the offer *in writing*. Just supposing Anne went sick from work for six months, or was 'rationalized' and changed jobs the day following her call, or some other disaster occurred? Don't be alarmed, but what proof have you at this stage that Anne made an offer to buy your book?

At its simplest, a letter with your offer will probably look something like this:

Dear Hope,

Subject to contract

I am delighted to be able to make you an offer for THE EGG-WHISK'S REVENGE which we propose publishing in our My First Book series in the Spring of 20XX. We all think this is a wonderfully imaginative and well crafted story.

I can offer an advance of ££$$ payable as to half on signature of the contract and half on first publication against royalties of X per cent of the published price on paperback copies sold in the home market, and X per cent on copies sold for export. We require World Volume rights.

I do hope this offer is acceptable and look forward to hearing from you. I will have the contract drawn up as soon as possible.

With best wishes,

Anne Eddittorre
Senior Commissioning Editor

It doesn't matter for the moment that you may not understand everything in the letter – the point is that an offer like the one above will *most likely* result in your work being published. Cancellations *do* happen for a variety of reasons, and it would be unfair of us to pretend otherwise – but they are rare and the great majority of publishers will behave in an honest and honourable way.

Money, money, money

What exactly is an 'advance'? Let us say your publisher offers you an advance of £1,000. The actual offer may say something like: 'an advance of £1,000 set against a royalty of 10 per cent of the published price of the hardback edition for home sales'. (Home sales means sales in the domestic market; export sales means sales of the book in the home language but in other countries, and foreign sales means sales of the book which has been translated into other languages.)

This £1,000 is the amount of money you will be paid in advance of any actual sales of copies of the book itself. You will be asked to sign a contract (more of that in a moment). The advance may come to you as, say, £500 when both you and the publisher have signed the contract, and a further £500 upon publication of the book itself. This money is paid in acknowledgement of the work you have already done in producing the book. So long as you fulfill your part in the deal as set out in the contract, this money is yours to keep.

Published price and royalties

The published price referred to in the offer is the recommended retail price. Say your book sells for £5 at 'home'. For every copy of your book sold at £5, you will be entitled to a 'royalty' of 10 per cent, in this case, 50p. *However*, the £1,000 advance you receive is an advance 'set against a royalty of 10 per cent'. That means you will not see any more money until enough 50ps have accumulated to cover the £1,000 advance. Which therefore means, in this case, that 2,000 copies of your book have to be sold before you will see any royalty money. Unfortunately, the deal outlined here is considerably less complicated than the real thing.

You have received the publisher's offer and having read the rest of this chapter carefully so you know what to look out for, let's say you're happy with the offer. You must then reply in writing and on paper to your editor, accepting the offer, and the basic wording should include the following:

Dear Anne,

Re: THE EGG-WHISK'S REVENGE

Thank you for your letter dated XXXX regarding your offer to publish the above title in your My First Book series. I am pleased to accept the offer as outlined, subject to contract.

I look forward to receiving and considering the contract in due course, and to working with you.

With all good wishes,

Hope ffulle-Author

Obviously every book and every offer letter is different, and you will reply accordingly, but the important basic wording you need to include is 'I accept the offer as outlined' and 'subject to contract'. This will give you an opportunity to examine the contract and perhaps negotiate some changes before you commit yourself. The same thing applies at this stage if you are being offered a 'flat-fee' payment (a flat fee is a single payment without royalties). In this case, the offer letter from the publisher may include wording along the following lines:

> *We would be delighted to include your text piece on THE HISTORY OF EGG-WHISKS in our* Encyclopaedia of Kitchen Utensils.
>
> *We will pay a flat fee of £$£ for your 800-word contribution upon delivery and acceptance of the text, for exclusive rights in all languages, all forms, editions, versions and adaptations throughout the world, and an acknowledgement will be given to you in the front of the book. We aim to publish in October 20XX, and will give to you one copy of the title upon publication.*
>
> *Please sign the attached copy of this letter where indicated as acceptance of our terms.*

In this case, the payment for your contribution is *all* the money you will receive. Because the publisher wants exclusive rights throughout the world, they can sell as many copies as they like, in whatever form, and you cannot sell that piece of text anywhere else. If you are happy with this, sign and date the copy of the letter and return it to the publisher.

'We all love it!'

Suppose the editor informs you that although everyone is very enthusiastic about your book, they would like you to do some revisions under editorial supervision before they are prepared to make you an offer. Anne Eddittorre's letter might say:

> *We all really loved your story about the little girl who didn't get the egg-whisk for her birthday, but we all thought it would work a whole lot better if she DID get the egg-whisk. And does the main character have to be a little girl? We all felt that a little gerbil would work much better. What do you think?*

You may well think, 'No way!' as this level of 'revision' will change your story almost beyond recognition. You are perfectly entitled to respond like that, particularly if you think the whole point of your story is about to vanish in a puff of editorial smoke.

However, you will probably find the editorial suggestions are much less drastic than those outlined above, and it surely would not do any harm for you to at least look at them? If it seems as if the editor has gone berserk all over your script with a red pen, or e-mails your book back covered in a rash of blue type, then you can still call it quits and leave with your authorial integrity intact.

Think long and hard before you choose this line of action. You will have your integrity – but who is going to benefit from that? Certainly not all the children who would have enjoyed your book had it been published. Be tough, be realistic. You want to be published: perhaps a certain amount of flexibility at this stage will prove to be of benefit in the long run.

Naturally you do not want to be published at any cost, but a degree of give and take and some carefully considered negotiations with your prospective editor may result in a compromise that will suit everyone. Do not be afraid to fight your corner, but beware of being too antagonistic. After all, at this stage in your career an interested publisher is worth more than none at all.

Revising your work

Let us assume you agree to take your manuscript away and do some revising. The editor will probably send you a letter or an e-mail outlining in general terms what they would like you to do. If your book is on a computer file, they will add their comments and suggestions in among the script – usually in blue or red type – and may even put lines through sections that they think should be taken out. If it is on paper, they may attach Post-it® notes to relevant pages or even make pencilled suggestions in the margins. Be sure that you understand precisely what is required of you. Sort out any ambiguities in advance. If there are comments which seem a little vague, then pin the editor down and ask *exactly* what they mean. A vague editorial comment is a sign of busyness or laziness: make sure they do their job and thus make your job of revising as painless as possible. And make sure you always keep your original version intact, either as a clean paper copy or as an unedited and unrevised file; editors will sometimes make minor changes to your book – especially if it's in the form of a computer file – without telling you, and you will need to have an unadulterated original to go back to if you find that an alien sentence has slipped in unannounced.

Rewrite and resubmit

Rewriting and resubmitting your work may not be the end of the road. It may well be that your editor is *quite* pleased with the results of your work, but that the book still is not *exactly* what they want. Are you prepared to take yet another look at it with yet another bunch of editorial comments? Their position may well be that they want to ensure that your book is as perfect as possible, bearing in mind that you are a new and unknown author. And it may well be that the book still has flaws in its construction. Try to keep an open mind about this: the editor may be starting to irritate you, but their job is to get as saleable a commodity into the marketplace as they possibly can, which is what you want too.

Development money

Before you re-revise any further, it would not be unreasonable of you to ask for some 'development' money. This is a payment which you get to keep should the publisher finally decide that after all your time and effort, your work is still not going to be accepted. If the publisher does finally accept your work after two or three reworkings, then that money will be deducted (or offset) from the advance or flat-fee offer they then make.

There is no guarantee that your editor will agree to your request, but if you are going to put in a lot of work, plus have your hopes raised, and the end result could be that the publishers still reject, then you are entitled to try for some sort of compensation.

Once everything is in writing and the editor is happy with your revised book, you will get a 'contract'. If you are working through an agent, they will be able to sort out all the fine print and do all the negotiations on your behalf, but it is still useful for you to understand a little of what goes on behind the scenes.

Contract time

Basically, when you are sent the official offer letter, the editor will then arrange for an appropriate contract to be sent to you. Depending on the publisher, the contract may be negotiated and drawn up by the editor, a contracts department or a freelance contracts consultant. You could wait some time before receiving the legal documentation. Progress could also be delayed by the type of contract the publisher uses. It could be a simple, single-page document or it could be an incredibly complicated, closely typed, 30-page wodge of paper, in which your book is called a 'media-neutral format product'. Those unfamiliar with legal terminology will rapidly find themselves totally bewildered.

Never sign anything you do not understand

If you do not understand legal jargon then we strongly suggest that you seek advice before accepting an offer, or signing a contract or contractual letter. The benefit of having an agent at this point is that part of the agent's job is to understand the small print and to ensure there are no sneaky little clauses very much to the benefit of the publisher at your expense. It happens!

There are books available on contracts and copyright, and information in writer's reference books and on the Internet, but unless you feel able to absorb this kind of information at speed, keep up to date on legal developments and become an expert, then you must seek the advice of published authors, authors' societies, writers' advice centres or groups. Best of all is to consult a book publishing and media contracts and copyright expert. It will prove good value to pay for advice now, rather than take any risks. Your family solicitor, incidentally, experienced as they will be in their own fields, may not understand the peculiarities of a publisher's contract, nor are they likely to know whether the terms you are being offered are fair even if they can unravel the jargon.

It is not easy for an inexperienced person to negotiate points in their first contract. You may even be so excited and thrilled at the prospect of getting into print that you will sign anything. Think carefully before you do this. What of the future? There may be a clause in the contract allowing the publisher 'first refusal' of your next work. ('First refusal' means they must be allowed to see your next work and consider whether to publish it before anyone else can see it.) What if you decide you never want to work with them again, and yet are legally bound to offer them your next work? The publisher may hang on to your next work for weeks, or make you a derisory offer, or they may even be a totally unsuitable publishing house for this second work. All these things need to be taken into consideration.

Your offer from the publisher could be a flat-fee payment to use your short story exclusively in an anthology for a specified period of time. The offer may be non-exclusive, which means you can sell the story again, say, to a magazine, even while it is still available in the anthology. The offer could be for an advance giving the publisher the right to sell your book in one language throughout the world, or it may be for all languages and all media throughout the world, beyond the world, and in perpetuity. You may or may not be entitled to a share of additional sales made from translation of your work into another language, audio versions, television, the movies and so on. Even if you do get a share, the proportions may not be as generous as they should be. If you do not know what is a fair and reasonable offer or contract, if you do not understand what every clause actually means, then you cannot be expected to make a good judgement.

We asked some contracts and copyright experts (including publishers, consultants and society advisers) for their comments:

The trouble with most authors is that they don't ask any questions about contracts. The usual remark is along the lines of, 'It looked so official I assumed it must be okay.' Alternatively, they consult their own solicitor who has never seen an author contract before and who asks a mass of niggling little questions. Some authors then try to change the basic terms of a contract once it arrives: 'Yes, I know I agreed to a 7 per cent royalty but I've heard that 10 per cent is more normal.' Please point out that such things should be agreed before contract stage.

No one ever asks me anything, except what 'special editions' means.

Children's authors often ask me why their royalties tend to be lower than those for other trade books. They also get confused over collaboration with illustrators, and the implications of electronic rights.

A contract is a legally binding document. Even if a publisher says, 'This is our standard contract' or the contract is (or appears to be) printed, contracts are negotiable. If in any doubt, consult a specialist. That almost certainly does not include your local solicitor.

Most authors will confess to never actually reading their contracts properly, if at all, when pressed!

We also asked these same experts if they could recount any interesting experiences negotiating contracts. Here are some of the more unusual:

The blind author whose contract expected him to read and correct proofs.

The Australian author who was expected to return corrected proofs to the UK publisher within seven days of their dispatch to the author.

The commissioned illustrator whose contract obliged her to deliver her material two weeks prior to the date of the contract (thus putting her in breach as soon as she signed it).

The agent whose contract provided for the advance to be on account of 'the aforementioned royalties' but the royalty clause came after the advance clause (the page was reprinted before the contract went off!).

The publisher's contract commissioning an author to write a work which contained a clause stating that the contract was null and void if the author had not delivered the typescript prior to signing.

Spend! Spend! Spend!

'When can I expect to see some money?' you might well ask. Let's go back to when your editor first sent you the offer. You now understand and have agreed the terms in the contract; you have signed and returned the contract. You may be required to supply an invoice along with your contract if you are being paid a flat fee. Your invoice should contain similar information to the following:

INVOICE no. 111

Date

To: Anne Eddittorre   From: (your name and address)
Senior Commissioning Editor
(address)

Payment due on delivery and
acceptance of short story
entitled WHAT IS IT WITH ALL THESE EARWIGS? by

B. Tell   £1,000

Total: £1,000

PAYMENT ON RECEIPT OF INVOICE

If you are registered for value added tax, or need to include any
other information, then do so at the bottom of the invoice.

It could take six weeks for the publisher's accounts department
to actually get around to sending you the cheque for the money
due on signature of the contract. Various people within a
publishing house may have to authorize a payment before it can
be made. If you are working with an agent, then add a week or
two on to this time, as your cheque will be sent to the agent first
in order that they can check the details, clear the cheque, note
their records system, and subtract their commission before you
get the balance.

The time-lag from when you are first told that the publishers are
interested in your work to the day when the advance cheque
arrives could be several months. If revisions are needed or
contract negotiations are lengthy, an unbelievable couple of
years could go by! This is not the way to get rich quick, by any
stretch of the imagination.

And things do not speed up very much once you have earned
out your advance payment. Publishers tend to make up their
accounts every six months. Some even do it annually,
particularly publishers of foreign editions. This means that the
50p coming to you for a book bought by a child in a store in
January, may not actually get to you until, say, October of the
same year, if the accounts are made up half-yearly, or, possibly,
March of the *following* year for an annual accounts system.

Royalty statements

Royalty statements are documents which will detail how your book is selling, and will show any other sales agreement payments the publisher has made. They will show a date from which the accounts are being calculated, but you may not actually receive the statement for up to four months *after* this date. This statement will include things like home sales and export sales, sales at a greater discount (to book clubs, perhaps), any other income from rights sales made by the publisher (for example, large-print rights), and possibly any deductions for copies you may have ordered for your own use. If you do not have an agent to check these statements for you, then you will have to do some careful checking yourself to ensure that you have received all the monies you are entitled to, and that they are the correct percentage shares.

For the most part, these statements of accounts will be honest and accurate, and any errors are genuine mistakes. If you have any doubts, your contract should entitle you, or someone on your behalf, to examine the publisher's books. If you have any other worries, including payment delays, an author's society may be able to advise you how next to proceed.

Rights

There are a variety of other ways in which you and the publisher can earn money from your book, and these include the selling of rights as we have previously mentioned. These are just some of the potential sales areas and rights which could ensue from that first hardback edition of your work:

- hardback, trade paperback, mass-market paperback editions
- anthology rights
- first serial rights (for newspapers or magazines)
- translation rights
- large print (books for those with impaired vision)
- audio (single-voice readings, or dramatized readings)
- radio, television, film, video and so on for dramatization
- animation
- merchandizing (everything from greetings cards to curtains)
- electronic (computer games, online, e-book and so on).

If you do not have an agent to sell these rights for you, or if you do not have a clue how you would go about selling them for yourself, then the best people to try and sell them are your publishers. If you have any helpful suggestions or contacts, the rights people would be glad to hear of them.

Surviving the edit

You will be working closely with an editor. This may not be the person you have been corresponding with thus far. (That person may well be the senior commissioning editor.) Once your work has been accepted for publication, you may find yourself liaising with an editor a little lower down the hierarchical tree.

You will be involved now in revising your work under this editor's guidance, or perhaps just doing a little polishing here and there. Your editor (let us call him/her 'Eddie' for convenience) may also be looking for an illustrator.

Illustrations

If your work is going to be very highly illustrated, you are likely to be sharing your royalties with this illustrator, usually on a 50/50 basis between yourself and the artist, depending upon the nature of the work, and sometimes the fame of the artist. By the way, if you are sharing royalties, the chances are that your contract is going to look even more complicated.

Some publishers will ask for your approval of a chosen illustrator, while others will assume they know best. The level of your veto should be outlined in the contract – if you have any veto at all.

Eddie may invite your comments on the work of several artists while a final decision is being made. You and Eddie will then be able to discuss which artist seems most suitable, but when it comes to the bottom line, unless you have an absolute contractual veto (highly unlikely!), Eddie will have the final say.

Once an illustrator has been chosen, the first thing you are likely to see are 'roughs' – sketches of the salient points in the book which it has been decided will benefit from illustration.

Book jackets

Your approval will probably be sought for the cover artwork and design. This is an area where the publisher will believe they know best and, with their experience and the input from their sales teams, they probably do. Your job will be to double-check that all the details of the artwork, design, cover 'blurb' and any biographical details are correct. (The 'blurb' is the text mainly seen on the back of a book which tries to sell the contents to the prospective purchaser.) You might also want to check at this point whether your name is being spelt correctly on the cover – and we're not joking about that, either!

Proofs

You may possibly not see anything until the 'proofs' turn up. Proofs are, or are like, photocopies of how the book will look with the final layout and all the illustrations in place. If you spot that your heroine has somehow metamorphosed into a gerbil, this is definitely the time to mention it.

The proofs will come with an accompanying letter asking for your comments and giving you a specific period of time in which to respond. It is important that you get your comments in before this deadline, or your silence could be interpreted as approval and the publishing process may continue without you being heard. Your editor will tell you how to correct the proofs, especially for when you spot any typographical errors.

By proof stage, the production costs are starting to rise, and your contract will probably stipulate that you are unable to make alterations in the text above (usually) $12^1/2$ per cent, due to the cost involved in such changes (unless you are prepared to foot the bill yourself). This is to stop you going into a panic that the whole book is totally wrong and needs thoroughly reworking now that you have had a few more months to think about it.

Edited scripts

You may receive a copy of your manuscript edited by a copy-editor and marked up for the designer or typesetter. The chances are that this is going to look like something out of your worst nightmare. Do not panic! The majority of the mess covering your script probably only consists of instructions to the designer or typesetter for the removal of typing errors and unwanted indentations.

Some of the scribbles may be grammatical corrections or minor improvements in the flow of the text. If some of the editorial changes go beyond simply tidying the text or making copy-editing alterations, you may find yourself having objections. If your book comes back via e-mail, there may be hidden changes, so read it very, very carefully – and cross-reference with your original if anything untoward catches your eye.

But before you blow a fuse over the liberties being taken with your book, take a deep breath, go for a walk or better still, leave the script overnight before you respond. Vent your frustration or outrage on your partner or a friend or on the mailman or the cat. Then write to Eddie or call or e-mail him in a calm and polite fashion to see if some compromise can be reached. Just as Eddie's changes may have put your back up, your angry dismissal of his ideas might do the same to him – and that's when things can start to get tricky. It may be that there is simply a difference of opinion between you and Eddie that can be talked through to mutual satisfaction.

On the other hand, if Eddie has spotted something in your text that is likely to cause offence to a large portion of the potential readership, then you would be well advised to take Eddie's advice and change the offending section rather than risk adversely affecting future sales. If it is practicable, you may well be invited to meet with Eddie (possibly not if you live in Vanuatu and Eddie works in Vancouver) and you may be introduced to other members of the production team. If you get on well with Eddie, you may find yourself in frequent contact with him as he fills you in on progress.

Authors are a curious, self-contained breed, most of whose work is done in solitary confinement, and to suddenly find their book in the hands of an outsider can be a traumatic experience. It will not endear you to the very busy Eddie if you are constantly ringing him up or e-mailing him to check on how things are going. Think before you make contact. Remember that Eddie will be dealing with several authors at once. Imagine what it must do to your efficiency to have several people calling you up for a chat every day of the week.

If you do have a problem or query and Eddie seems always to be in meetings when you call, then write, fax or e-mail if you really do require a response. You may need to be patient and to learn to cope with what seem to you to be breath-takingly unbusinesslike practices in the world of children's publishing.

Troubleshooting

If something to do with your book has gone wrong and you have enough confidence, then speak to the individual concerned. If the problem is particularly emotive, or if you are unable to reach a compromise verbally, then write to or fax the publisher so that your concerns are made perfectly clear. You would probably be wise to put such important concerns on paper – e-mails can all-too-easily get deleted or lost, and a hard copy is going to ensure that closer attention is paid.

If the reaction to this is not satisfactory, then write to the managing director and send a copy of your letter to the person with whom you are having the disagreement.

Be firm in your letter, but also try to be as fair and as objective as possible. Make sure the point you are pursuing is of direct relevance to your book, and not simply the product of a clash of personalities or some misunderstanding that has blown up out of all proportion. If even this level of complaint does not bring things to a satisfactory conclusion, then you should seek help according to your needs.

This help may come in the form of an authors' or illustrators' society, an advice centre, a book trade periodical, a media contracts expert, an agent or even a solicitor with the relevant experience in the publishing world. This advice could end up costing you money, so be sure the point you are arguing is worth it.

Just remember that publishers have a large investment in keeping their authors happy. After all, they are spending a lot of money to get that first book of yours off the launch pad, and hopefully providing the initial impetus for what could be a glittering career. If you and your publisher get on well, this first encounter could be the start of a mutually rewarding, lifelong involvement.

12

publication day – and afterwards

In this chapter you will learn:
- what happens when your first book is published
- about publicity and promotion
- how to deal with tax demands
- about self-publishing.

So, you have climbed Mount Everest, you have walked on the moon, you have won an Olympic Gold medal and your first book has a publication date. What do you do now?

Go into tax exile? Probably not. Write another book? Well, you should already have done that. Try to get another book published?

Getting to publication day means you have already jumped two of the Big Three hurdles:

1 Getting a publisher to read your first work.
2 Getting a publisher to publish your first work.
3 Getting a second (and third and fourth and …) piece of work published.

There is no need to become depressed right now, but it is said that getting your second book published is more difficult than your first. It does happen that some authors throw so much into their first work that they have nothing left for any subsequent projects. This is understandable. You want to present the very best of yourself to a potential publisher; you may have spent years polishing and honing your first book. A publisher may ask, 'What else have you got?' Panic! What *else* have I *got*? The publisher needs another book. You write something quickly. The publisher rejects it, saying it is not as good as the first one. Of course it isn't! You spent two years over the first one; you rushed this out 'on demand' in six weeks. Welcome to the world of the published author.

Publication

Back to the day-to-day practicalities for a moment. You have seen and corrected the proofs. You have been given a publication date. The title of your book will probably have appeared, along with a picture of the cover, in your publisher's sales catalogue some six months in advance of this date. The date will have been chosen by your publisher to maximize its sales potential: for instance, a wintry tale might come out in October to attract Christmas sales. There are also peak seasonal publication periods – spring and autumn – and traditional publishing days: Thursdays in the middle of the month, for review and accounting reasons. However, publishers are now far more flexible about choosing dates.

Advance copies

A finished copy of your book will usually be sent to you about six weeks in advance of the actual publication date. Thus it is called an 'advance' copy.

Check it thoroughly, but keep calm if you find that things are not absolutely perfect. You may find some 'minor' errors: misspellings in the blurb, or your biography may even be missing. These things may seem like major nightmares to you, but a publisher is unlikely to recall all the books and start again to correct that sort of mistake or omission – it would be too expensive. These 'minor' problems probably won't be corrected until a second print run – if there is one, and that won't happen unless all copies of the first print run sell out. *However*, if you spot that the book jacket has been attached upside down, that pages of the text are missing or out of order, or your name has been misspelt, then these books will definitely need to be reprinted. Call the publisher immediately in case no one else has noticed.

These faults *do* happen although, thankfully, not very often. And it may well be that the author, who is usually the last person to see the finished article, is the first to spot the problem. One agent said this:

> *I have seen book jackets upside down, names spelt correctly on the front cover, and incorrectly on the spine. But I once got a call from an author to say, 'Thank you for my advance copy, but the last page containing the climax of my story is missing!'. Three thousand copies were promptly reprinted, at the printer's expense!*

Gratis copies

Your contract will stipulate how many copies of your book you are entitled to receive free upon publication day. *Always* keep at least one copy of every title and edition of your work in a safe place for the future. If you have given all your copies away, it may be difficult to track down your books if they are no longer on sale in 10 years' time. You will also be entitled to purchase further copies at probably the lowest trade discount a publisher would offer to a retailer. (Bear in mind, though, that you are not supposed to sell these copies and keep the profit yourself, unless you are a bookseller. Check with your publisher if you need copies to sell at, say, a school author visit.)

Lead titles

In the publishing world, a 'lead title' is one which is going to be promoted in preference to all other titles being produced by the publisher. It seldom happens that the first work by an unknown author is going to get this sort of attention. We know of one new author whose first 32-page picture book was published at the same time as a biography of a very famous person which captured world media attention for weeks. He could not understand why his title was not receiving the same attention.

You need to get things into perspective. To you, the publication of your first book may be the climax of a lifetime of ambition, but to the publisher it is just another book on their list, another chocolate Santa on the conveyor belt, another piece of the corporate jigsaw. To the wholesale buyers, it is one more title amongst the tens of thousands published in a year.

Sales and publicity

By publication day, you should have been sent a publicity questionnaire. If you are under the wing of a large publisher, you may already have spoken to someone in the publicity department to discuss ways in which your book can be promoted.

It is one of the unfortunate aspects of the general tendency towards cutting costs to the bone that the publicity departments are often the first to suffer. This cost-cutting is particularly noticeable in the publicity departments that deal with children's books: some publishers will employ freelance publicists for special titles or a new series of titles.

Your publisher's sales team, both directly employed and freelance, will also have been attending sales conferences and pre-selling titles (including yours) to bookshops, wholesalers, library buyers and so on. They will have been provided with advance information sheets to distribute, sometimes nine months in advance of publication day. Hundreds or even thousands of copies may be pre-sold or subscribed (known as 'subbed') prior to the big day. You should know, however, that these copies are not definite sales until the copies pass from the retailer into the hands of a paying customer.

Returns

Retailers sometimes return unsold copies of books to the publisher, which will show up as negative amounts on your royalty statement. Publishers will bear this possibility in mind and will 'hold back' a certain amount of royalty money to cover this likelihood. It is known as a 'reserve against returns', and the exact details will be found in your contract.

Reviews

As well as getting your book into the stores, your publisher should also be sending out copies to appropriate people for 'review' purposes. One of the best things you can hope for upon publication of your book is that it gets a glowing review in a magazine, newspaper, online bookseller or children's book website read by potential purchasers, particularly booksellers, teachers and librarians. It is said that no publicity is bad publicity, and any review will draw attention to your title.

A critical review, although depressing, is in the vast majority of cases only a matter of one person's opinion. Your book must have had *something* about it to have attracted the reviewer's attention in the first place.

You cannot please everyone all of the time, and the fact that your book is now in the public domain and in a position to be criticized is proof that a good many people have faith in your work.

Most publishers subscribe to a 'cuttings' service, provided by a firm specializing in scouring all printed material for reviews, comments or whatever of books published by a particular organization. All such pieces of printed publicity are then sent to the publisher, who will forward copies to you. They may range from coverage in a local paper to mentions in national newspapers and magazines. The problem is that you will be sent the reviews whether they are good or bad.

Keep a publicity file. Good reviews and publicity can later be put to use, perhaps when approaching a different publisher a few years down the line.

The space available for reviewing children's books is notoriously limited, and it would not be unusual for your book to get no reviews at all. This is not the end of the world. Children's books, particularly the 12+ titles, have become bestsellers through word of mouth, and if children latch onto a particular book, it can quickly become a vital fashion accessory. Children also like to collect: so, if they like one title in a series, they are quite likely to buy and read the whole lot.

You may wonder why your publisher seems not to have invested much time, money or effort into making sure that people know your book is out there. Where are the billboards? Where are the full-page ads? Unfortunately, most of a publisher's publicity budget will go on books that they expect to be sure-fire bestsellers – books by authors who already have a large following, or books that have some 'angle' that gives them a pre-determined appeal. This 'only-push-at-an-open-door' attitude can be very frustrating for a newly published writer, but unfortunately in a word dominated by quick profits, your book probably won't be seen to warrant a large publicity budget. On the other hand, they might see you as the next Big Thing – in which case prepare yourself for a roller-coaster ride of magazine interviews, TV appearances and nation-wide book-signing tours.

Prizes and awards

Many prizes and awards are granted each year to children's books. Your publisher will be aware of these, and will know the appropriate time to make submissions. You could ask your editor, or publicist if you have one, where they are sending copies of your books for reviewing purposes and whether there are any suitable prizes for which your book can be entered. Depending on timing, any such prize could be awarded in the year, or even two years, after the publication of your book. In any event the press attention and publicity surrounding the presentation of an award is guaranteed to increase sales.

Self-publicity and promotion

Does your book have some topical angle which could attract publicity? Is there a 'hook' upon which to hang some PR (public relations: another way of saying publicity)? Is there something in or from your life that will make the publication of your book of particular interest to the media? Does your book connect with some anniversary, event or topical issue? Most books, whether fiction or non-fiction, contain something in them which can be used to advantage. Something may happen by coincidence in the news to which you can link your book for some useful publicity.

Speak to your publisher's publicity department and see what ideas they can suggest. If you find that your publisher does not have the time or the budget to do all that they might, then have a go yourself. Local newspapers are often very willing to write about a local celebrity ('Local Person Makes Good!'), and may even publish a photograph of you signing books at a local library or book shop. Local radio stations may also be interested, particularly if there is an extra newsworthy angle. If your publicist is unwilling or unable to produce a press release or information sheet on your book, then consider writing or designing one yourself.

Visit your local bookstore or make an appointment to meet with the person who runs the children's department. Suggest that you would be willing to visit the store and sign books for customers. If it is a story or poetry book, you could also read from it. Many local booksellers would be only too happy to accommodate you, and would be glad of the local press publicity such an event would be likely to promote. You may have to make personal arrangements if you want a photograph taken, and in some cases, you may even be asked to do the write-up (the article) yourself for the local newspaper if a reporter cannot attend.

Such signing sessions need not be limited to bookshops, either. You could also generate some publicity for yourself by signing copies of your book at a school fair, a garden centre, supermarket or boat/ferry trip; anywhere, in fact, where books are being sold.

Signing sessions can have varying rates of success for no readily apparent reason. You could sell out copies of your book in half an hour, or find that a huge local media blitz only results in half a dozen sales in an entire day. Still, what have you got to lose? It all means more sales, more publicity and eventually, more money.

Your library may also be interested in a visit from a local author if you are prepared to read your story book to a group of children at a story-telling session. Contact the children's librarian for your area.

These days many authors have their own websites – so you might like to consider setting your own site up, where you can give information about yourself, update fans on your writing activities and maybe even have a questions and answers page.

Unless you are a computer nerd, you will probably have either to get a knowledgeable friend to set the website up for you, or pay a professional to do it – but you may find the long-term benefits are worth the expense.

And while we're talking about the Internet again, you could always go into one of the online bookshops such as Amazon and write your own review of your book.

Visiting schools

You may find that local schools would be interested in you visiting them to talk to students, to read to them or to work with them, say, on a book project or as part of a book sale/fair. While some schools cannot pay you for such visits, others can, and you can learn the appropriate fee to charge by contacting any one of the authors' societies. This fee could also include expenses and you may find that some schools are able to pay you quite well for a day or two's work. For some established authors, the fees from school visits make up a worthwhile percentage of their income.

Ask the headteacher if it is permissible for you to sell signed copies of your book to the students. Ask your editor or publicist if they can arrange for you to have copies and any promotional material, but make sure you give them plenty of notice. Check, too, that the students to whom you wish to sell your books are alerted to the fact that they should bring in some money on the day.

If you have arranged this visit yourself and it's a non-paying event, it may still be worth approaching your publisher to see if they are willing to pay some travelling expenses for you. They may also be able to provide you with promotional material, such as posters, postcards, badges, leaflets or bookmarks that feature your book, especially if it's part of a series which the publisher is promoting as a whole.

You may find that your publisher has produced a press release which they can give you, or perhaps a mail-order leaflet. Make your publisher aware that you are available and eager to do publicity work – this is likely to add impetus to any of the PR department's promotional ideas. If you are really keen and able to self-promote your work, then some research into publicity and marketing will help you with ideas. (There are books available to guide you in this area.) Help your publisher to help you.

Tax and accounts

Whatever your circumstances, whether you are a taxpayer or not, or wherever you live, the tax situation for authors can get complicated. Your local tax inspector or an accountant may be able to provide helpful advice. There are also media accountants who specialize in the vagaries of author taxation. If in doubt, seek expert advice.

We invited London Chartered Accountants H. W. Fisher & Company to provide the following for UK-based authors. Please note that the following is for guidance only, and does not purport to give professional advice.

Who is an author?

For tax purposes, someone is a professional author if they are writing regularly with a view to making a profit. Their taxable income is the amount receivable, either directly or via an agent, less expenses wholly and exclusively incurred in exercising their profession. If expenses exceed income, the loss can generally either be carried forward and set against future writing income, or set against other income in the same or previous year. If a writer receives only occasional payments from books or stories, it may not be possible to argue successfully that these are profits from a profession. In this case, only expenses directly incurred are likely to be deductible.

Allowable expenses

The following are expenses that can normally be claimed. Note that it is essential to keep detailed records, including receipts wherever possible.

- agent's commission
- secretarial, proof-reading and research
- telephone, postage, stationery, printing
- periodicals and books
- research assistance and materials
- photographic expenses
- software, CDs, Internet charges
- travelling and accommodation
- car hire, car running expenses or mileage allowance
- publicity and advertising expenses

- illustrations
- subscriptions to societies
- rent, business rates, mortgage interest, council tax, lighting, heating, etc. in proportion to the number of rooms used exclusively for the profession – most authors do not claim exclusive use of rooms and restrict their claim to a portion of home expenses in order to avoid capital gains tax upon the sale of their home
- accountancy and legal costs (incurred in the course of the profession)
- TV and DVD/video rental, and relevant cinema and theatre admission
- capital allowances can be claimed for business furniture and equipment as follows: cars – 25 per cent in year of purchase, and 25 per cent of reducing balance each year; other business equipment – 50 per cent in first year and 25 per cent of reducing balance
- courses and conferences
- copies of own books for publicity.

Setting up in business

There are a number of important matters that new (and existing) businesses should be aware of. These include:

- registering to pay National Insurance or claim exemption or deferment
- registering for VAT including joining the Flat Rate Scheme and Cash Accounting – it is almost always beneficial to register for VAT; the compulsory registration income limit is £60,000 in any consecutive 12 months, including reimbursed expenses
- preparation of VAT returns
- preparation of tax returns
- preparation of accounts.

Delays with any of these matters attract penalties.

Increasingly, authors are coming to realize the tax and National Insurance advantages of trading as a limited company. However, incorporation is an important matter, and it is essential to take professional advice.

Averaging income

Anyone who is new to the writing profession should take expert advice about the date to choose for their accounting year end. An author may average earnings over two consecutive tax years if the net profit in one year is 75 per cent or less than the other year. It is also possible to average income within the terms of a publisher's contract. Income is the amount earned in the year rather than the amount received.

UK and overseas tax

If an author is resident in the UK for tax purposes, all income from literary work, whether domestic or foreign, is subject to UK income tax. The UK has double taxation treaties with most countries. After completion of certain formalities, no tax is usually deducted by the overseas publisher or other payer, but is taxable in the UK in the ordinary way. Where tax is withheld abroad, this can be offset against UK tax.

Grants and prizes

Certain Arts Council grants and literary bursaries are deemed to be taxable, but most prizes and awards are not.

What next?

And what of that next published project?

You *are* a new author. It is more than likely that your publisher will be waiting to see how the sales of your first work are going before committing themselves to publishing anything else by you. Before broadcasting your next work around the publishing community, check your contract. If you have a first refusal clause committing you to giving your present publisher your next book, it may include a timescale within which the publisher must come to a decision. If your publisher rejects your work, then the clause automatically fails and you are free to show your book to whoever you choose – as well as any subsequent work.

Chances are your editor will already have asked you what you are working on, or what you plan to work on next, or may even have made some suggestions as to where you might like to go from here. As long as you and your publisher have a good, stable working relationship, it makes sense for you to submit your work to them before showing it to anyone else. Your publisher will be just as anxious as you to build a lasting, profitable relationship, and it could take some years for an author's name to start registering with people.

Depending upon the type of market for which you are writing and the size of the publisher's list, your publisher might be hoping for between one and four new titles from you per year – assuming your material continues to suit them. On the other hand, you may be the sole author of a major series with a new title every month. In that case, you are likely to be working flat out and to daunting deadlines. Always allow yourself enough time before agreeing to a delivery date; add in some emergency time in case of a booked holiday, illness or other unforeseen problems such as a hard-drive crash which stops you working for a week or so.

If you are more prolific than your publisher can cope with, you may need to make some alternative arrangements. Could you branch out into fields which might interest different publishers? If you are able to broaden your scope by writing for different age-groups or by writing on different subjects, then you will increase your marketability and you could find yourself working for several publishers at the same time without competing with yourself, and without upsetting your first publisher.

Self-publishing

Say you are absolutely convinced of the worth and value of a work that you have produced, yet the publishing world seems stubbornly blind to its merits. You are sure many people would enjoy your work if only they were given the chance to actually read it. What do you do when all the obvious options have been closed off?

Should you self-publish? First, ask yourself whether there really is a viable market for your book. A non-fiction title which covers a particular neglected subject, or which supplies an as yet undernourished need, is more likely to be successful than a typical novel or collection of poetry. A self-published book of which we heard, which explained the intricacies of croquet, sold out its initial print run and made a profit in no time – and of course the Internet is a great way of letting the world know that your book is out there, especially if you can plug into an existing worldwide market. An instruction manual on croquet? Make contact with every croquet website on the Internet and soon you could find yourself spending most of your spare time packaging and mailing books to every corner of the world where croquet is played.

Assess whether the rejection of several publishers has been on economic or technical grounds: is it a good book, but with a potentially limited readership, or is everyone telling you that the book is poorly written or ill conceived? If the general assessment is that there is something technically or stylistically 'wrong' with the book, then you should think very carefully before plunging into the world of self-publishing. Could it be that they are right and that you really need to spend some time polishing your skills? Consider this point carefully before committing time and money to a process that may result in you trying to find storage space for hundreds of unsold books starring Eric the Earwig.

Let us suppose you do decide to go for self-publishing. Fortunately, with the existence of desktop publishing facilities and highly competitive printing prices, it is far easier now to publish yourself and less expensive than you might imagine. But do you have the time to learn the business? And do you have the necessary capital to cover the initial production costs? Self-publishing may not cost the earth, but it is a time-consuming business, as you need to absorb everything from how to get an International Standard Book Number (ISBN; you will find one on the back of every book published since the 1970s), to supplying copies for copyright registration, to finding a distributor for the finished product.

Given the requisite time and money to set up the business, your next biggest headache will be figuring out how you are going to get your book in front of your potential customers in sufficient quantities to cover your costs and maybe even make a profit.

There are good books available on how to go about publishing your own work and, as with everything in this business, you will want to do some thorough research before you make a final decision. You will also discover the existence of small publishers (known as 'small presses') who may be able to help you publish and distribute your book if you can 'sponsor' them (that is, help out with the costs). It is helpful for publicity and distribution purposes if you can have your book on a publisher's list, no matter how small that publisher might be.

We asked someone who had successfully entered the world of self-publishing for suggestions based on his own experiences:

> *The first thing to do is get yourself an ISBN number. These come in sets of 10 consisting of a publisher prefix followed by numbers for individual publications, and are issued in the UK from the ISBN Agency, Midas House, 62 Goldsworth Road, Woking GU21 6LQ. The Agency also arranges for your book/s to be listed by Nielsen BookData, a database which is used by bookshops and libraries. After you've found a typesetter and/or designer and printer, you need to think about distribution. You can either use your own direct sales methods (e.g. via a website) or find a distributor who will supply bookshops. Finally, you need to organize a publicity leaflet/press release and send out review copies to relevant people, newspapers, magazines, organizations etc. ... addresses for which can be found in a current edition of* The Writer's Handbook. *If you want to track reviews then you need to subscribe to a cuttings agency, but beware, because this can be an expensive undertaking.*

There are now print-on-demand companies which can take your work from a disk, design the typography and page layout, help with jacket design and make your work available electronically. In this way, your book will be printed on demand; the main sales area for this will be via the online bookstores, to which most print-on-demand companies can arrange listings and the relevant links. It works this way: your potential reader finds your book on the web, orders it, and hey presto that order connects to the print-on-demand publisher who then prints a copy and sends it to the customer. At present, to keep their costs down, many print-on-demand publishers are only interested in larger numbers of titles, and deal only with professionals within the business rather than with individual authors. However, authors are now beginning to see the value in banding together to exploit the possibilities afforded by this new technology. If this is an area you wish to investigate, you would be wise to seek the opinion and recommendation of someone in the know – otherwise you might not end up getting quite what you had hoped for.

Also, before you are tempted to publish a teaser sample of your work on your own or another website (or chapters or even whole books online), ask yourself 'How am I going to make any money from this exercise, and is my work safe from theft and corruption?' These are important questions.

Before you self-publish also ask yourself the following questions:

- Why am I doing this?
- Is there a real market for my book?
- Is it the best it can be, or would it benefit from the hand of a professional (potentially expensive) editor?
- Have I the time and resources to learn the business?
- Can I afford the costs and the risk of making a loss?
- Will I be able to promote and sell the book to anyone other than my friends and family, who will expect free copies anyway?

Vanity publishing

A cautionary word on 'vanity publishing'. These people advertise regularly in magazines and newspapers, and you need to be careful about how you approach them. Vanity publishers always praise your work, no matter how unmarketable it really is. Vanity publishers are willing to publish *anything*, provided you come up with the money, but do you want your work published for the sheer vanity of it? Be very careful about your dealings with such operators and ask an author's society for advice or knowledge about any such company you may contact. At any given time, several vanity publishers will be under investigation for fraud. Writer beware!

You may also spot deals advertised sometimes in newspapers and magazines, etc., where you can get your book published for a fixed fee. But be careful of these offers – the quality of the finished product is often very poor, and once you have your books, you still need to come up with a method of getting them out to potential buyers/readers.

The bottom line

Now you've read this book, does the life of a published author still look interesting to you? Even after everything we've warned you about? Are you kidding? You *still* want to go ahead with it?

In that case, at least you're now armed with a lot more information than you were 12 chapters ago. The things we've written about here only scratch the surface of writing and publishing books. In many places we've recommended that you go and look out books that detail specific aspects of the business of writing and getting published. Remember – the more research you do, the better your chance of hitting that elusive target.

Hopefully, we've given you a few pointers about how to go about collecting and organizing your ideas, producing a product which will attract a publisher and dealing with all the failures and successes that may come from your desire to see your name or your work in print. Over the years we have learnt the hard way, and made all the classic mistakes. With the aid of this book, your learning process should be much faster than ours was.

In the end, it is all down to you. We can only provide the signposts: it's up to you to make the journey. And for that journey you will need persistence, determination, stamina, talent and a good deal of luck. Just keep one thing in mind: for an author, there is nothing more satisfying or fulfilling than actually holding your first published book in your hands.

What are you waiting for? Publishers are crying out for new talent. Go and get that book published! Oh, and when you're rich and famous and living in tax exile, remember we had faith in you all that time ago when everyone else thought you would never make it.

Endnote

It took dozens of letters, faxes and e-mails, hours of phone calls, months of time and research and many drafts and revisions of the script to complete this book and deliver it to our publisher, in between our normal day jobs, sleeping, eating, parenting and putting the cat out. We also used and abused friendships and family above and beyond the call of duty and are forever in their debt. One of the authors questioned added the following to the bottom of his returned questionnaire:

> *The question that really interests me is: how to write <u>my own</u> children's books – the satisfying and necessary ones – <u>and</u> to make contact with an audience. There are plenty of books and evening classes which only talk about market research and how-to-please-the-little-brats. (Don't write one of those, will you? I know you won't.)*

Sorry, but there's only one way to sign off:

> *… and they all lived happily ever after.*

THE END

taking it further

Listings for UK-based authors

Books

Bann, David (2006), *The All New Print Production Handbook,* Hare: RotoVision, ISBN: 2 9403 6138 X.

Books in Print 2005–2006 (2005, published annually), New Providence, NJ, USA: R R Bowker (8 vols), ISBN: 0 8352 4732 5.

Clark, Giles N. (2000), *Inside Book Publishing* (3rd edition), London: Taylor & Francis, p 264, ISBN: 0 4152 3006 3.

Crofts, Andrew (2002), *The Freelance Writer's Handbook*, London: Piatkus Books, p 224, ISBN: 0 7499 2309 1.

Finch, Peter (1997), *How to Publish Yourself*, London: Allison & Busby Writers' Guides, p 144, ISBN: 0 7490 0301 4.

Legat, Michael (2002) *Understanding Publishers' Contracts*, London: Robert Hale, London, p 192, ISBN: 0 7090 7289 9.

Legat, Michael (1995), *An Author's Guide to Literary Agents*, London: Robert Hale, p 128, ISBN: 0 7090 5572 2.

Legat, Michael (1995), *Writer's Rights*, London: A & C Black, p 128, ISBN: 0 7136 4018 9.

Literary Market Place 2006: The Directory of the American Book Publishing Industry (2005), Medford, NJ, USA: Information Today, p 2200 (2 vols), ISBN: 1 5738 7228 0.

Poynter, Dan (2001), *The Self-Publishing Manual: How to Write, Print and Sell Your Own Book* (13th edition), Santa Barbara, CA, USA: Para Publishing, p 432, IBSN: 1 5686 0073 9.

The Publishers Association (2005), *Directory of Publishing 2006* (31st edition, published annually), London: Continuum, p 216, ISBN: 0 8264 8753 X.

Ross, Tom and Ross, Marilyn (2002), *The Complete Guide to Self-Publishing* (4th edition), Cincinnati, OH, USA: Writers' Digest Books (F&W Publications), p 432, ISBN: 1 5829 7091 2.

Turner, Barry (ed.) (2005), *The Writer's Handbook 2006* (19th edition, published annually), London: Macmillan, p 864, ISBN: 1 4050 4154 4.

Warhurst, Caroline and McAuliffe, Juliette (2005), *Prizes & Awards* (3rd edition), Stockport: Dewi Lewis Publishing, p 319, ISBN: 1 9045 8716 X.

Writers' & Artists' Yearbook 2006 (published annually), A & C Black, London, p 848, ISBN: 0 7136 71734.

Periodicals

The Author
(in-house membership magazine of the Society of Authors, see below)
E-mail: theauthor@societyofauthors.org
Website: http://www.societyofauthors.net/soa/page_id.php4?-pid=16&sectid=16urlsection=Publication
Manager: Kate Pool (Deputy General Secretary)

Bloomsbury Magazine
Bloomsbury Publishing Plc, 36 Soho Square, London W1 3QY
Tel: 020 7494 2111; Fax: 020 7434 0151
E-mail: alert@bloomsbury.com
Website: http://www.bloomsburymagazine.com
Manager: Stephanie Duncan

Books for Keeps (BfK)
1 Effingham Road, Lee, London SE12 8NZ
Tel: 020 8852 4953; Fax: 020 8318 7580
E-mail: enquiries@booksforkeeps.co.uk
Website: http://www.booksforkeeps.co.uk
Editor: Rosemary Stones

The Bookseller
Fifth floor, Endeavour House, 189 Shaftesbury Avenue, London
WC2H 8TJ
Tel: 020 7420 6006; Fax: 020 7420 6103.
E-mail: firstname.lastname@bookseller.co.uk
Website: http://www.theBookseller.com
Editor-in-chief: Neill Denny

Carousel
The Saturn Centre, 54–76 Bissel Street, Birmingham B5 7HX
Tel: 0121 622 7458; Fax: 0121 666 7526
E-mail: carousel.guide@virgin.net
Website: http://www.carouselguide.co.uk
Editors: Jenny and David Blanch

Directory of Writers' Circles 2006
Tel: 01525 873197.
E-mail: diana@writers-circles.com
Website: http://www.writers-circles.com
Editor: Diana Hayden

Publishing News
7 John Street, London WC1N 2ES
Tel: 0870 870 2345; Fax: 0870 870 0385
E-mail: firstname.lastname@publishingnews.co.uk
Website: http://www.publishingnews.co.uk
Editor: Liz Thomson

Publishers Weekly
360 Park Avenue South, New York, NY 10010, USA
Tel: 00 1 646 746 6758; Fax: 00 1 646 746 6631
E-mail (general enquiries): itaylor@reedbusiness.com
Website: http://www.publishersweekly.com
Editor-in-chief: Sara Nelson

Times Educational Supplement
Admiral House, 66–68 East Smithfield, London E1W 1BX
Tel: 020 7782 3000; Fax: 020 7782 3200
E-mail: firstname.lastname@tes.co.uk
Website: http://www.tes.co.uk
Editor: Judith Judd

Contacts and societies

Arvon Foundation

Website: http://www.arvonfoundation.org

- National administration: 2nd floor, 42a Buckingham Palace Road, London SW1W 0RE
  Tel: 020 7931 7611; Fax: 020 7963 0961
- Lumb Bank – The Ted Hughes Arvon Centre, Heptonstall, Hebden Bridge, West Yorkshire HX7 6DF
  Tel: 01422 843714; Fax: 01422 843714
  E-mail: l-bank@arvonfoundation.org
- Totleigh Barton, Sheepwash, Beaworthy, Devon EX21 5NS
  Tel: 01409 231338; Fax: 01409 231144
  E-mail: t-barton@arvonfoundation.org
- Moniack Mhor, Teavarran, Kiltarlity, Beauly, Inverness-shire IV4 7HT
  Tel: 01463 741675; Fax: 01463 741733
  E-mail: m-mhor@arvonfoundation.org
- The Hurst – The John Osborne Arvon Centre, Clunton, Craven Arms, Shropshire SY7 0JA
  Tel: 01588 640658; Fax: 01588 640509
  E-mail: hurst@arvonfoundation.org

Association of Illustrators (AOI)

2nd floor, Back Building, 150 Curtain Road, London EC2A 3AR
Tel: 020 7613 4328; Fax: 020 7613 4417
E-mail: info@theaoi.com
Website: http://www.theaoi.com

Author's Licensing and Collection Society

Marlborough Court, 14–18 Holborn, London EC1N 2LE
Tel: 020 7395 0600; Fax: 020 7395 0660
E-mail: alcs@alcs.co.uk
Website: http://www.alcs.co.uk

Booktrust

45 East Hill, London SW18 2QZ
Tel: 020 8516 2977; Fax: 020 8516 2978
E-mail: firstname@booktrust.org.uk
Website: http://www.booktrust.org.uk

Children's Book Circle

Evening speaker meetings most months at venues around central London for anyone involved with or working in children's books (including, annually, the Eleanor Farjeon award in the autumn and the Patrick Hardy Lecture in November each year).
Tel: 020 7761 3699
E-mail: nwilkinson@euk.egmont.com
Website: http://www.childrensbookcircle.org.uk

Contracts for Publishing Limited

Unit 2 MSL, Headcorn Road, Staplehurst, Tonbridge, Kent TN12 0DS
Tel: 01580 890777; Fax: 01580 890781
E-mail: info@contractsforpublishing.co.uk
Website: http://www.contractsforpublishing.co.uk

Federation of Children's Book Groups

2 Bridge Wood View, Horsforth, Leeds, West Yorkshire LS18 5PE
Tel: 0113 258 8910; Fax: 0113 258 8920
E-mail: info@fcbg.org.uk
Website: http://www.fcbg.org.uk

H. W. Fisher & Company, London Chartered Accountants who prepared the tax and accounts summary in Chapter 12 would be glad to hear from authors who would like more information. Barry Kernon, who heads the firm's Authors and Journalists Team, can be contacted by e-mail on bkernon@hwfisher.co.uk, or telephone 020 7874 7875.
Website: http://www.hwfisher.co.uk.

International Board on Books for Young People [IBBY] (British Section)

PO Box 20875, London SE22 9WQ
E-mail: ann@lazim.demon.co.uk
Website: http://www.ncrcl.ac.uk/IBBY/ibby.htm

Public Lending Right

Richard House, Sorbonne Close, Stockton-on-Tees, Teeside TS17 6DA
Tel: 01642 604699; Fax: 01642 615641
E-mail: enquiries@plr.uk.com
Website: http://www.plr.uk.com

The Publishing Training Centre
Book House, 45 East Hill, Wandsworth, London SW18 2QZ
Tel: 020 8874 2718; Fax: 020 8870 8985
E-mail: publishing.training@bookhouse.co.uk
Website: http://www.train4publishing.co.uk

Society of Authors
84 Drayton Gardens, London SW10 9SB
Tel: 020 7373 6642; Fax: 020 7373 5768
E-mail: info@societyofauthors.org
Website: http://www.societyofauthors.net

Society of Young Publishers
c/o The Bookseller, Fifth floor, Endeavour House, 189 Shaftesbury Avenue, London WC2H 8TJ
Website: http://www.thesyp.org.uk

The Writers' Advice Centre for Children's Books
16 Smiths Yard, Summerley Street, London SW18 4HR
Tel: 07979 905353
E-mail: info@writersadvice.co.uk
Website: http://www.writersadvice.co.uk
Contact: Louise Jordan

Writers' Guild of Great Britain
15 Britannia Street, London WC1X 9JN
Tel: 020 7833 0777; Fax: 020 7833 4777
E-mail: admin@writersguild.org.uk
Website: http://www.writersguild.org.uk

biographies

Allan Frewin Jones

I am born. I deeply resent the fact that the cat stays at home while I have to go to school. I grow up. I deeply resent the fact that the cat stays at home while I have to go to work. I resolve to discover some way of avoiding going to work. I write 12 children's books in tea breaks, lunch hours and evenings. They're all rotten. I write children's book number 13. It is better. I rewrite it 30 squillion times and it gets published. About 70 books follow. Most are published. Some in different languages. I stay home writing books. Ha! All I need to do now is find some way of getting that cat out to work.

Lesley Pollinger

I studied arts and literature at college and joined the police. After eight years and an unfortunate incident involving myself, a brick wall and two paratroopers, I had to do something more sedentary. So I had two children, acquired other people's children (as a foster parent) and joined the family firm. I studied a lot more, joined various publishing organizations, and developed a strong children's authors' client list. My daughters, cats, clients and company demand as much time as they ever did, but no day is ever dull. If I have any spare time, I get on my bike, garden, or sing karaoke at my local pub.

creative writing
dianne doubtfire

- Do you want to know more about the writing process?
- Are you eager to develop your talent and improve your skills?
- Do you want to find out about the industry and getting published?

Creative Writing is the ideal practical handbook for any aspiring author. Using exercises to explore topics, it will encourage you to develop, direct and edit your creative ideas in addition to giving you invaluable guidance on how to present work for publication.

The late **Dianne Doubtfire** was a successful author of both fiction and non-fiction. This edition has been fully revised and expanded by Ian Burton, a former pupil of Dianne's and a published author and lecturer in creative writing.

how to write a blockbuster
helen corner & lee weatherly

- Would you like to be the next Dan Brown?
- Do you want to write pacy action?
- Would you like tips on finding an agent?

If you've always wanted to write popular fiction, like a romance, thriller or historical saga, this book will tell you how. From developing a gripping plot to creating emotionally engaging characters, it gives lots of practical advice and insider tips on how to polish your script, find an agent,and when to quit the day job!

Helen Corner is the founder of Cornerstones, a leading literary consultancy. **Lee Weatherly** is an editorial consultant and the author of a number of contemporary novels for teenagers.

teach yourself

writing a novel
nigel watts

- Do you want to turn your ideas into a novel?
- Do you need to overcome writer's block?
- Are you looking for advice on getting published?

Writing a Novel takes you through the whole process of writing a novel, from the germ of an idea, through developing plot, character and theme, to preparing it for publication. This fascinating analysis will appeal to both new and experienced authors alike.

Nigel Watts, PhD in Creative and Critical Writing, taught from 1989, the year in which he published his first award-winning novel, *The Life Game*. He went on to publish four further novels for adults, two children's stories and an anthology of spiritual poetry.